ABANDONED MANSIONS OF THE NORTHEAST

RUSTY TAGLIARENI
AND
CHRISTINA MATHEWS

AMERICA
THROUGH
TIME

AMERICA THROUGH TIME®
An imprint of SUTTON PUBLISHING INC.
www.through-time.com

First published 2025
Copyright © Rusty Tagliareni and Christina Mathews 2025

ISBN 978-1-63499-545-0

Typeset in Trade Gothic 10pt on 15pt
Printed and bound in England

CONTENTS

Introduction 5

1 A Forgotten Farmhouse 7

2 The Cenacle 15

3 Little Flower Orphanage 25

4 Reflective Silence 35

5 Greed 45

6 ELDA Castle 53

7 Selma Plantation Manor 61

8 Modern Ruins 73

9 The Burned Remains 81

10 An Unquiet Silence 93

11 The Cryptic Keep 103

12 Lynnewood Hall 113

INTRODUCTION

For decades we have traveled the United States documenting overlooked relics of our collective past. Abandoned properties, left to weather away, cast off by a society that no longer has use of them. They stand today as shadows, forms that resemble their former selves, but only superficially. The lives that once congregated here have sunken into the umbra of our modern era, all but lost in obscurity. They linger still, though, just faintly behind peeled paint and cracked plaster—an anemic beating of many hearts, of many lives, all slowly turning to dust.

Simply put: The subject of this book focuses on abandoned mansions. Properties that are simultaneously grand in scope but incredibly personal. Lives unfolded here, families grew, festivities were had, and memories forged. That was the past though, and these walls and halls have long fallen silent, but they remember.

Left without use, we can use these abandoned structures as points of reflection, seeing a place clearly without the distraction of daily life which once consumed its halls. Abandoned homes contain in them incalculable unseen things. From the very moment they come to exist, they slowly absorb the histories and personal tales of each and every person who has resided within its walls. Over decades, the architecture slowly comes to serve a far deeper purpose than that of its initial design, holding time itself within its geometry.

This awareness of generations, of our own very fleeting moment in history, is far easier to perceive when a place has fallen silent. It can be strange at first, but when left alone in the gloom-soaked corridors of these abandoned homes one is able to clearly see the forest as well as the trees.

Rusty Tagliareni and Christina Mathews
www.AntiquityEchoes.com

1

A FORGOTTEN FARMHOUSE

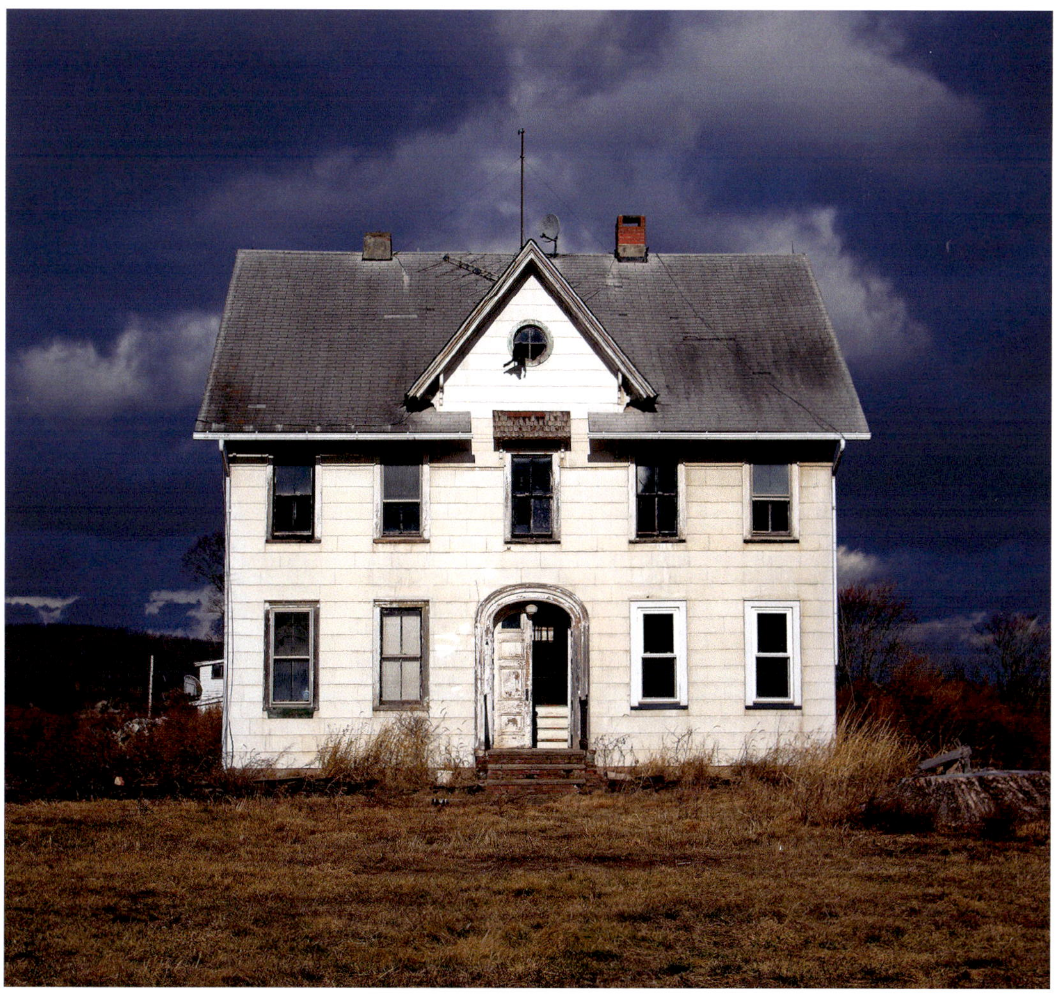

We felt it was appropriate to open this book with the humble charm of a seemingly unremarkable farmhouse. At first glance, it may appear less grand compared to the other properties showcased within these pages. Yet, therein lies its significance: This farmhouse embodies the universal lesson that "appearances can be deceiving." If one spends the time, there is often a profound beauty in all things, though it is sometimes hidden just below the surface.

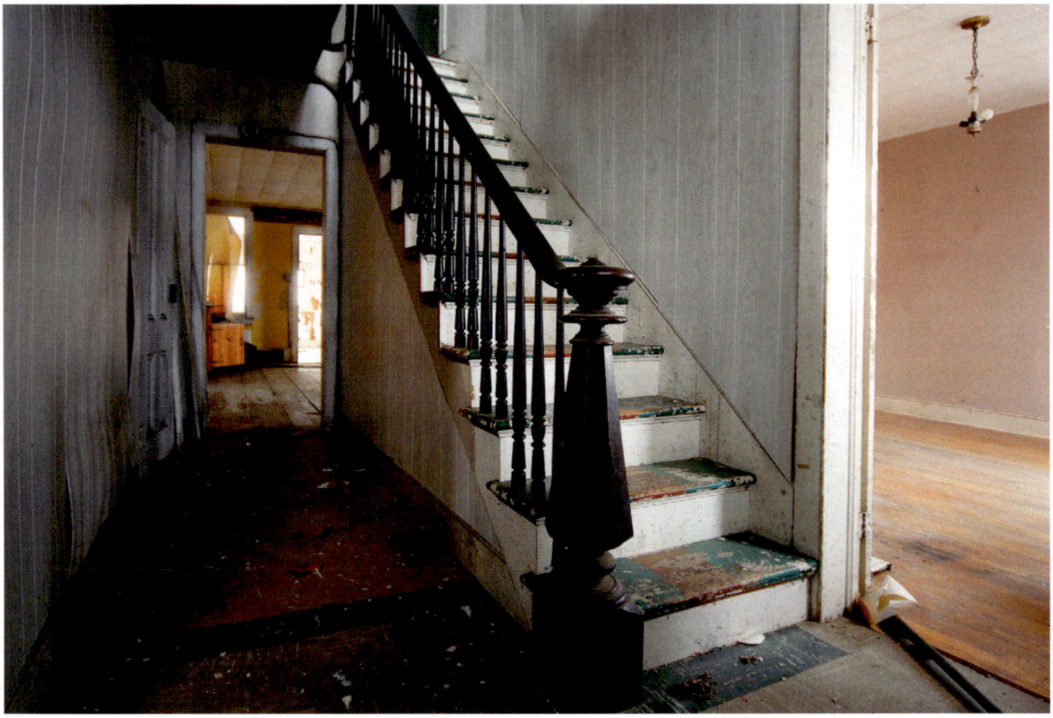

When you first enter the old house, it becomes immediately apparent that the previous residents stripped away nearly all traces of their presence, leaving the vacant property mostly barren of personal belongings and furnishings.

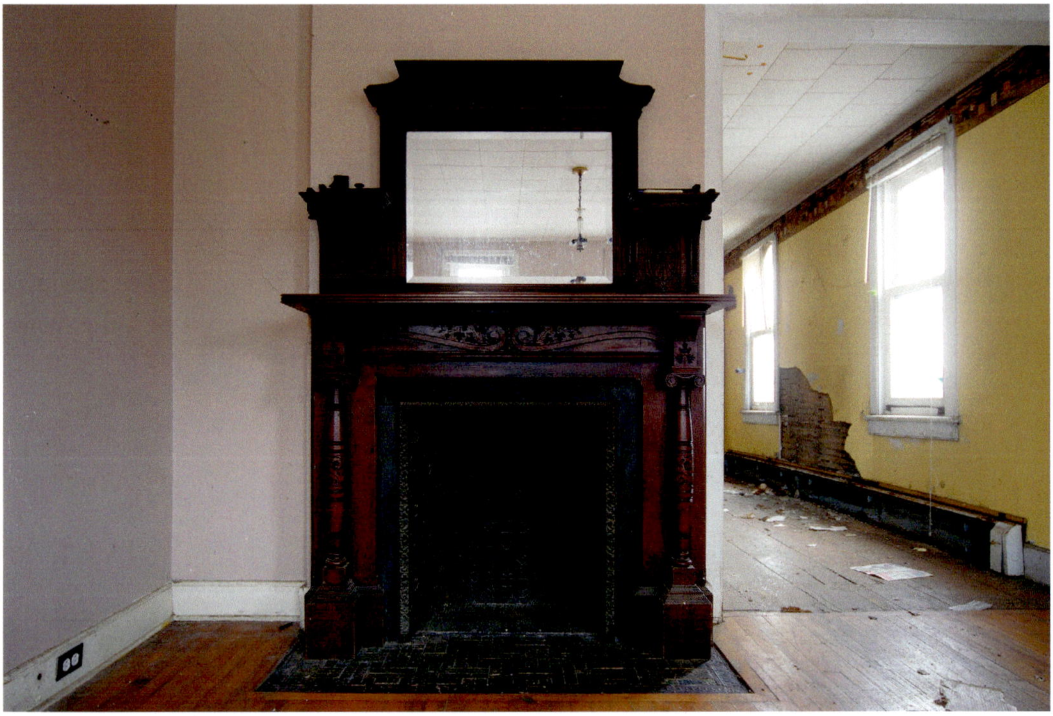

However, what few items did remain offered a beautiful peek into what once was.

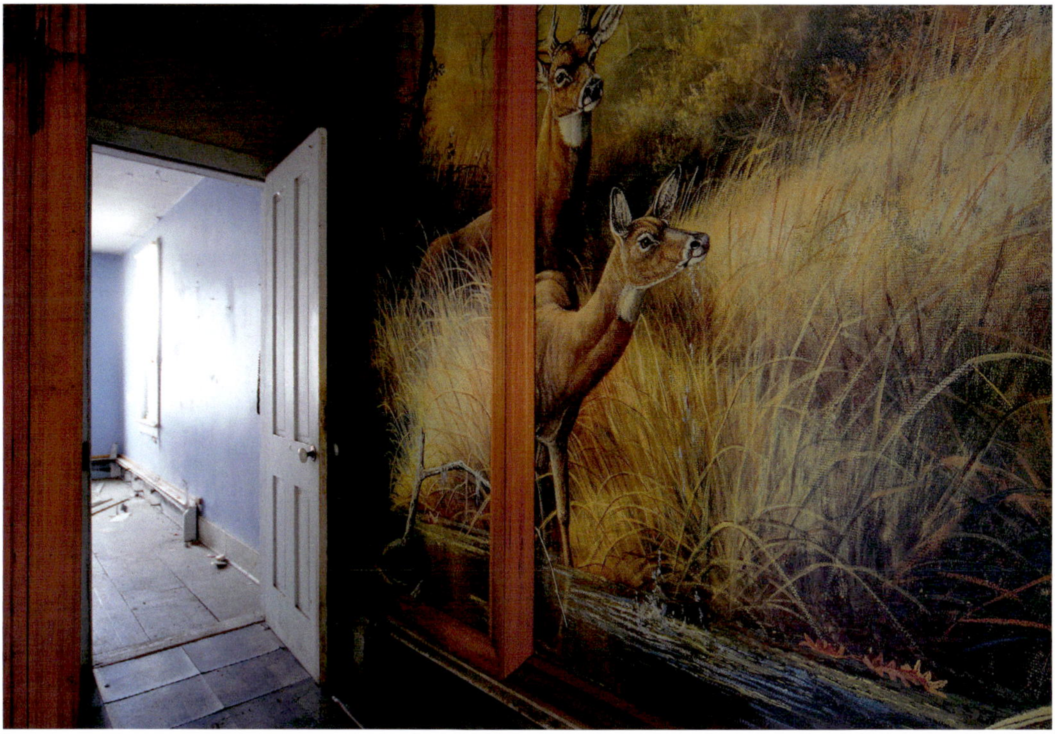

Above and below: This room served as a bathroom and through-way between the kitchen and the living room. A strange floor-plan made even more bizarre by the unique choice of mural. Life-sized deer stare out at you, a guest in their halls.

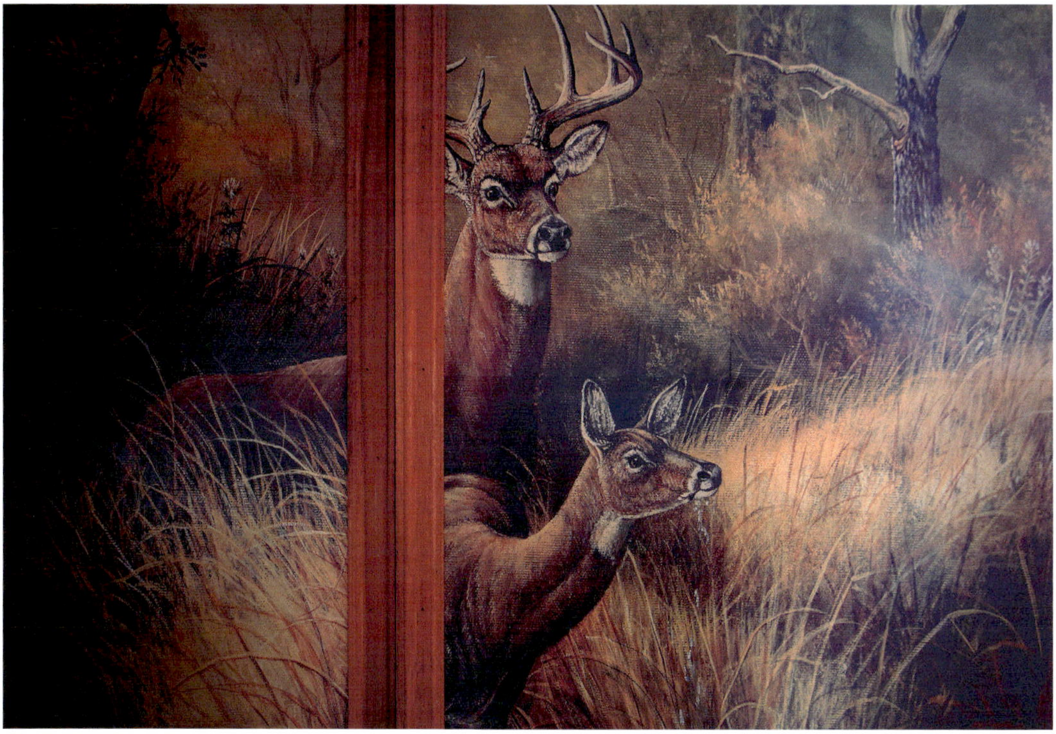

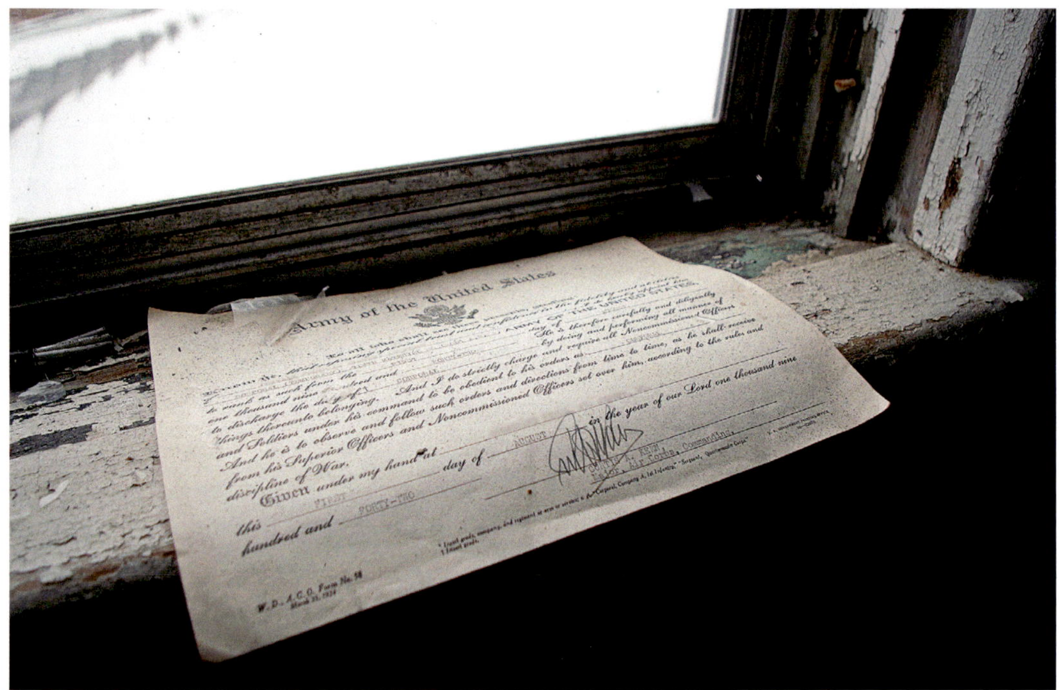

An appointment paper from the United States Army, dated August 1, 1942. Relics like these are what weave the seemingly disjointed items found throughout an old house into a story. A tale spoken without words.

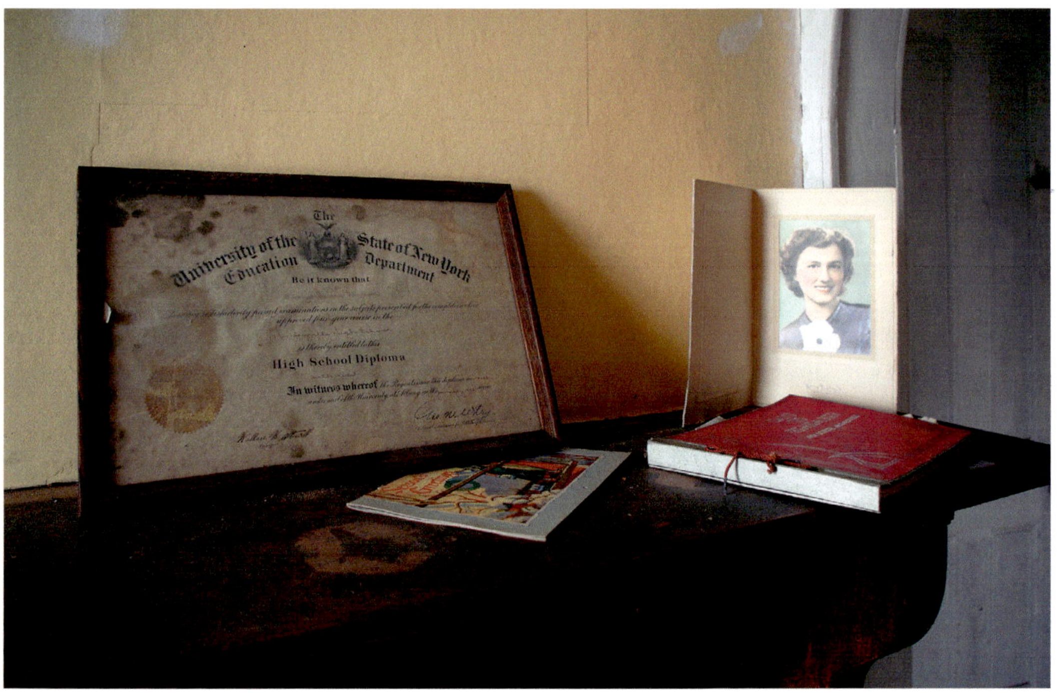

A high-school diploma from 1932, a woman smiling out from an antique hand-colored portrait. What did this graduate go on to do? Who was she? These are questions that conjure the imagination while also invoking an empathy to the real-world walls that now crumble around you. This was truly a home once, now it wastes away with its secrets.

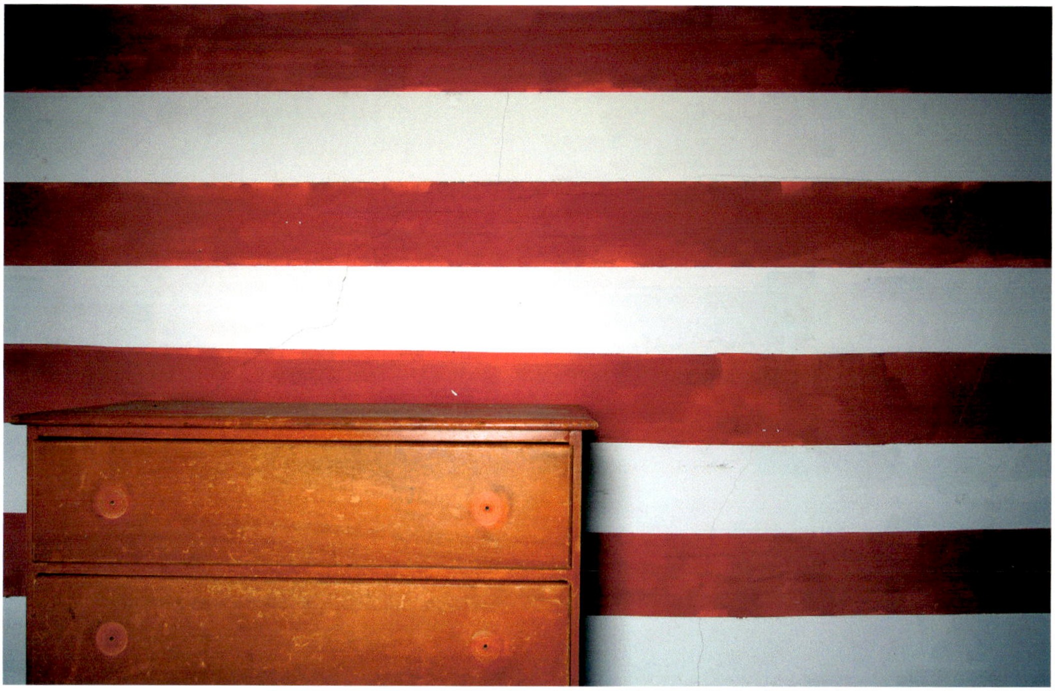

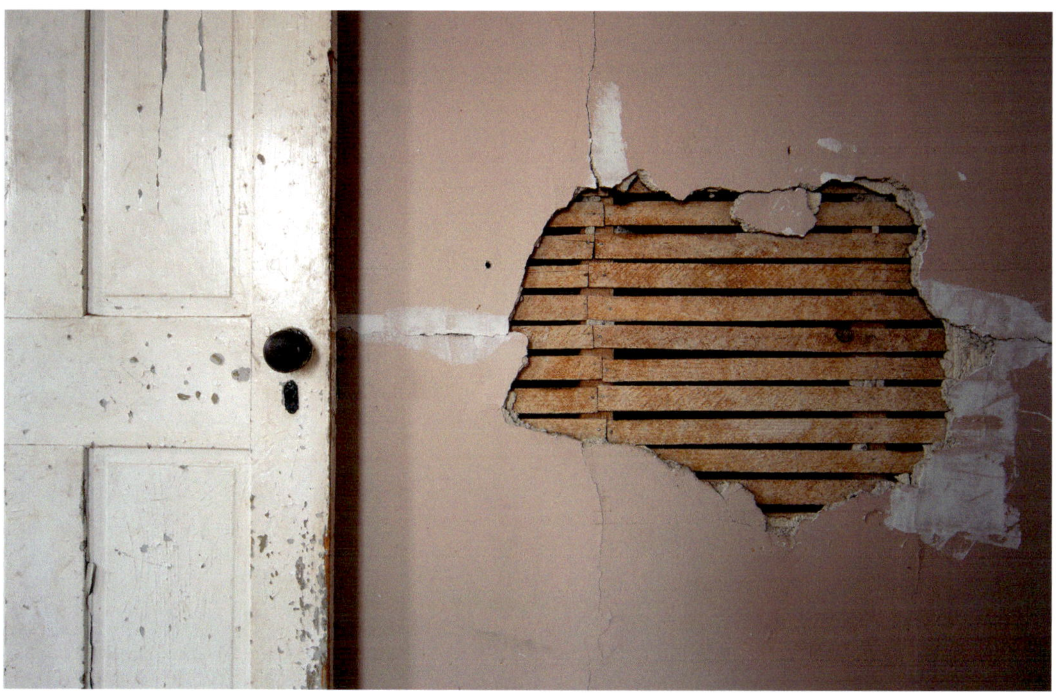

This red and white striped wall is an example of something that seems unusual at first but makes sense through context. Through the items left behind, the house reveals that its former residents had ties to World War II-era military.

Another wall, another story. Not one of personal insight, however, but the history of the physical house itself. The plaster fallen away from this wall reveals wood lath underneath, a construction technique that had all but vanished by the 1940s.

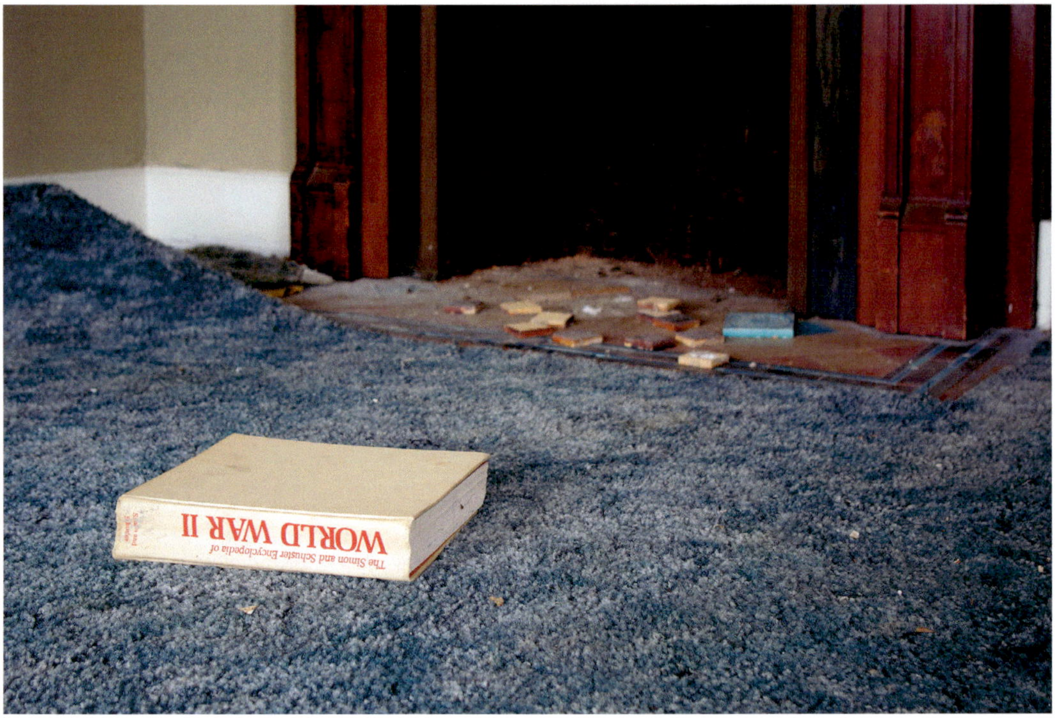

A thick encyclopedia volume about World War II lays, upside down, in front of a fireplace that likely predates that war by half a century. A distilled sampling of the timeline this house has witnessed.

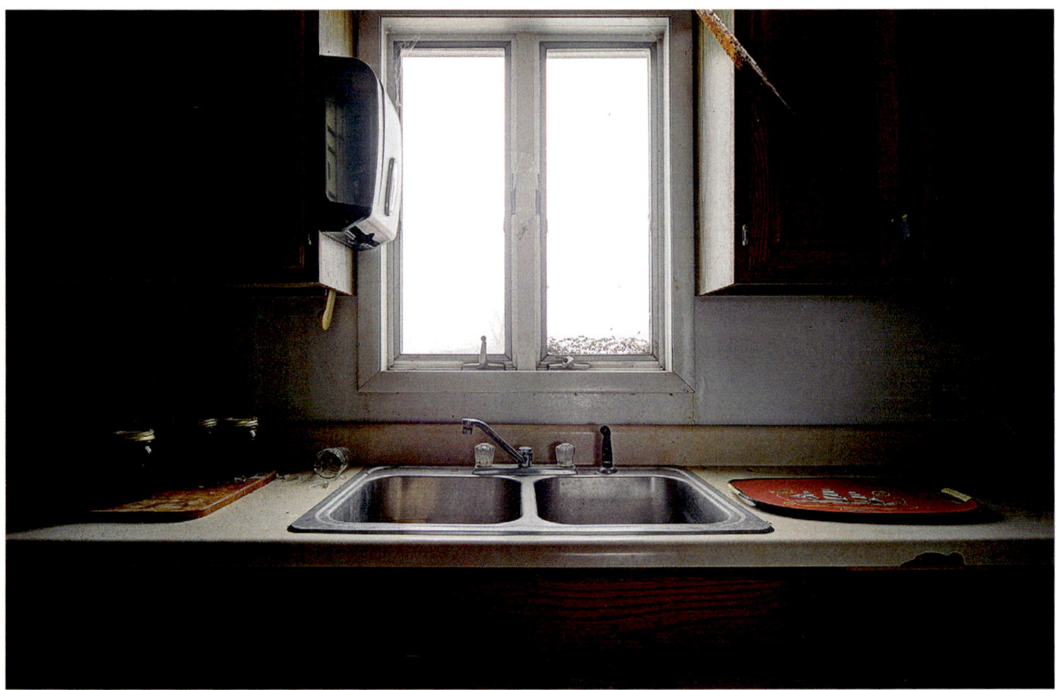

In the kitchen, only fly-tape and jarred preserves remain. How many have stared out this window, lost in thought as they went about their daily chores?

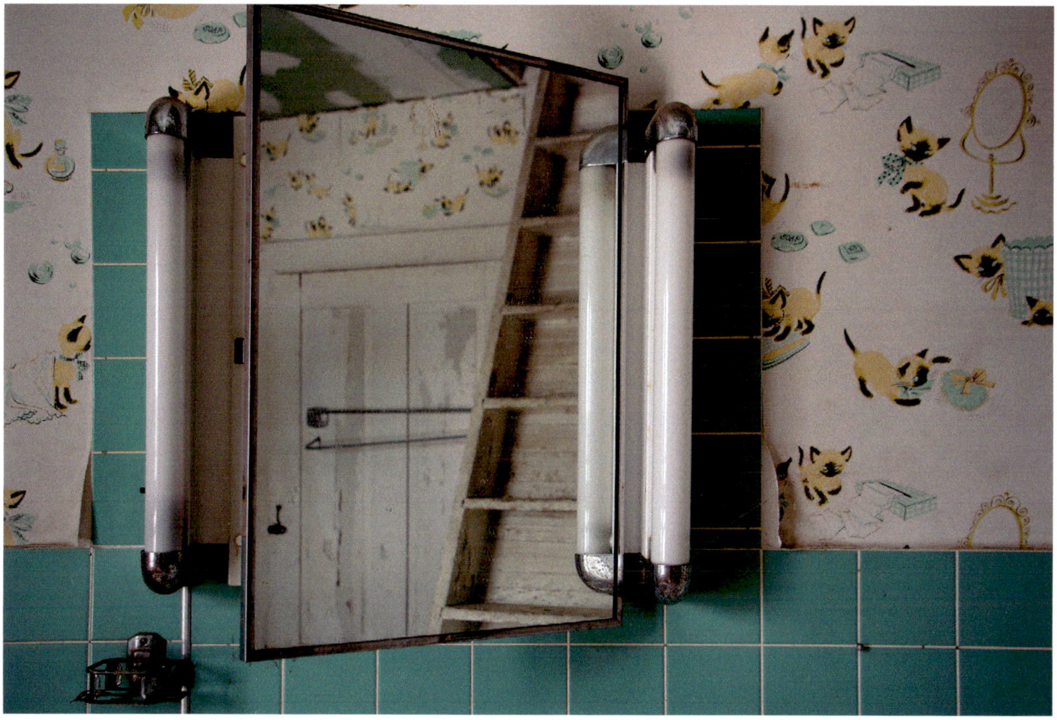

Above and below: A bathroom can be surprisingly informative regarding the tastes of the families who once lived here, as well as the last time the home was updated. In this case, between the color pallet, wallpaper pattern, and style of fixtures, this room was likely last updated in the 1950s or early 1960s. A time capsule of sorts.

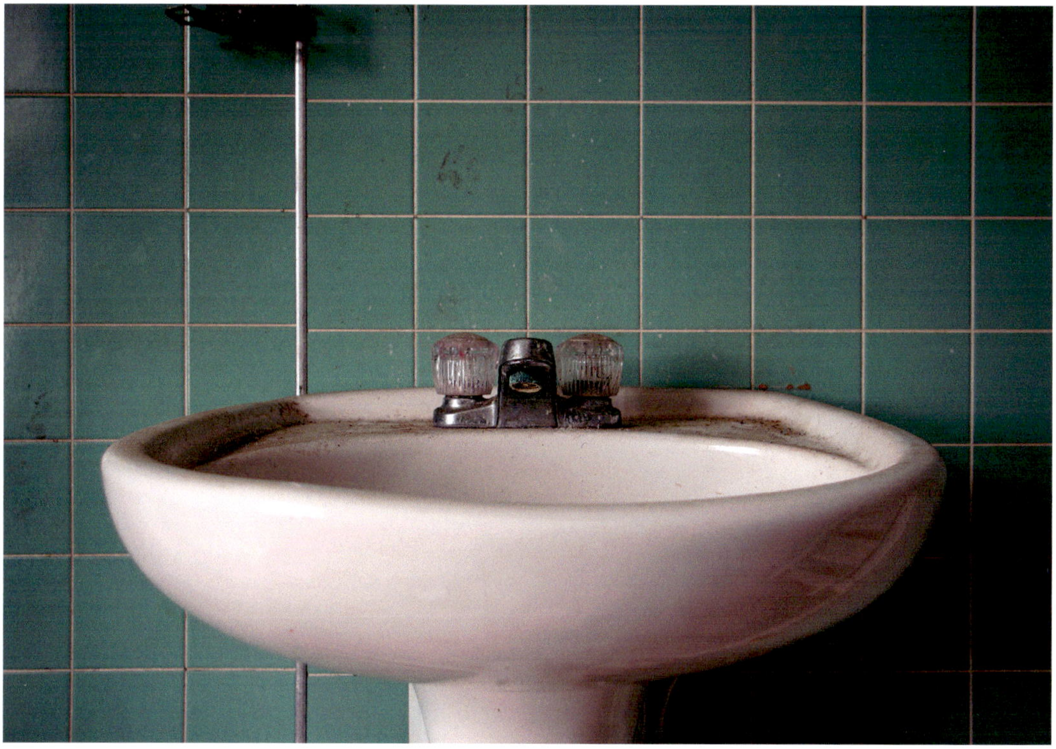

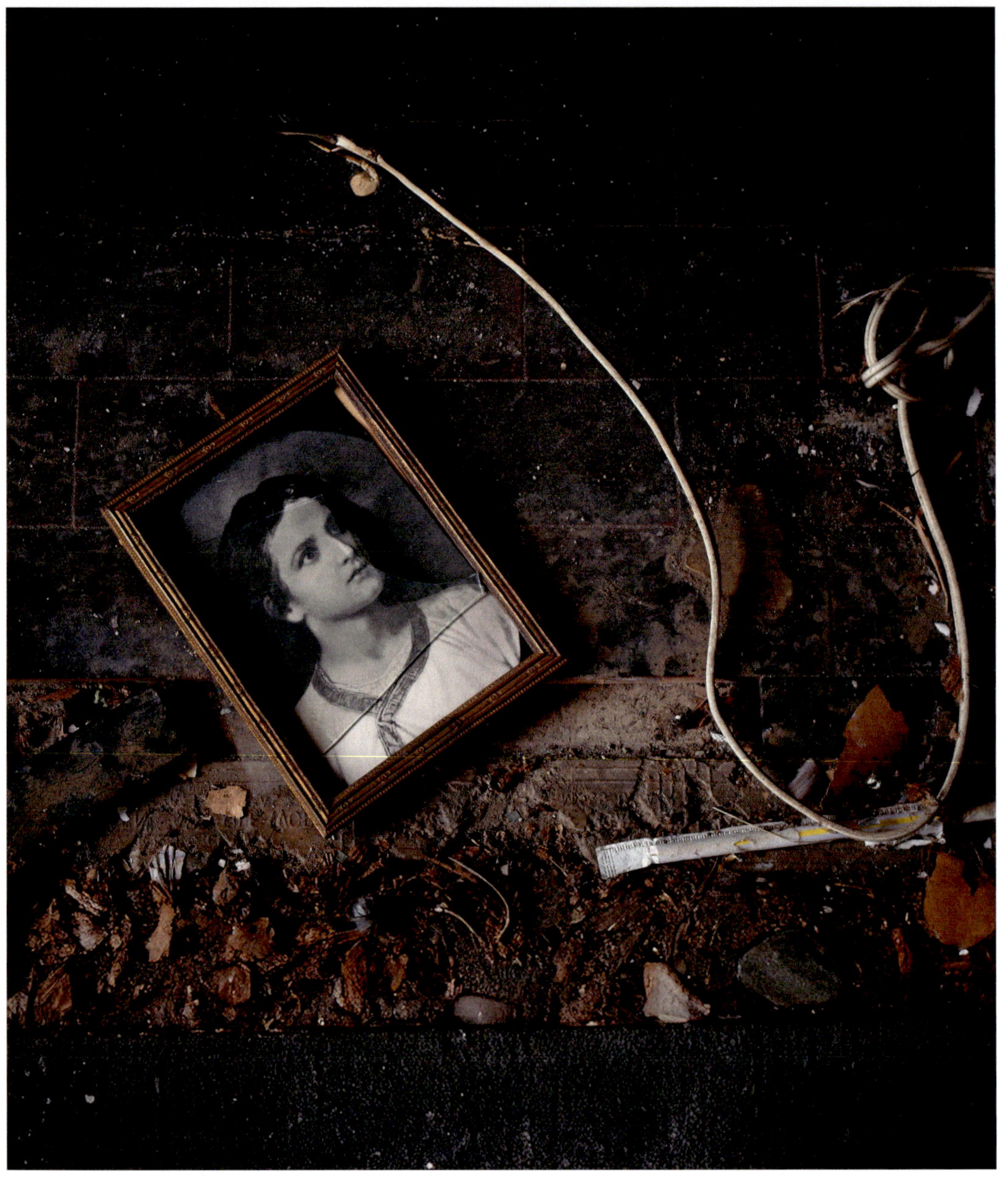

Scenes such as this are uniquely upsetting. A woman, once the subject of a cherished portrait, now lies shattered on the floor alongside garbage and debris.

2

THE CENACLE

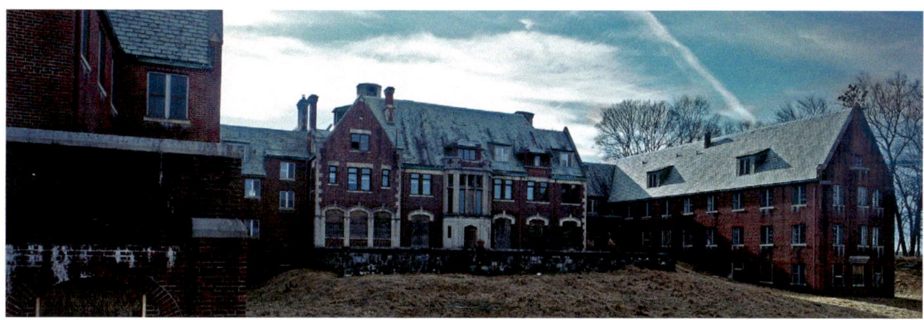

This grand convent began its life as a far smaller building, though small is relative in this case. The roots of this winged structure spread outward from the central mansion, which once stood alone on this wooded ridge, its name was Rose Hill. The original manor was constructed atop a rolling parcel of land in 1904, eventually becoming home to famous showman of the day Billy Rose, who bestowed upon it the name "Rose Hill."

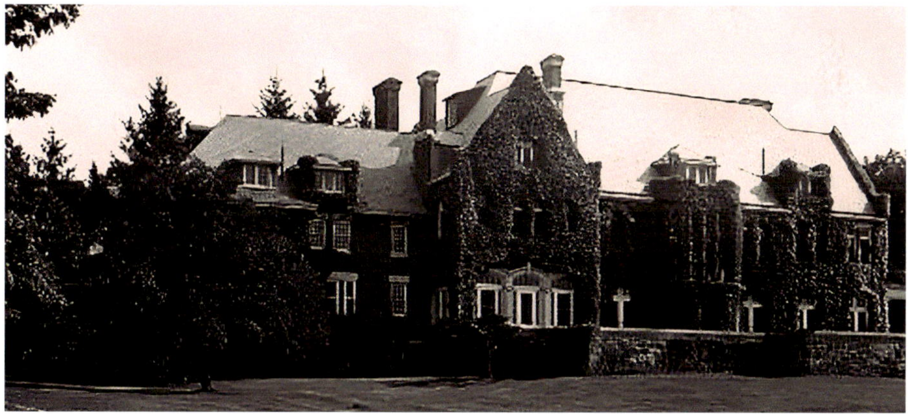

In 1956, a massive fire ravaged the estate, gutting a majority of the structure and decimating the personal effects of Billy Rose. When interviewed by a local paper after the ordeal, Billy plainly stated: "I lost a lot of things that can't be replaced with money." Some time thereafter, the property was sold off to The Convent of Our Lady of the Retreat in the Cenacle, who rehabilitated and expanded the initial mansion for use as a convent with a final size of some 70,000 square feet. Much of the additional space was utilized for classroom and dormitory-style living quarters. The most notable portion of the '50s expansion was the creation of a beautiful chapel which came to be a hallmark of the property. However, as we previously mentioned—everything is temporary. (*8mm Film Scan—Courtesy of the Library of Congress*)

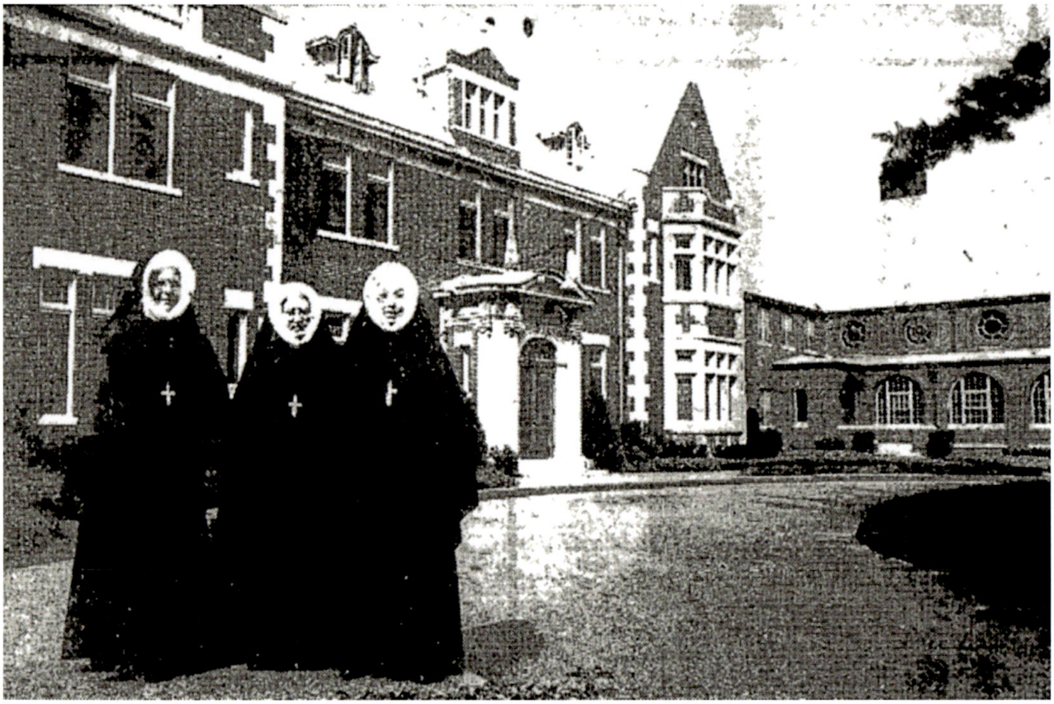

The convent eventually sold off the property as well, and it changed hands several times throughout the decades. Always, though, officially or not, the property retained the moniker of "The Cenacle." (*Digital scan of a newspaper article—Original source unknown*)

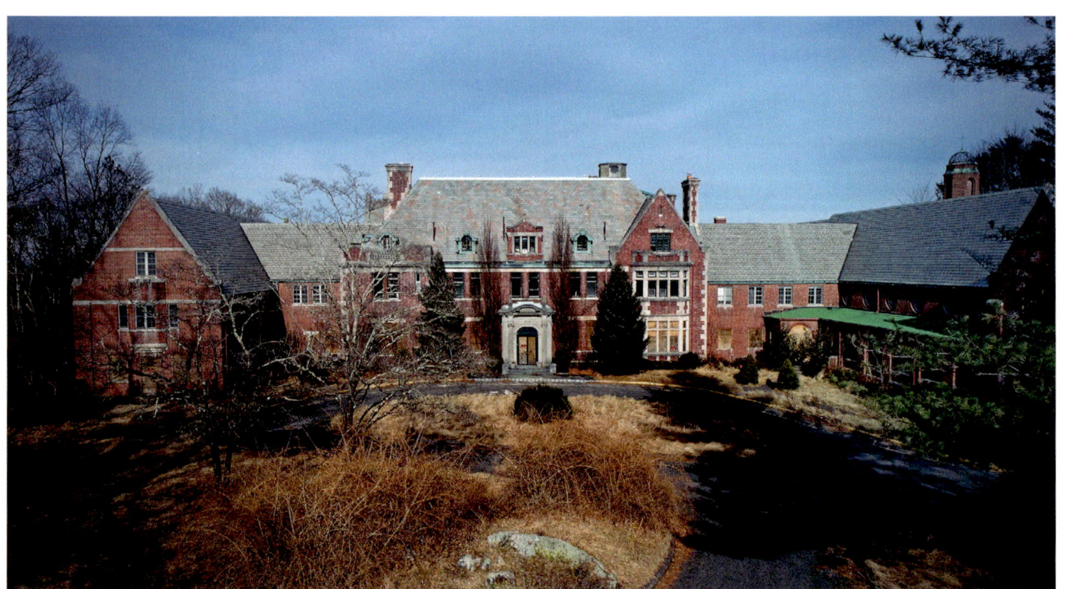

During a period of vacancy in the late 1970s, David Krebs, manager for the band Aerosmith, organized the rental of the entire building, with the hopes of utilizing it as a sanctuary away from the influence of drugs, so that they may compose with clear minds and bodies. This proved futile, however, as Steven Tyler comments upon in his autobiography *Does the Noise In My Head Bother You?*: "Drugs can be imported, David … we have our resources. Dealers deliver! Hiding us away in a three-hundred room former convent was a prescription for total lunacy."

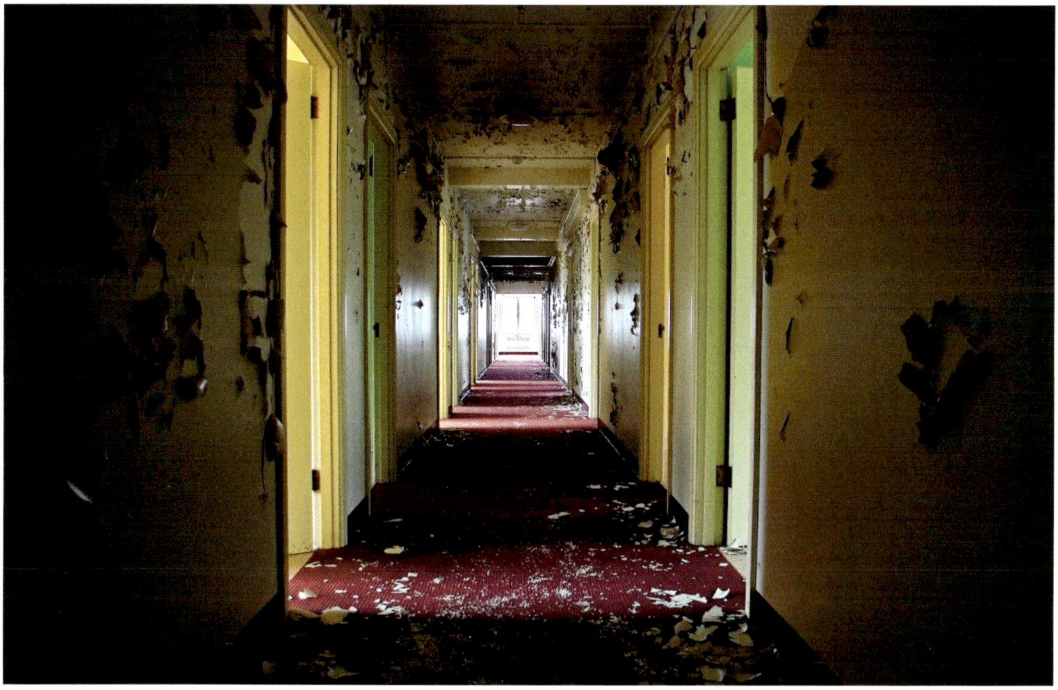

Above and below: Long dark halls reached out limbs of cold brick. In the air floated a strange aroma, an uncomfortably sweet mixture of carnations and a damp decomposition. Off of the central corridors were chambers as large as they were empty, and within them ornate mantles framed massive fireplaces. Caked in dust, long extinguished, and from which cold winter air flowed. The chill was biting and stung any exposed skin it caressed.

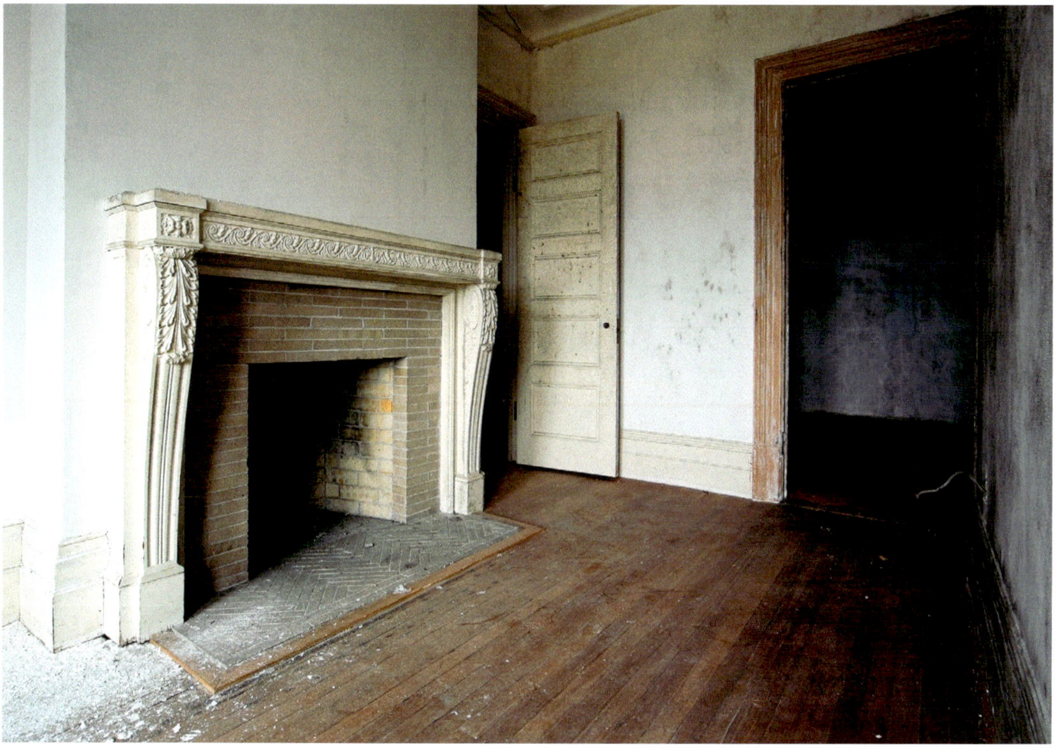

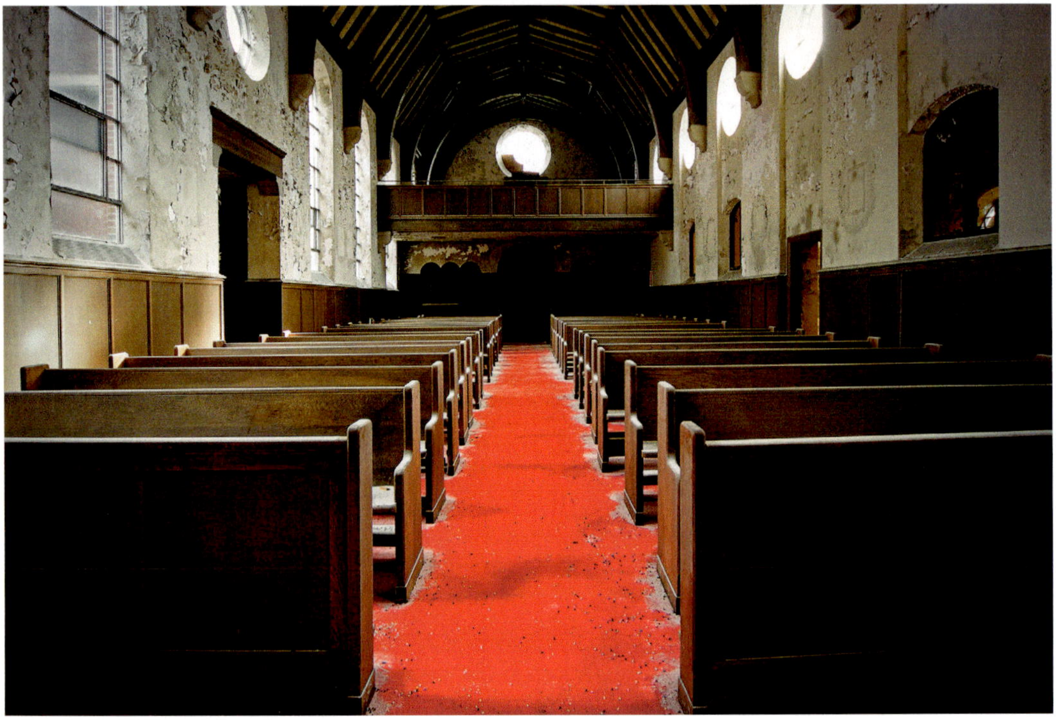

Down through more shadowed halls stood a singular point of light: the chapel. Once magnificent and proud, now as forsaken as the rest of the estate had come to be.

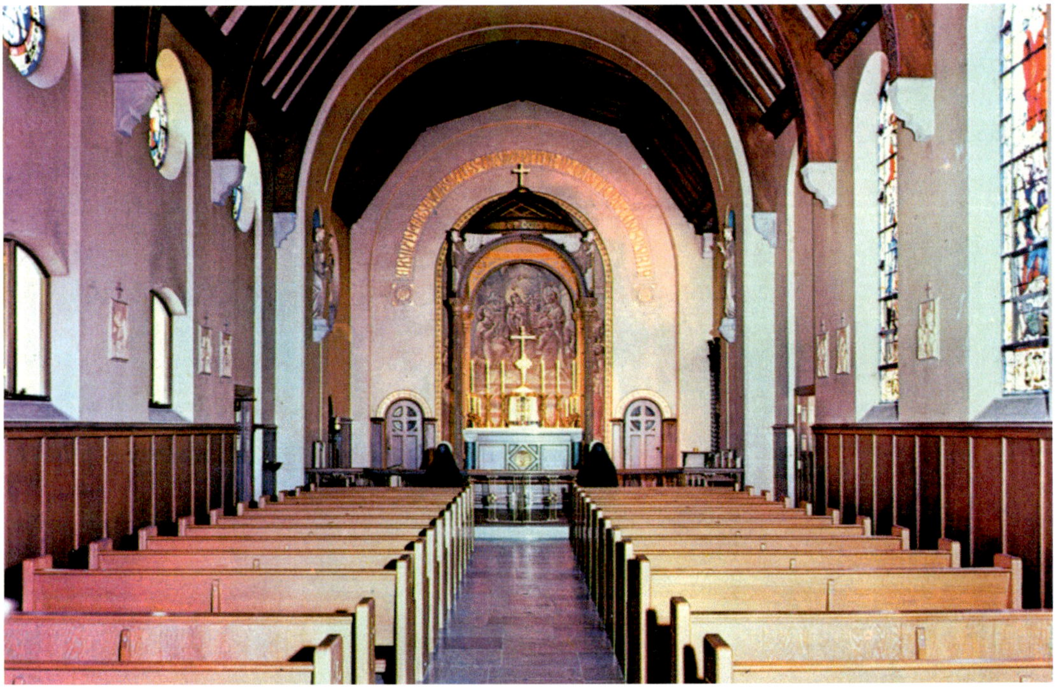

A reverse view of the previous image, as seen in a postcard from The Convent of Our Lady of the Retreat in the Cenacle. (*Digital scan of a postcard—Personal archive*)

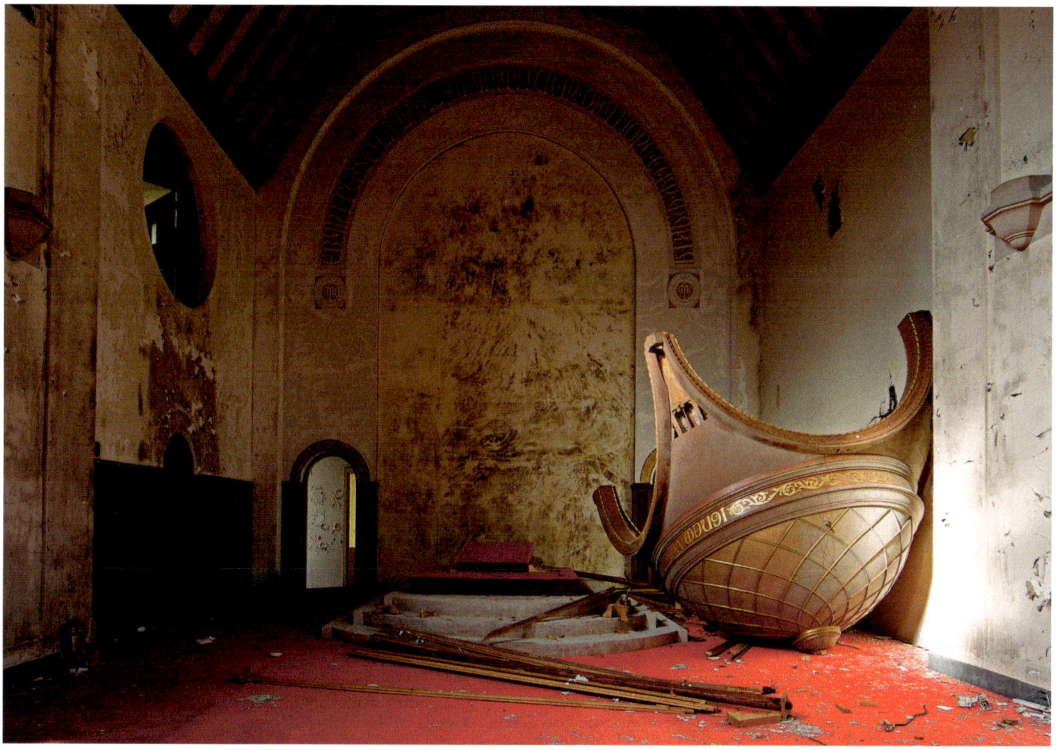

The chapel, a once sacred space now left in utter ruin.

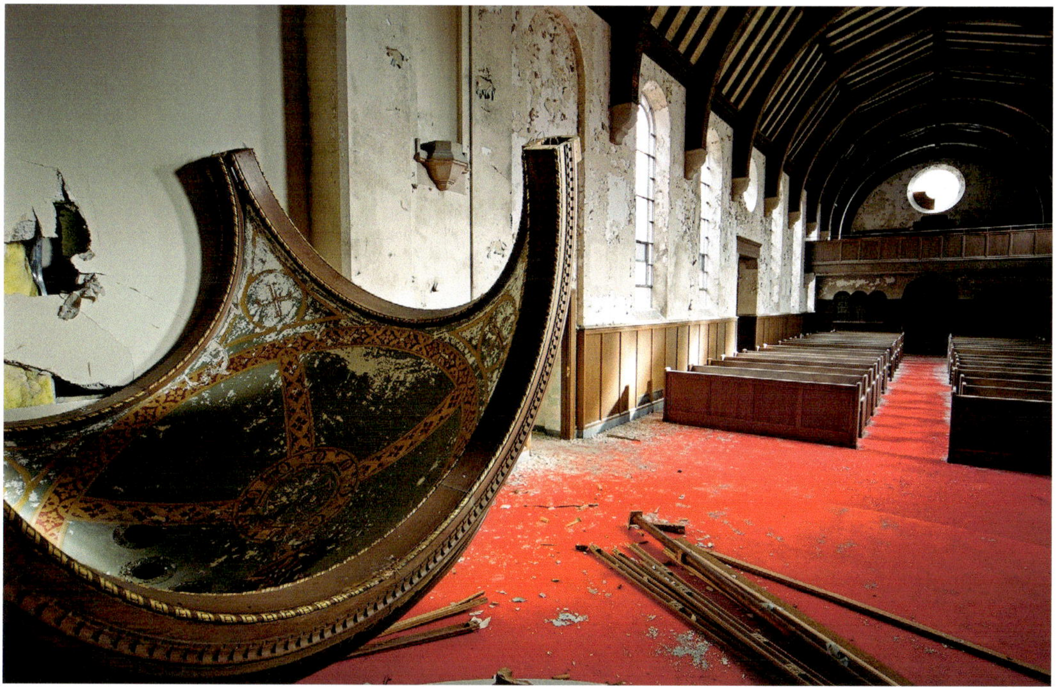

Looking outward from where the alter once stood, its ornate dome toppled and broken.

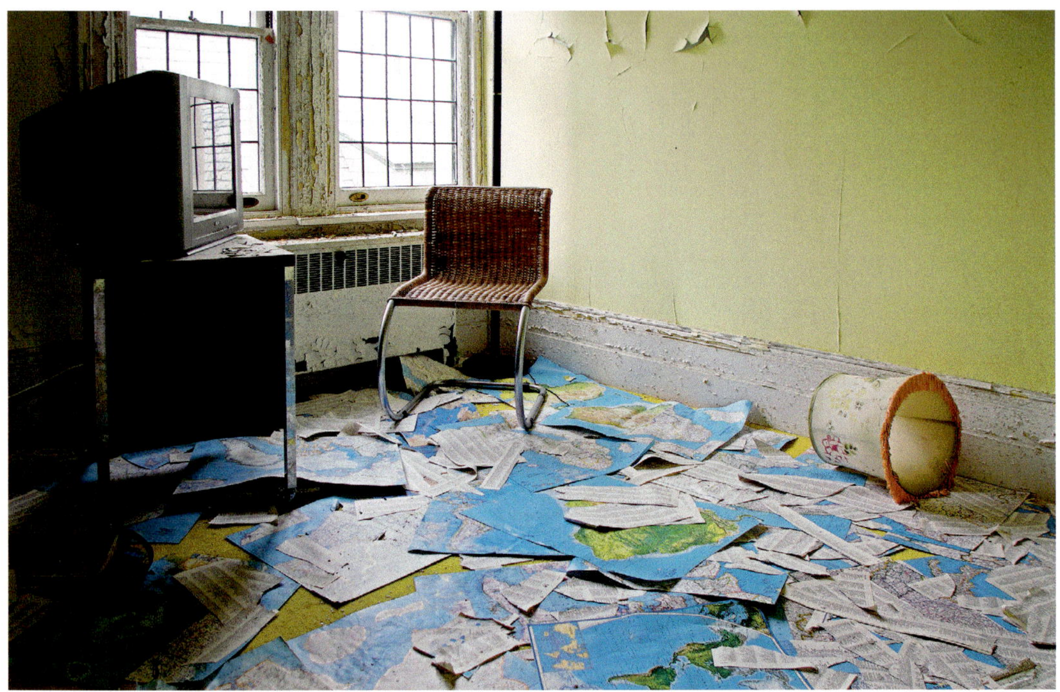

The last organization to call The Cenacle home was Our Lady of Mount Kisco, who operated the grounds as a retreat center. After they vacated the building in 2011, the grounds sat more or less without use.

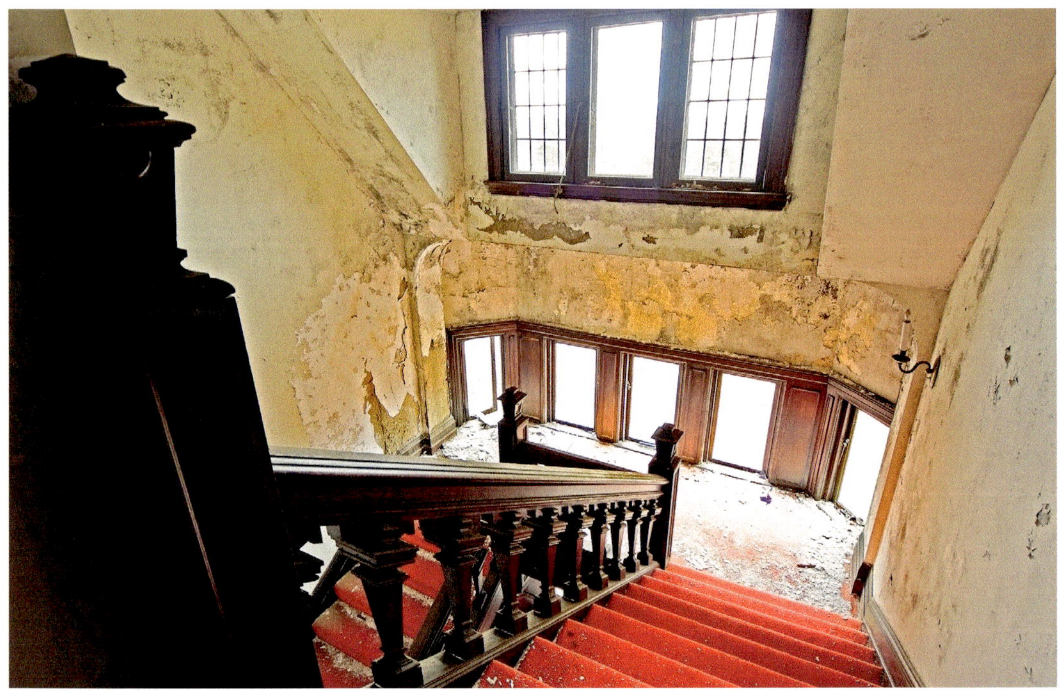

There were some grand redevelopment plans which would pop up from time to time, stirring up a bit of fanfare before disappearing into the void from which they came. All the while The Cenacle sat, its century of stories, memories, and lessons moldering away in the woods.

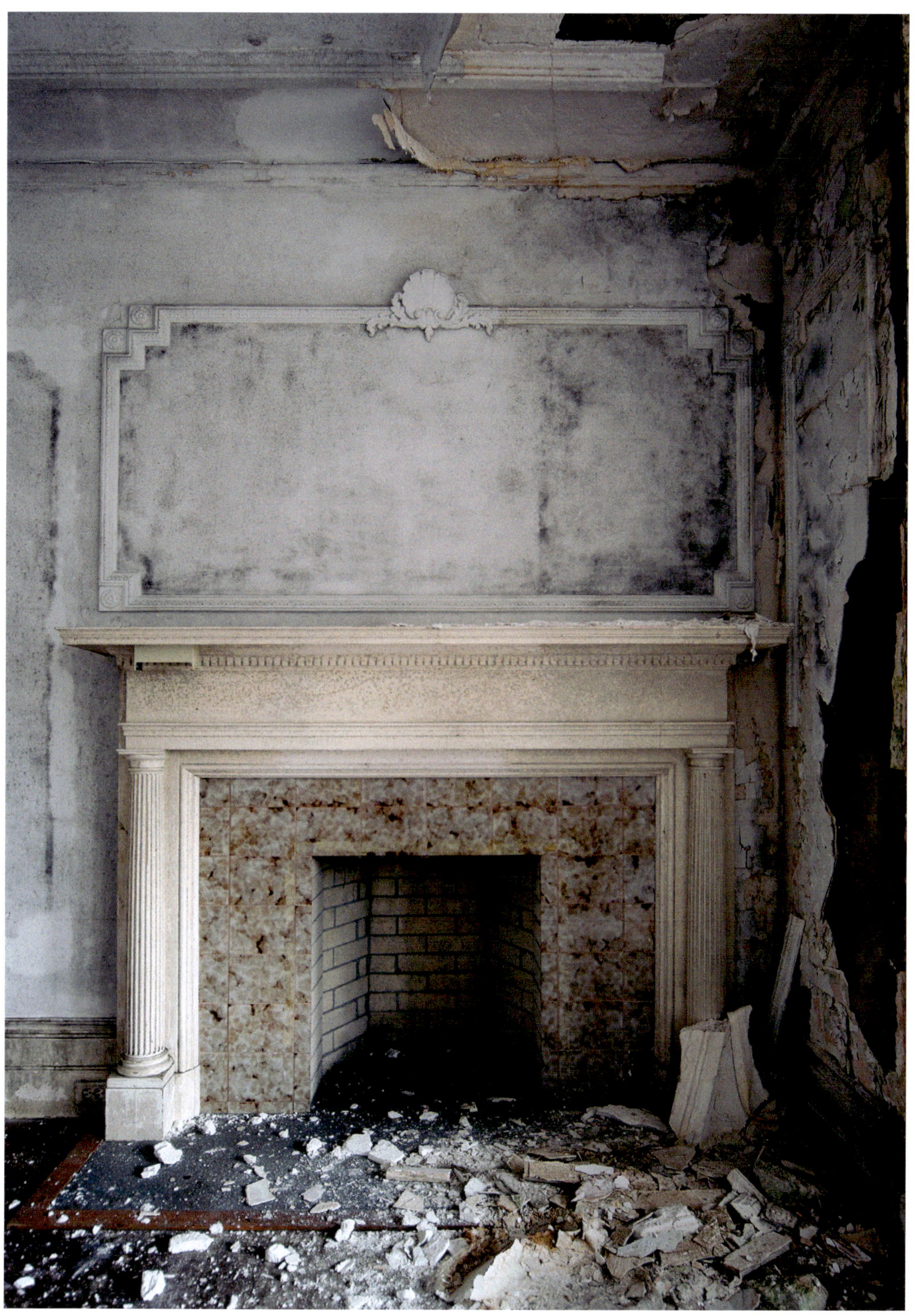

A beautifully appointed fireplace, crumbling away through the seasons. Its plaster turning to dust with every cycle of freezing and thawing.

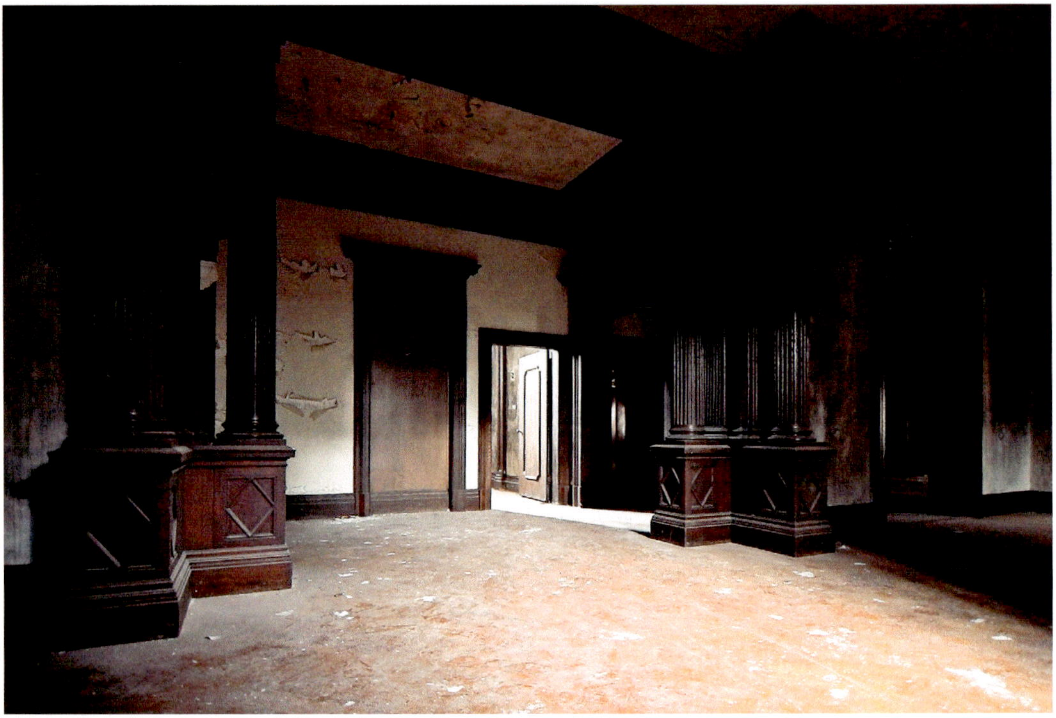

Above and below: Buildings grow wise with age, and they are not selfish with the knowledge. An old building will freely impart what it has learned to whoever may care enough to pay listen. It is a mutual exchange, though, where one may glean knowledge, and the building may garner respect. And with this respect may come safety. Safety from neglect, from being forgotten, and hopefully from being lost altogether.

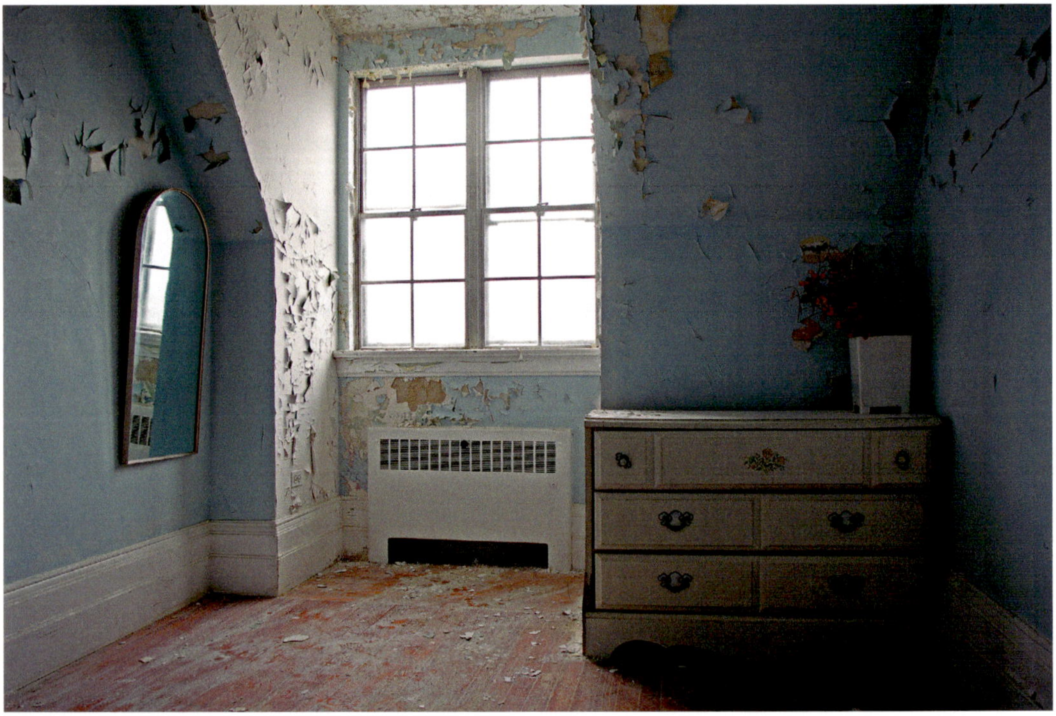

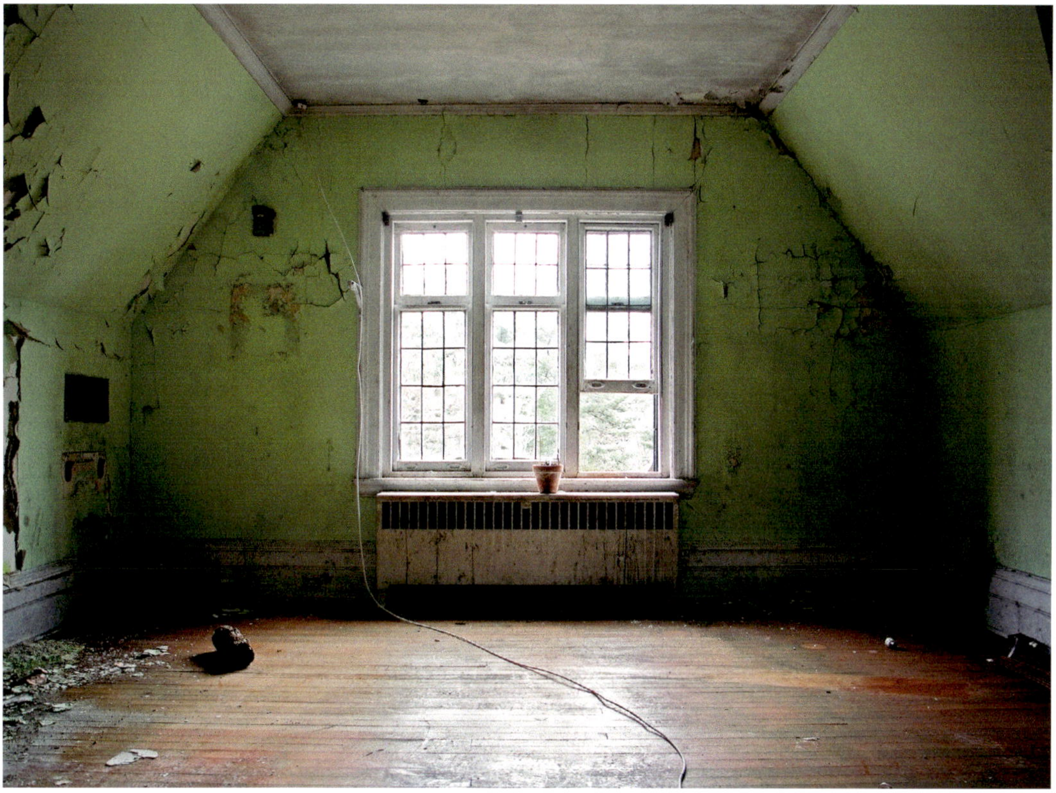

Unfortunately, any stories or lessons which The Cenacle had to share were lost.

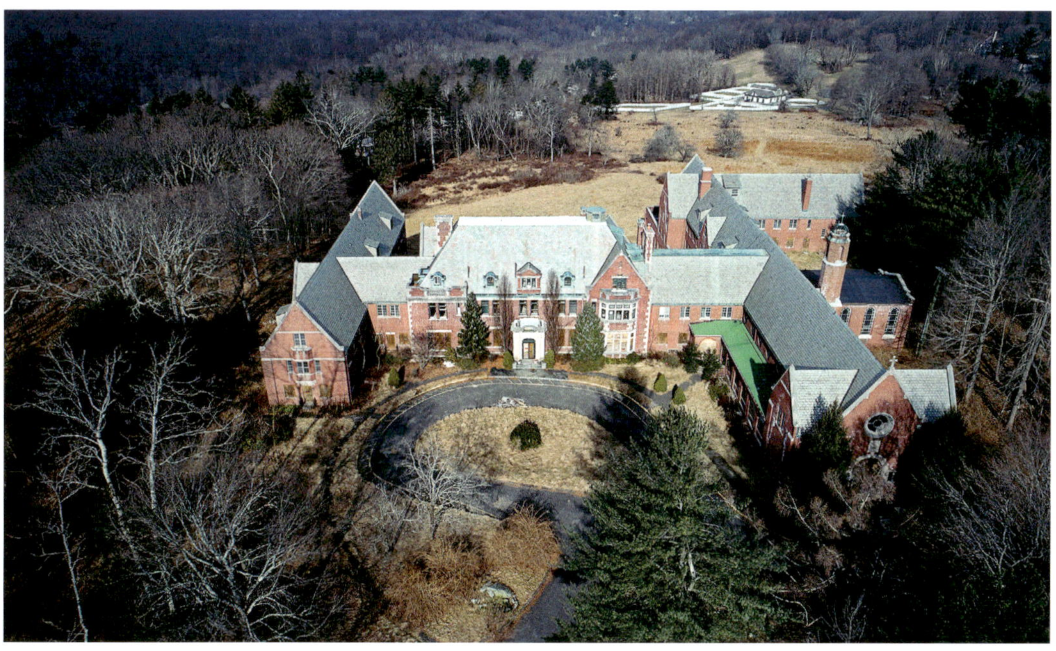

In the spring of 2019, the entirety of the property was quickly and unceremoniously leveled to make way for a proposed housing development that will one day sprawl across the hilltop.

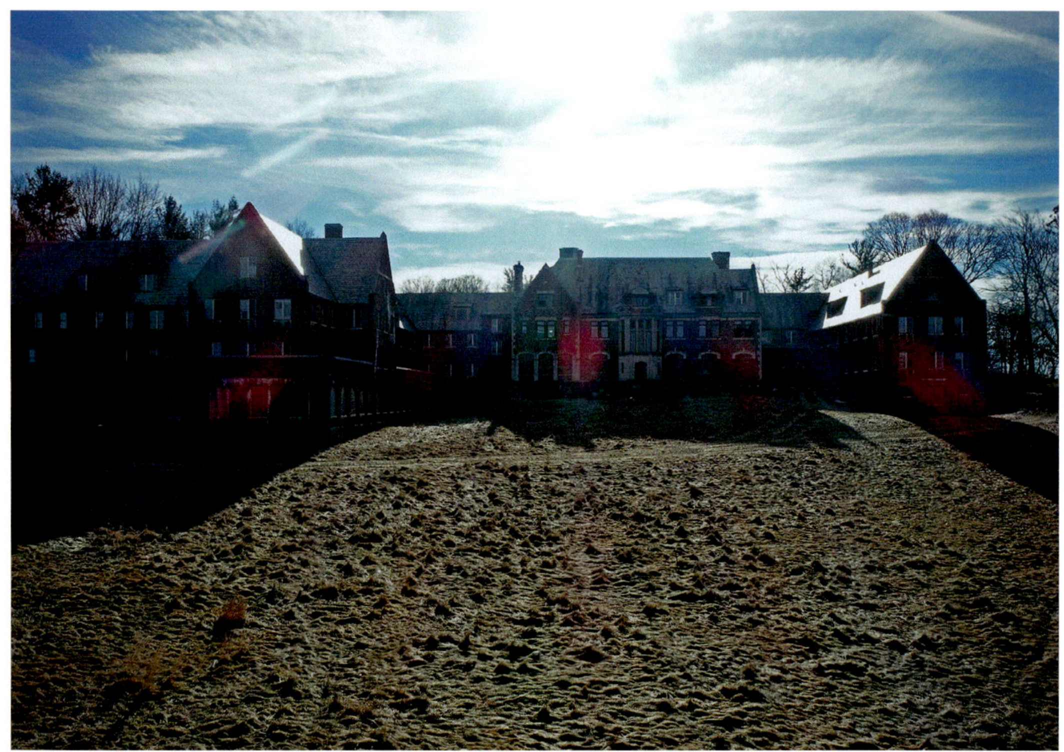

The Cenacle of Mount Kisco, New York, is a place that will forever exist as a reminder to how dramatically time can shape a place and, perhaps more significantly, just how fleeting it all is.

3

LITTLE FLOWER ORPHANAGE

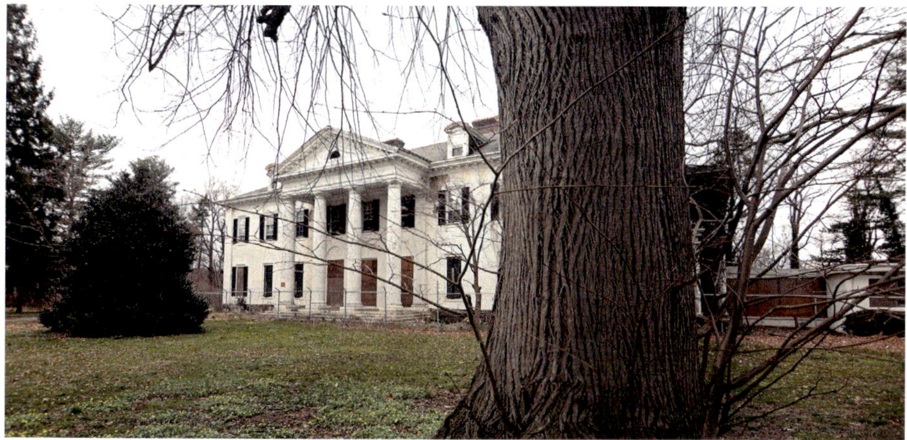

Above and below: To see this weathered husk, with its stained and crumbling halls and rooms, as anything but the ruin before you can be difficult to envision. It is truth, though; nearly every ominous-looking abandoned hose was at one point a warm and inviting home. The duality between past and present is haunting at times, as the past lingers, almost painfully, draped along decayed curtains and along rotten ceiling beams. In that strange juxtaposition of illustrious past and shameful present is where we find the Woodburne Mansion—or, as it would later be known, The Little Flower Orphanage.

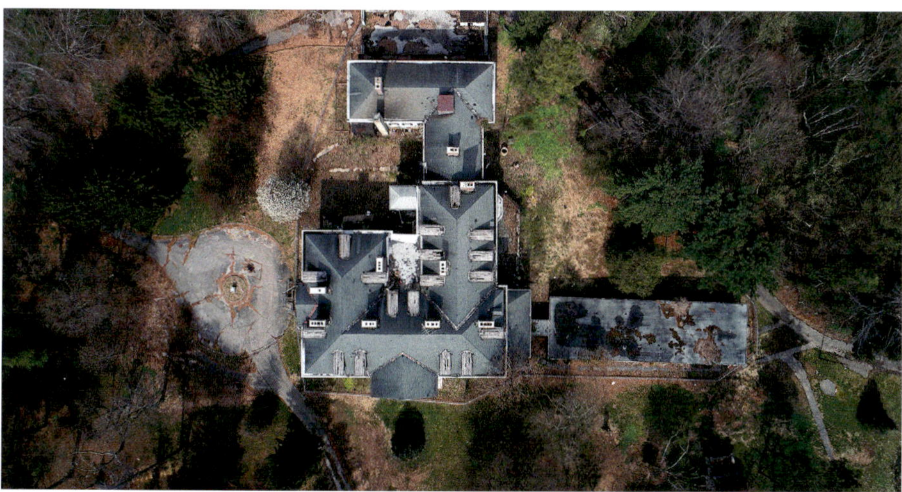

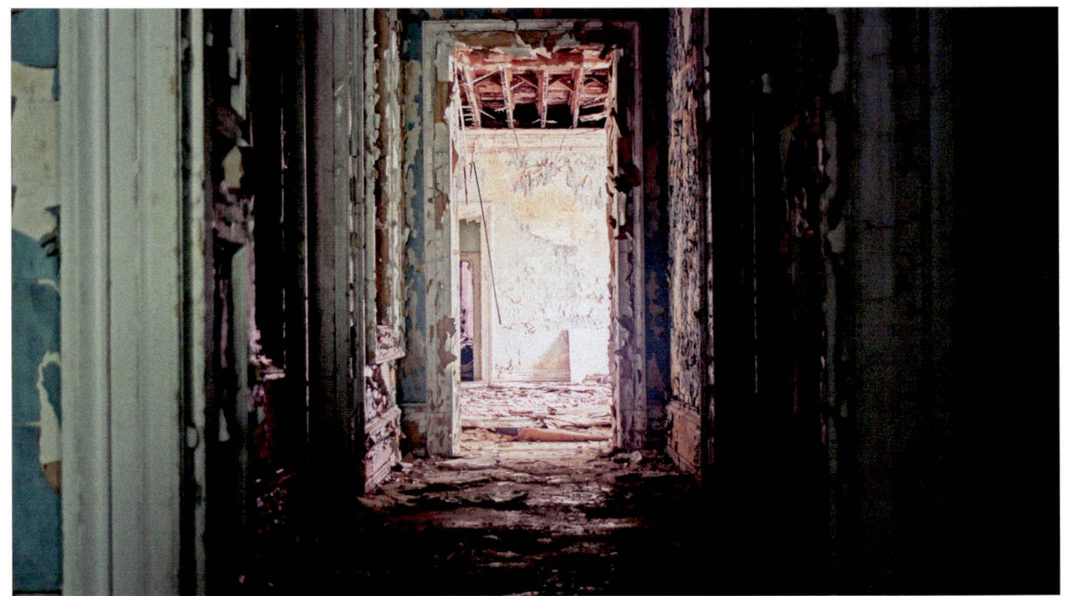

Above and below: Paint hangs loosely along the walls of cracked plaster before you. Walls which frailly form the chambers and corridors of this weathered estate. Long before you stood here, this building was bright and alive. It molders now, stretching out into shadows and ruin. A flake of dust flitters to the floor, disturbed by your presence. It flashes for a second in the sunlight passing through a fogged windowpane, before being lost. The dust spoke as it fell, as do the walls, pillars, and hand-carved trim above your head. They all speak at once, the disordered words of a building standing long beyond its life. They tell you of life, of death, and of how nothing is truly yours. How nothing can ever be owned, only borrowed. Finally, the tumultuous choir of voices reduces to a singular phrase. A sharply pointed message reciting over and over; the voice of time itself: "What's yours is mine."

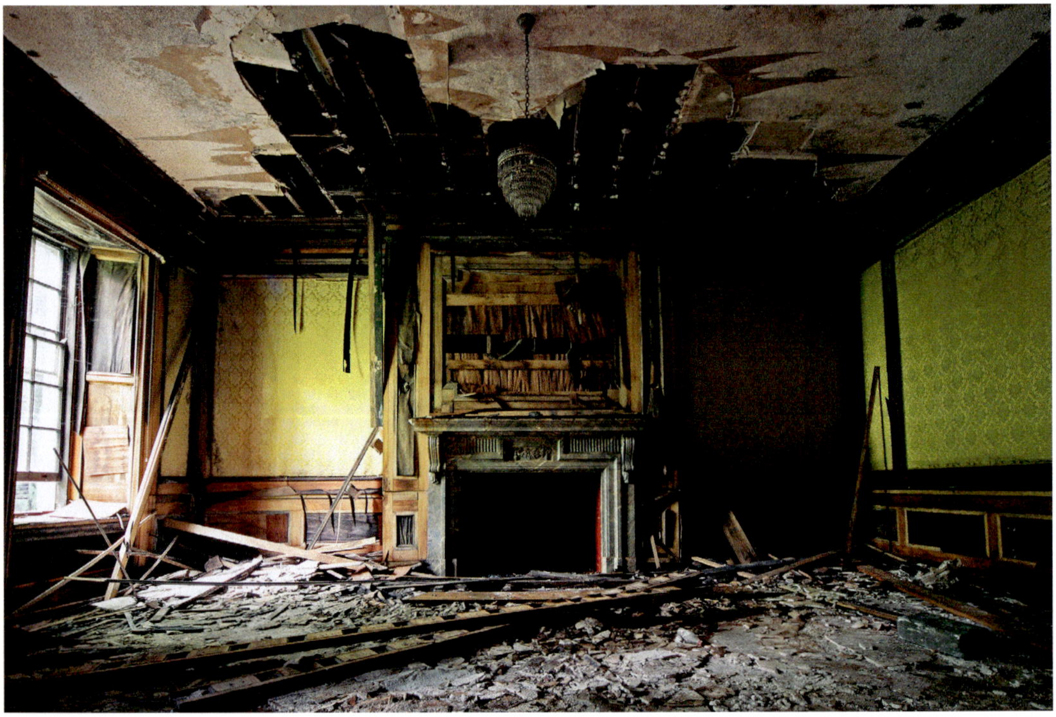

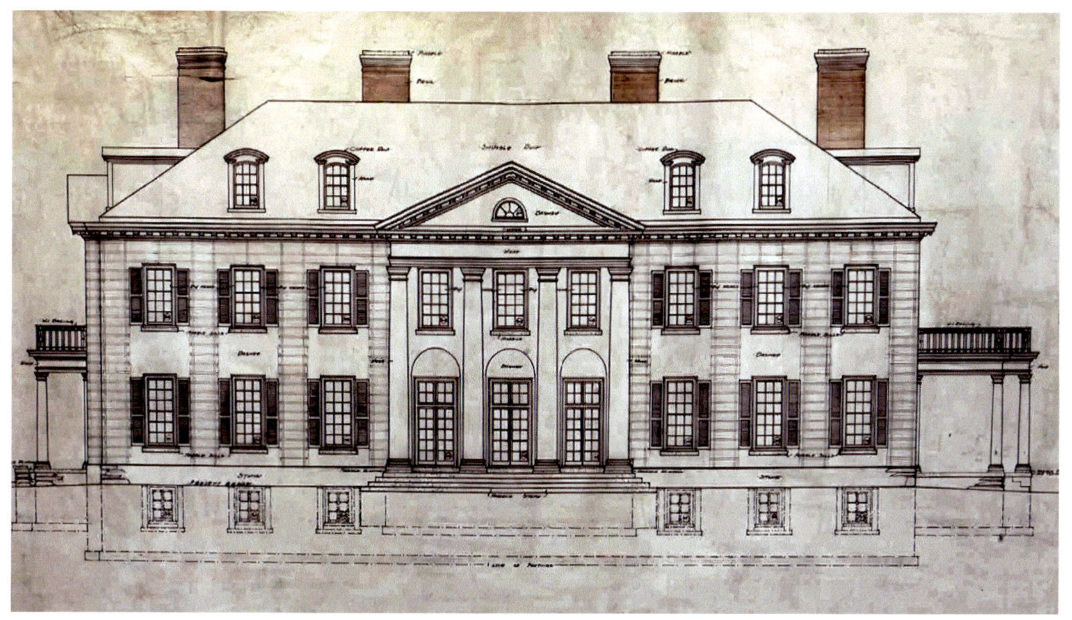

Construction of Woodburne was completed in 1906, a grand fifty-five-room Greek Revival mansion tasked by Edgar Thomas Scott to architect Horace Trumbauer. It served as a beautiful home, situated on a wooded bluff over Darby Creek in Darby, Pennsylvania. In the 1930s, the home was sold to the Sisters of the Divine Redeemer, who converted the home into an orphanage of high reputation called the Little Flower Orphanage. (*Building plans for Woodburne—Original source unknown*)

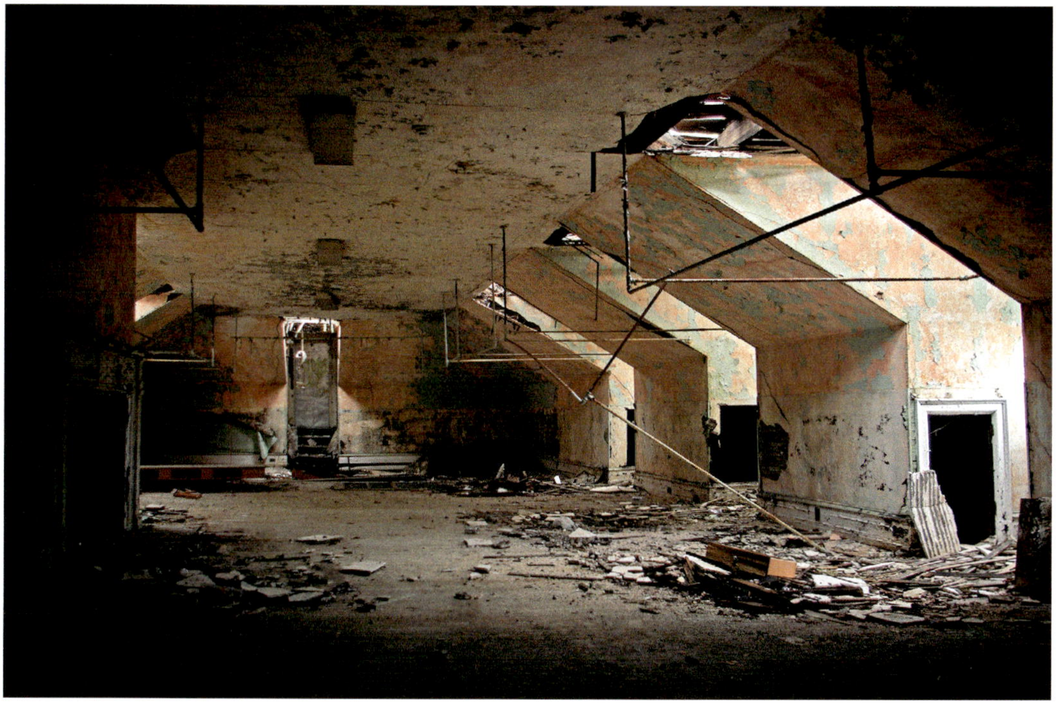

An upstairs space in what was essentially the attic of the Little Flower Orphanage. This large area would have been lined with beds during the orphanage days, serving as a communal bedroom for the children.

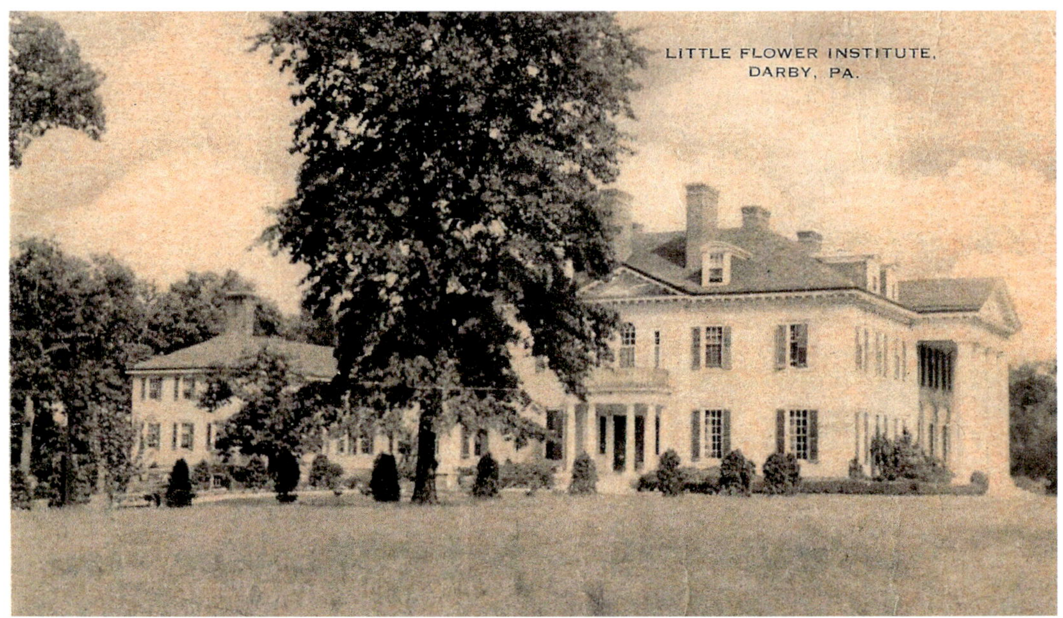

The *Chester Times* from May 31, 1956, ran a praising story about the facility and the hard work of the nuns who had devoted themselves to the children they were charged with: "Snuggled away in a spacious home on a hilltop overlooking the Darby Valley are 36 girls ranging in age from 4 to 15, happy and content. In some cases they are orphans. In others, they are children not wanted by their parents. And other children whose parents simply cannot afford to care for them. But here at Little Flower Institute on Springfield rd., they have found a home and loving care."

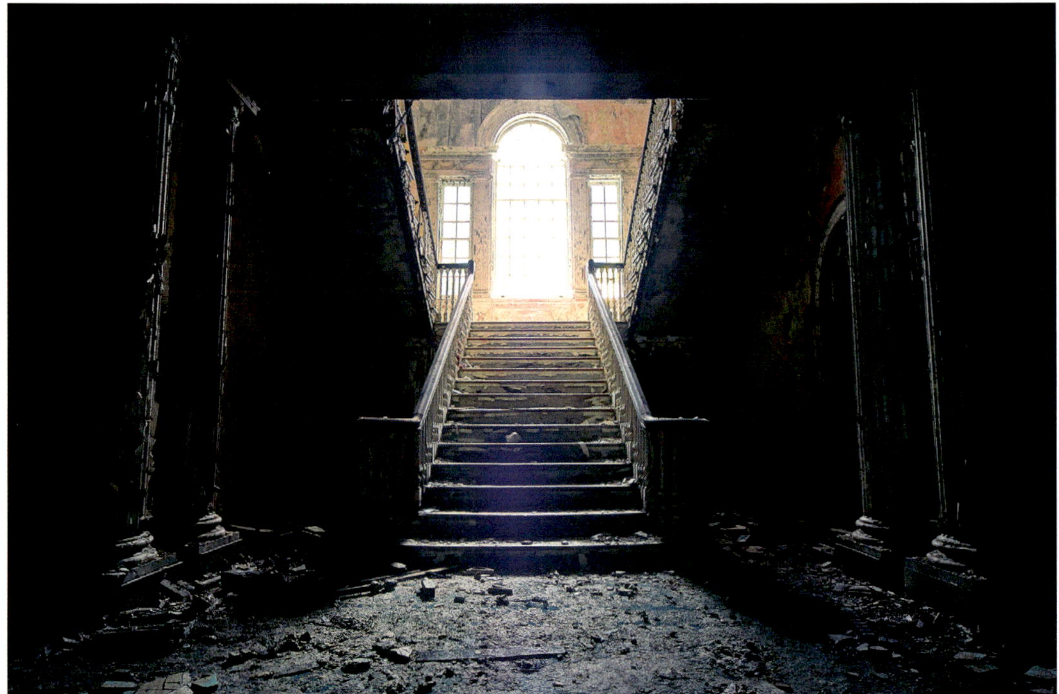

The crumbling master staircase of Woodburne, its broken heart.

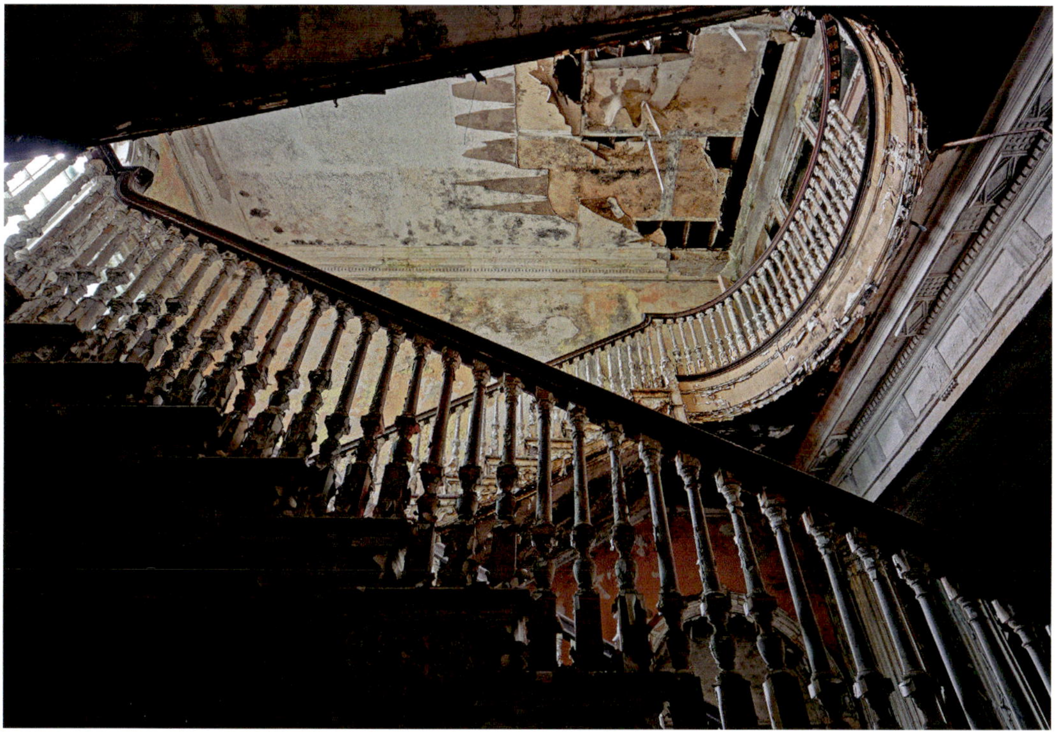

The scope and space of the master staircase is difficult to convey, both in written words or photograph.

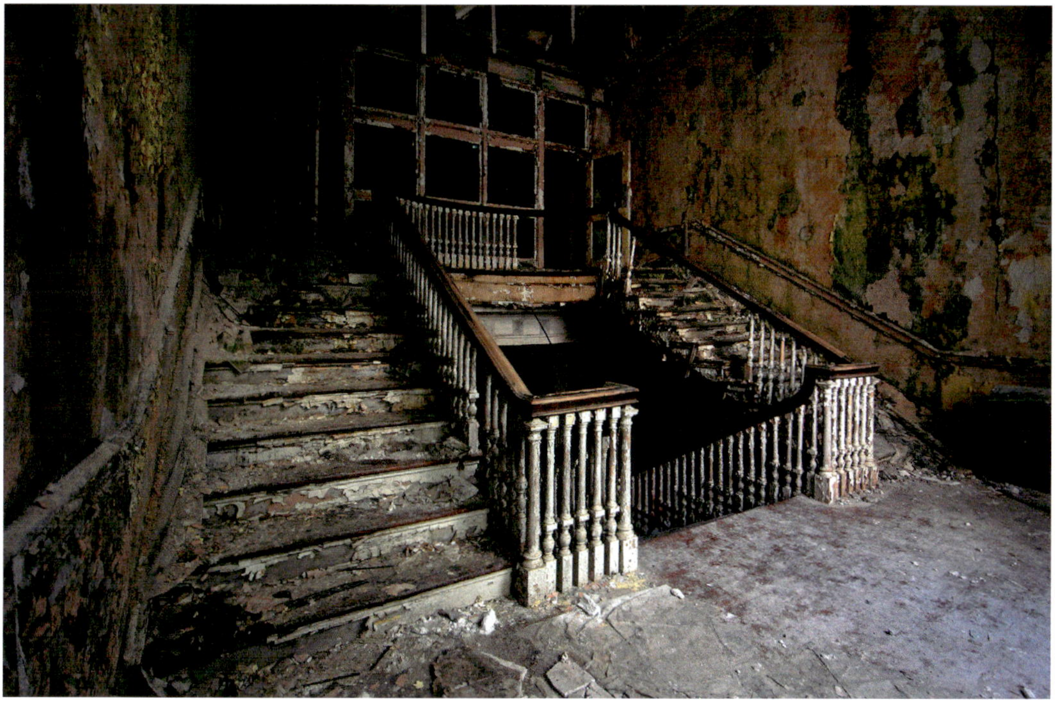

These stairs were not simply crafted to serve as a way to access the upper floors, they were fully intended to serve as a showpiece of the manor as well as the craftsmen who created it.

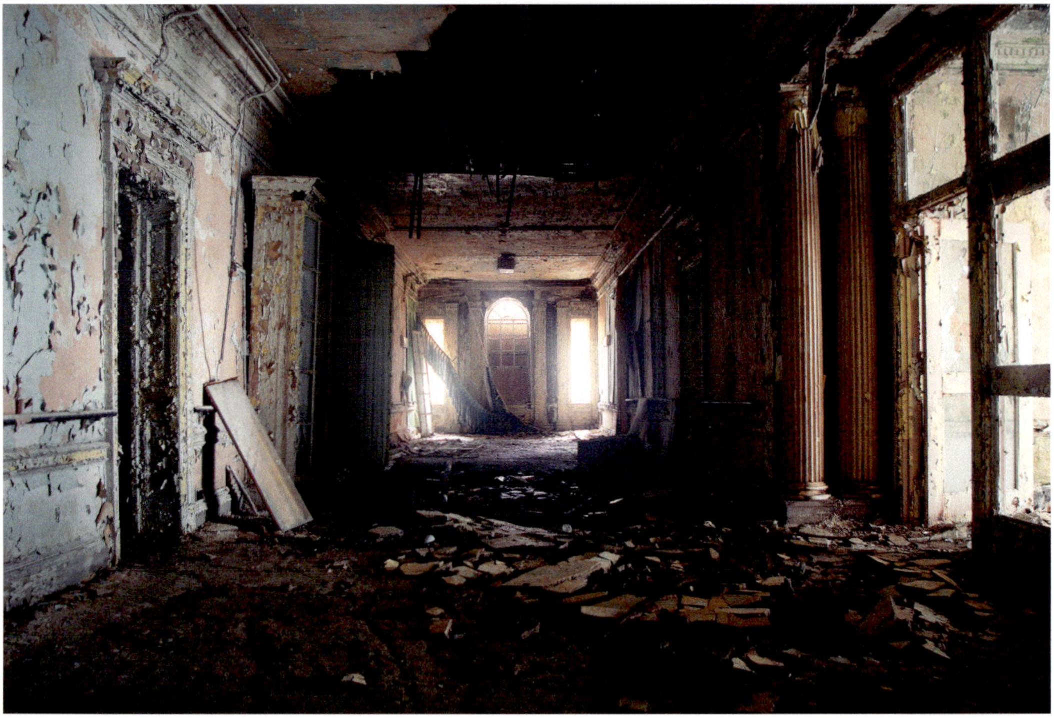

Even in utter decay, the elegance of Woodburne shines through.

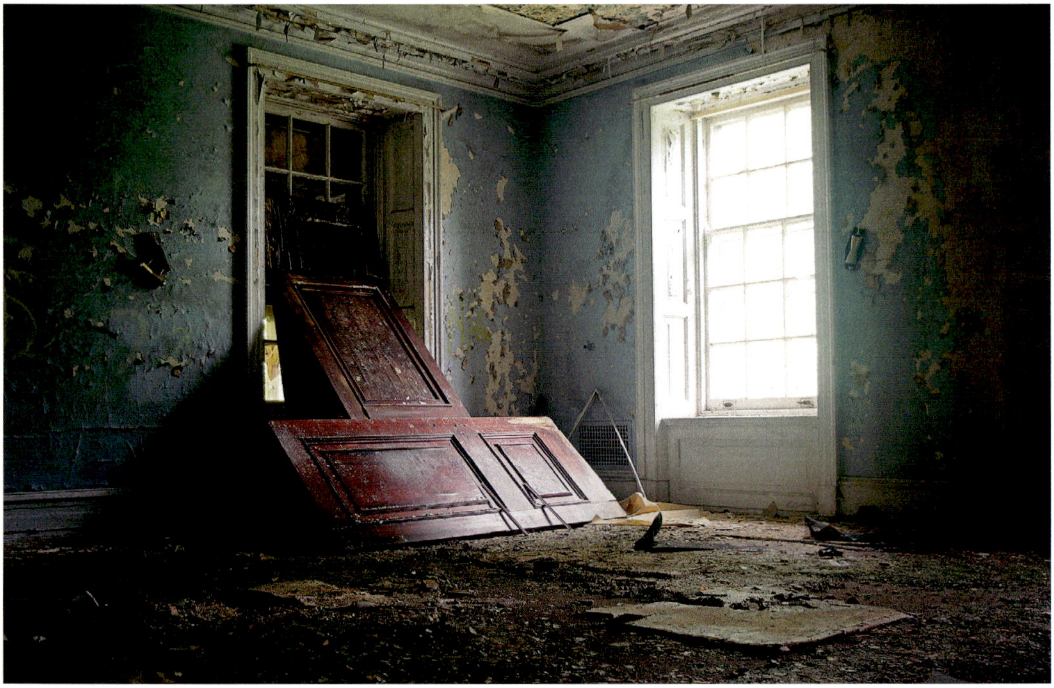

Old doors lay against boarded windows. Scenes like this do well to illustrate the dramatic fall from grace.

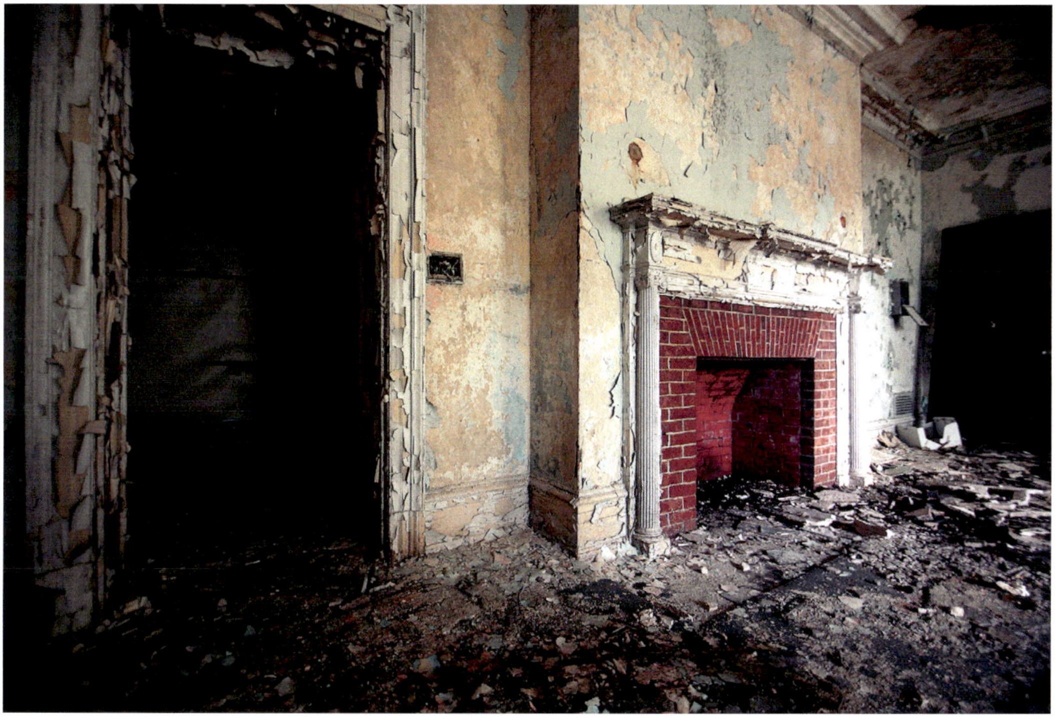

An upper-floor fireplace, long extinguished. One wonders what types of gatherings once took place around it during better times.

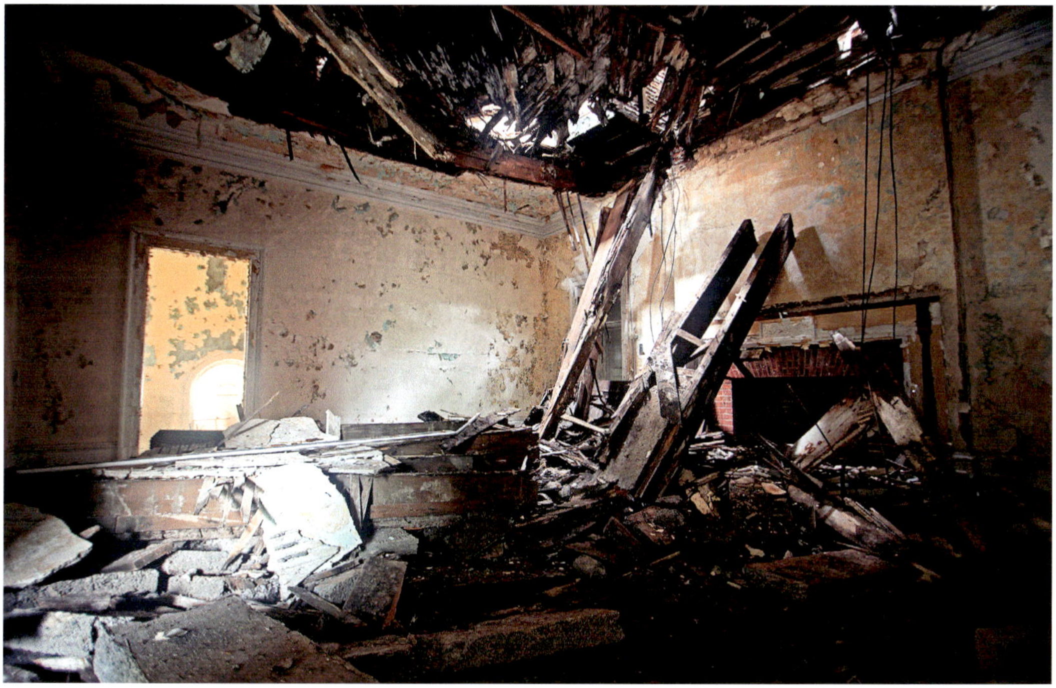

Upstairs, some portions of the roof have given up entirely, collapsing in creating weak points in the already fragile structure.

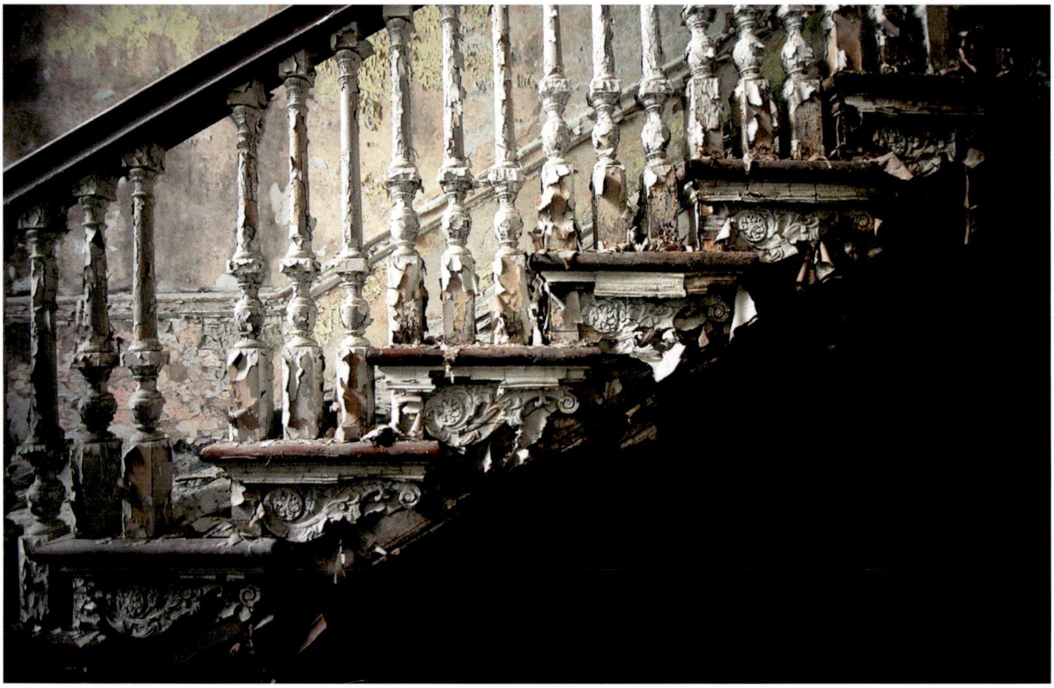

Detail of the staircase side; care and skill were evident everywhere you gazed.

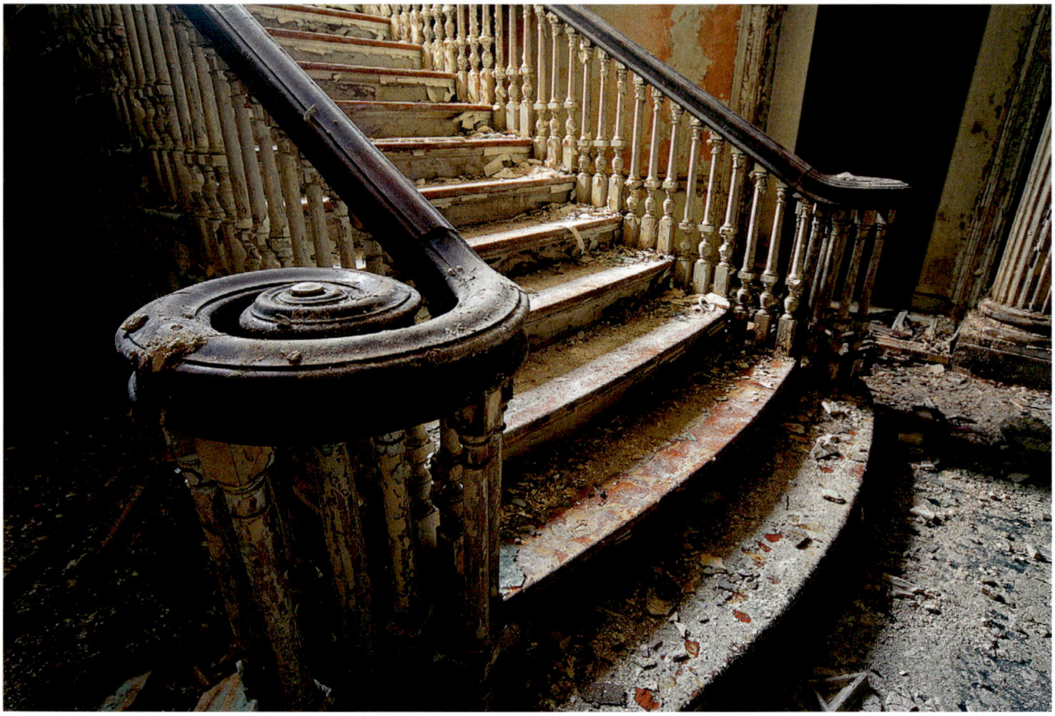

The handrail at the base of the master stair. It is strange how such a simple element of a house can become so deeply personal when you reflect upon what it is seen and who may have run their hands upon it.

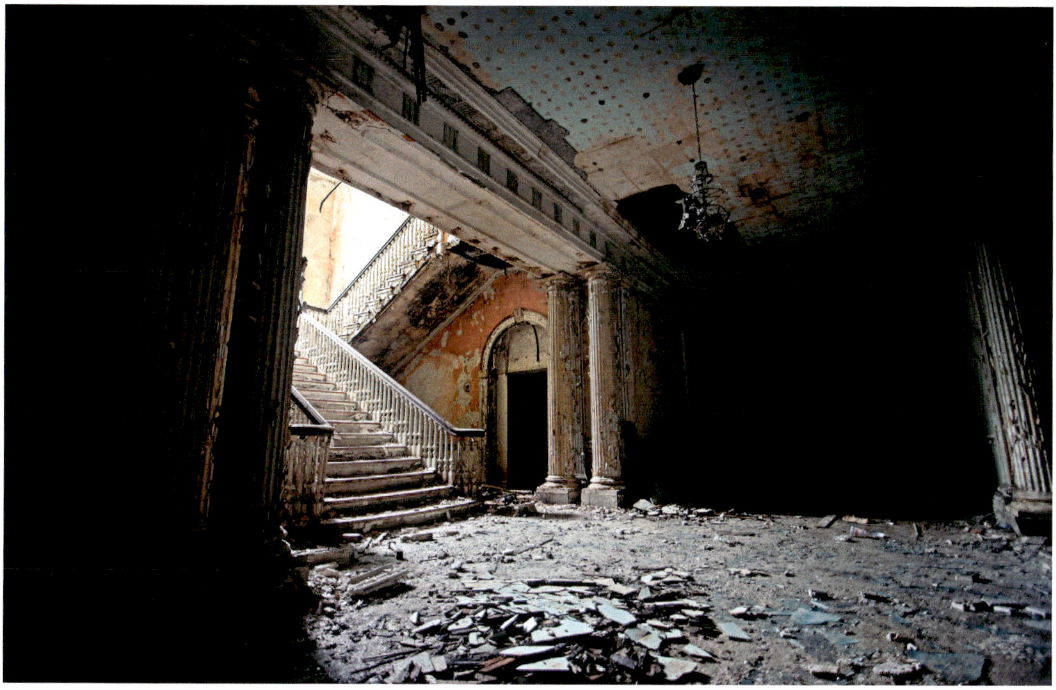

In time, the orphanage transitioned to an assisted living facility, and it was eventually shuttered for good in 2005 when a much larger, modern facility was completed on the property in front of Woodburne.

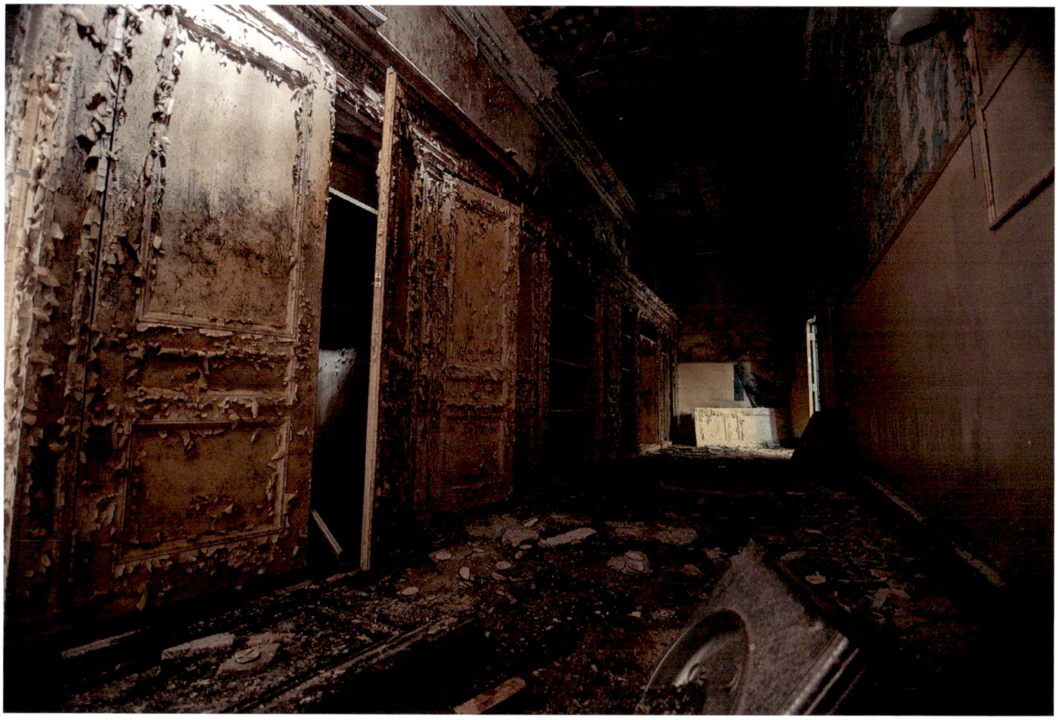

In the years since abandonment, various attempts have been made to preserve, or at the very least prolong the life of the old mansion, with few plans gaining much traction.

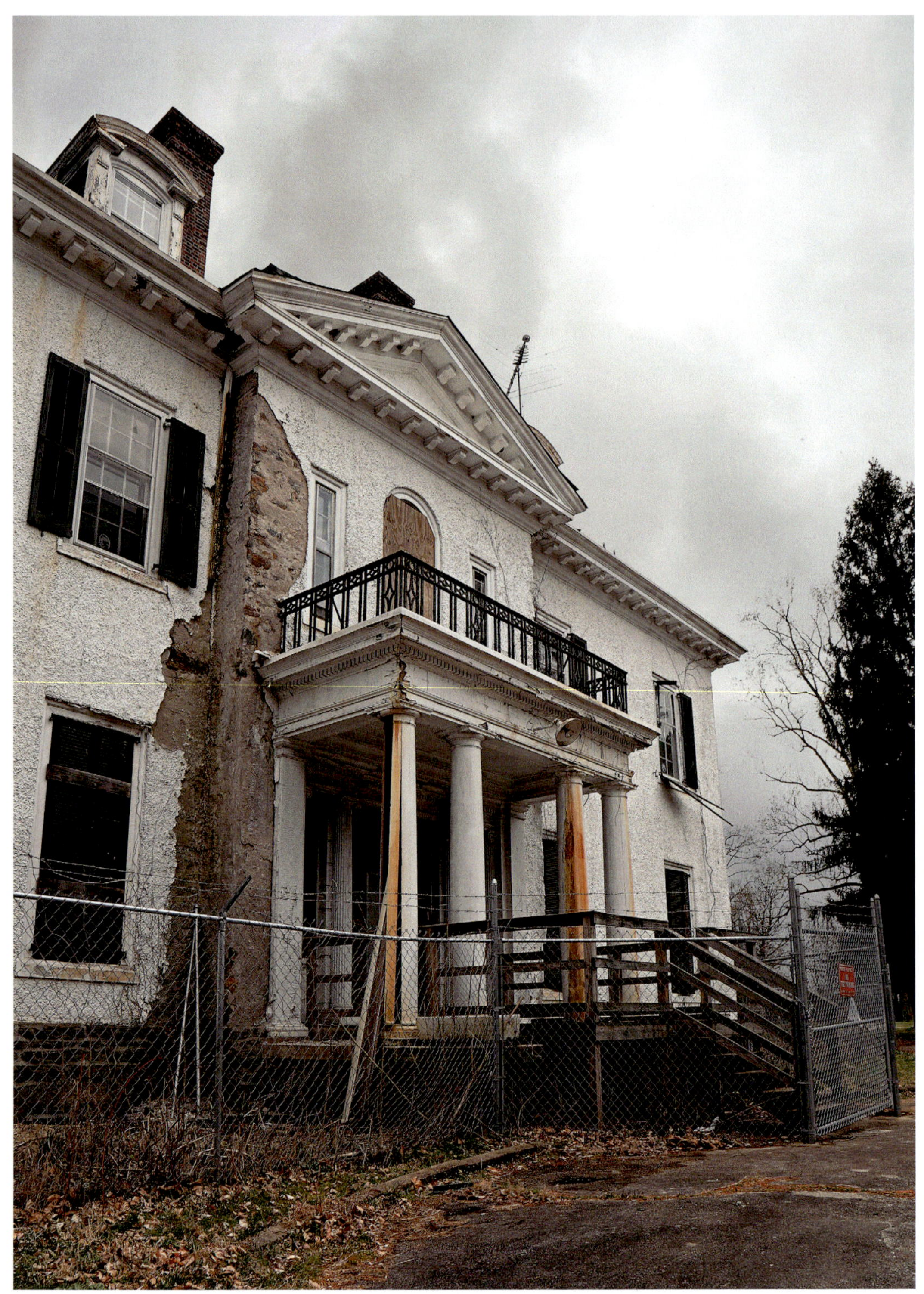

Perhaps there is still hope for Woodburne. Maybe this is simply a dark chapter in an otherwise unfinished story, one with an incredible rise from ruin. That, or these ever-weakening walls, will finally surrender completely to the neglect they have been forced to endure. Time will tell.

4

REFLECTIVE SILENCE

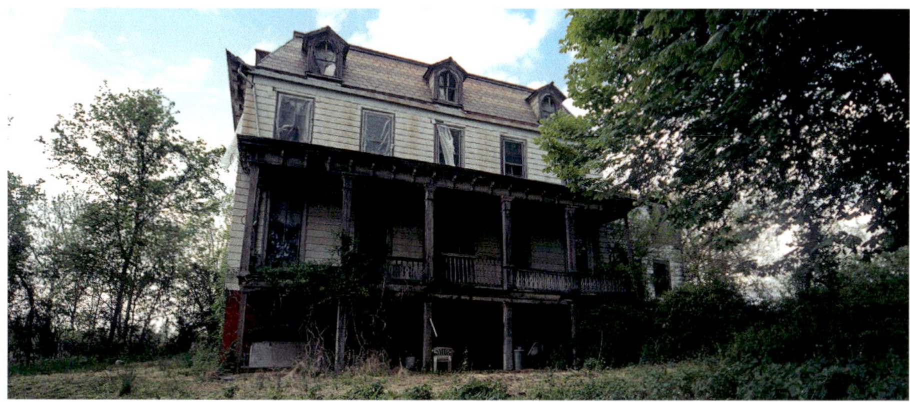

Above: At what point does a house become a home? Is it simply when we familiarize ourselves with it? Perhaps, but we feel it's more profound than that.

Below: We like to think the answer is this: A house becomes a home when we entrust it with enough memories that it knows us as well as we know it.

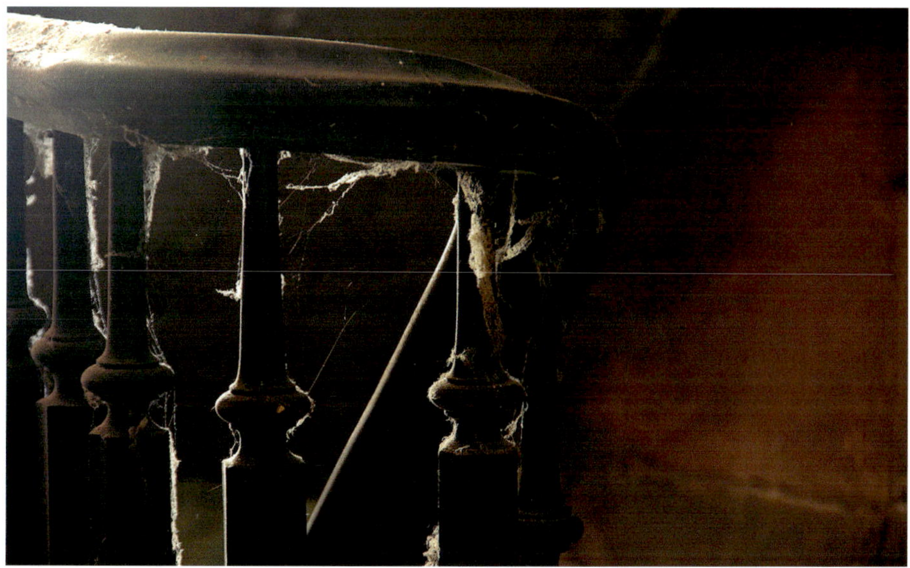

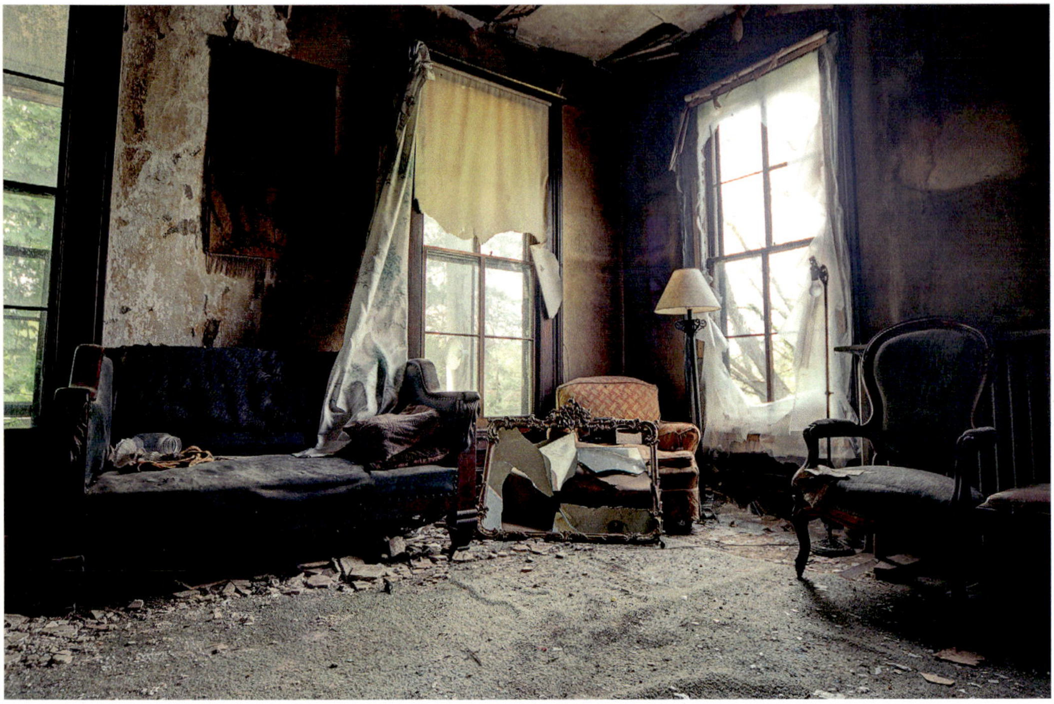

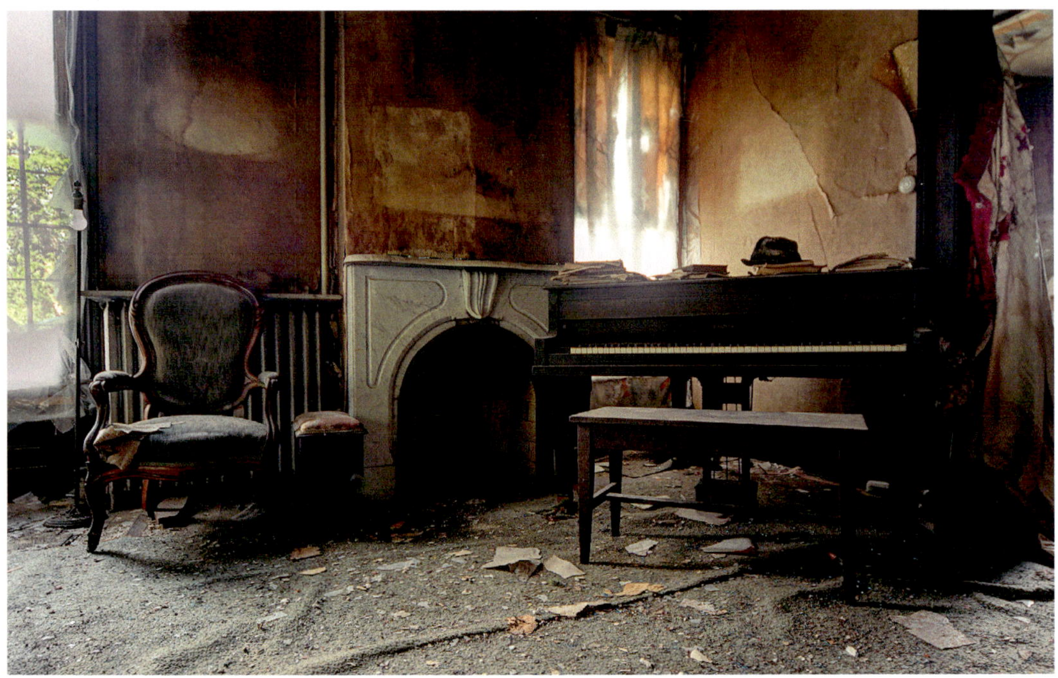

However, this begs another question: After everyone leaves, and a house no longer has someone to watch over, does it cease being a home?

This question is not so easily answered. Unless, of course, you have personally spent time in an old house, especially one that had known generations of families. If you have, then you know the answer: Once a house becomes a home, it never forgets.

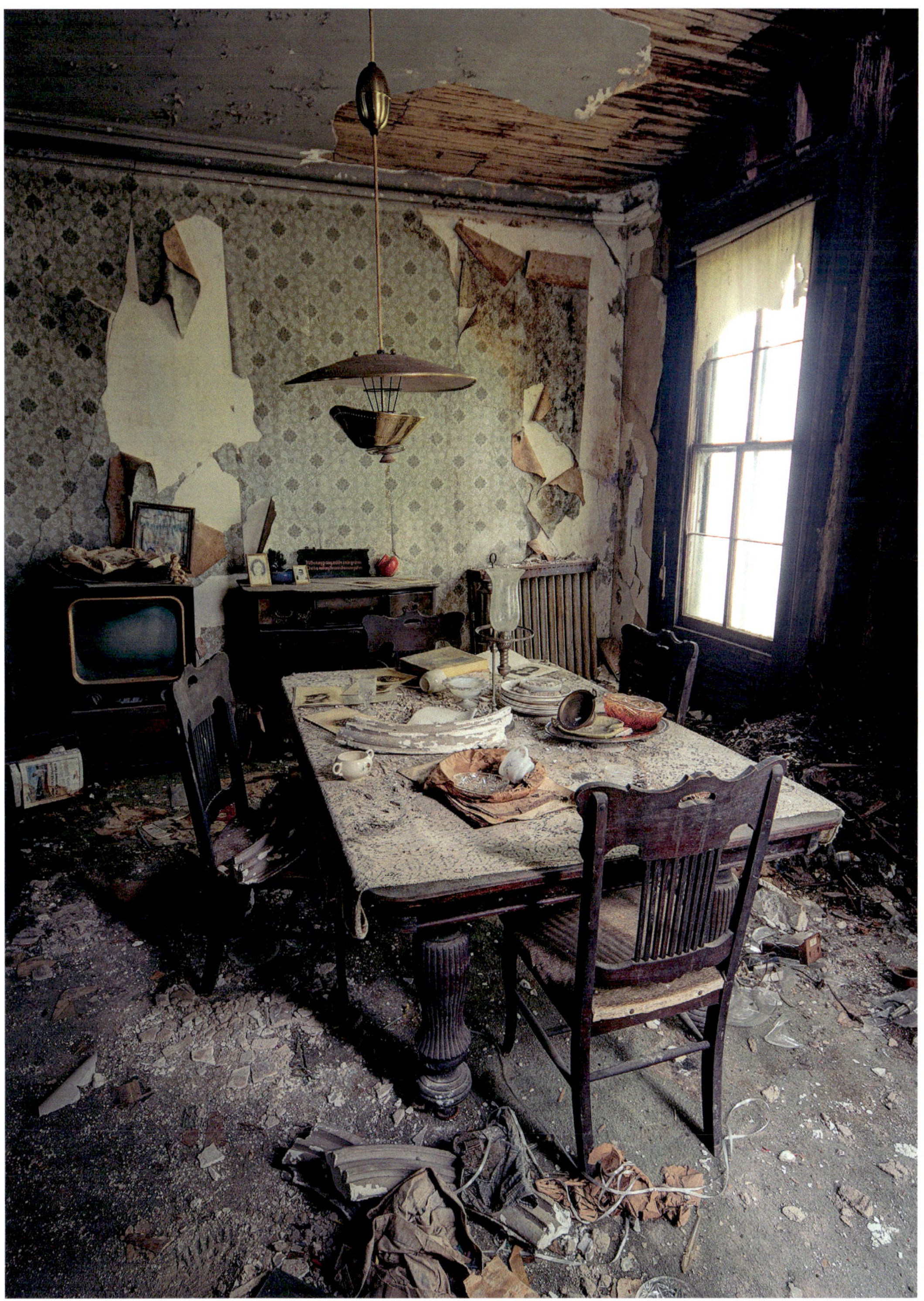

The humidity of summer made the air within the mansion uncomfortably hot and still, and as we moved through the rooms, the aroma of water-damaged wood swirled around us. A bitterness emanating from some unseen rot festering away in the walls. A terminal cancer.

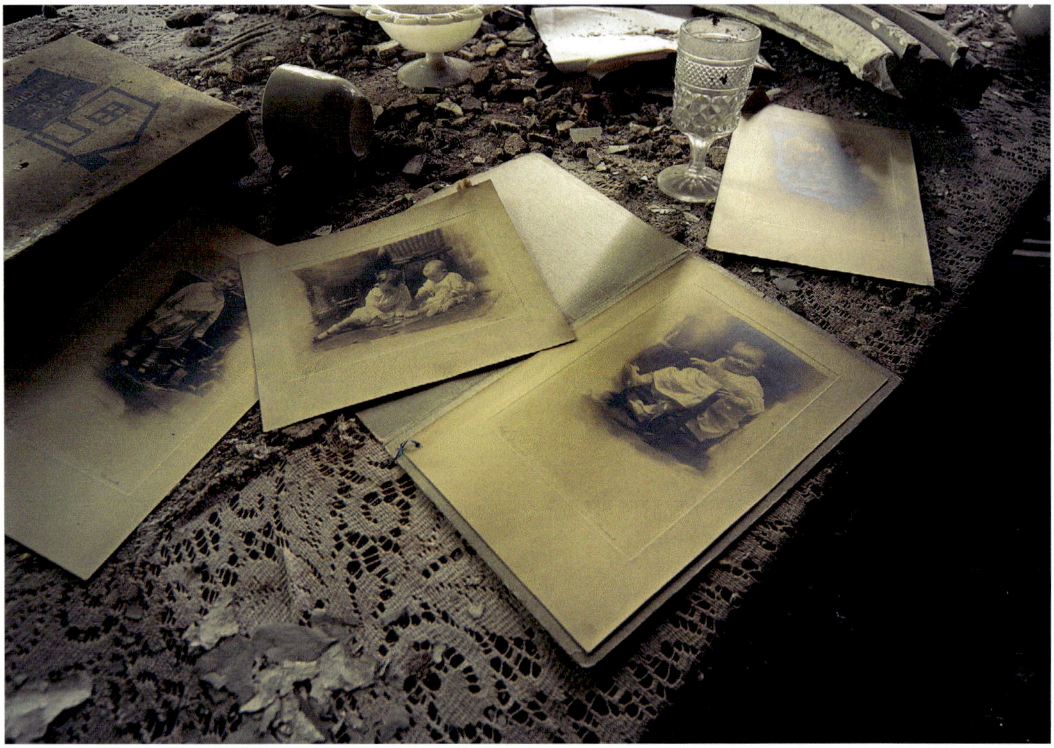

Above and below: Patches of sunlight entered through tattered curtains and ripped plastic, illuminating not just the rooms, but decades of family photos strewn across the floors and tables in nearly every chamber of the home.

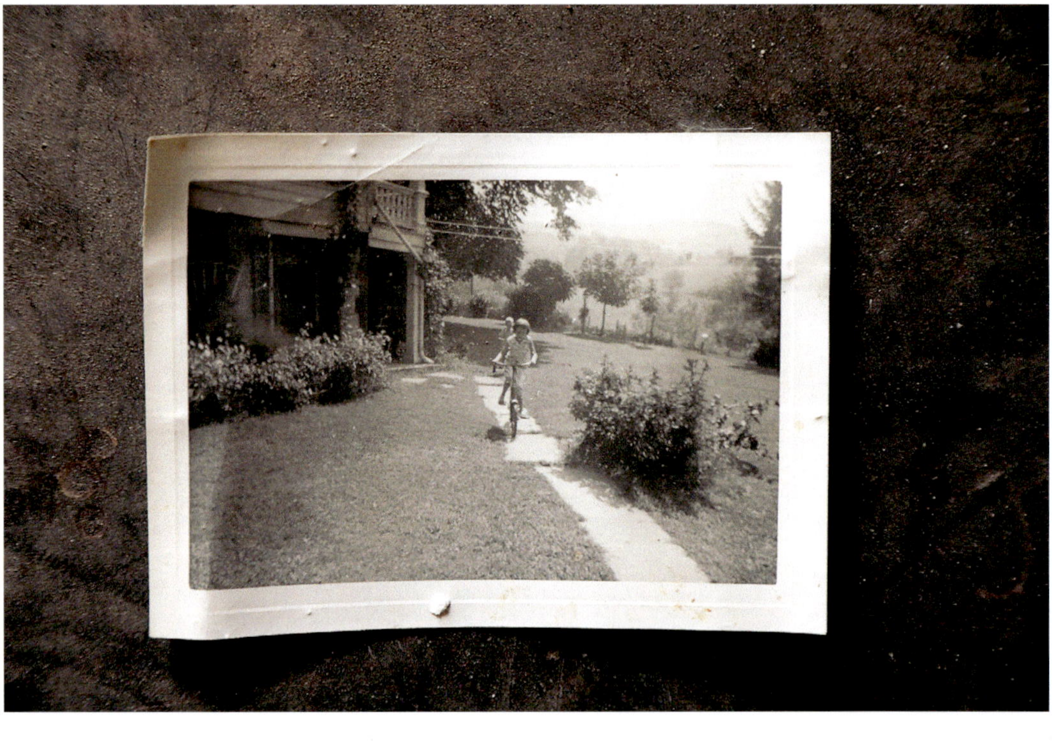

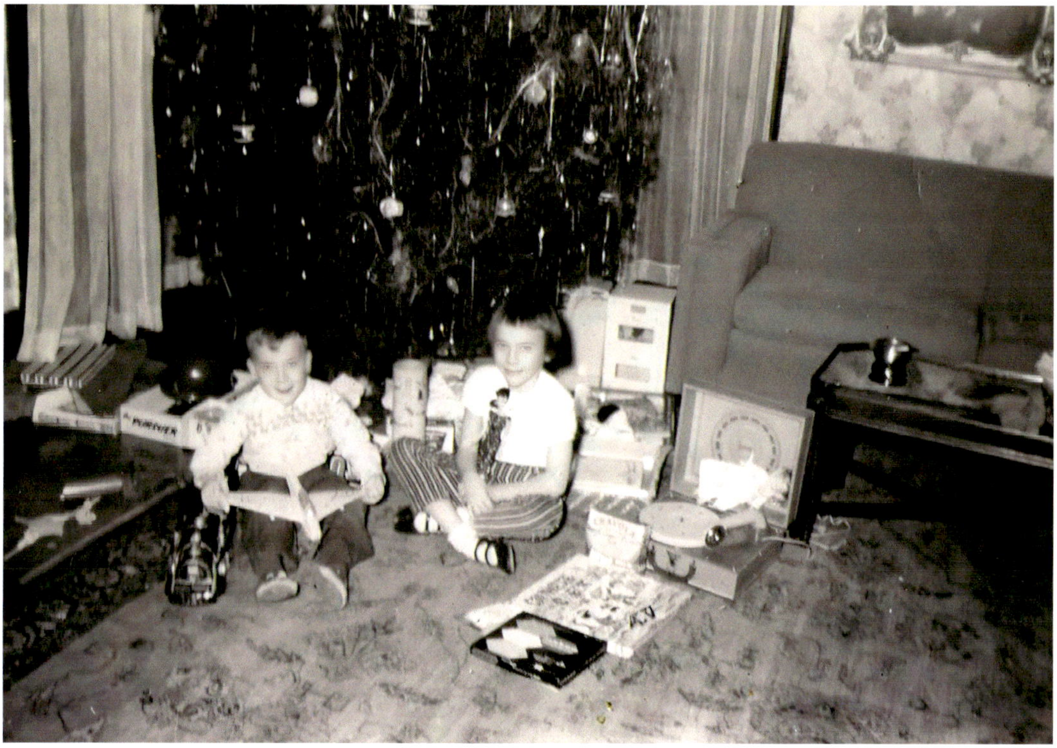

Above and below: The memories of the house, scattered and out of sequence like the thoughts of a failing mind. "Look at what I am … at what I had," it professes loudly through the debris. (*Photograph found on floor—Faces blurred to protect identities*)

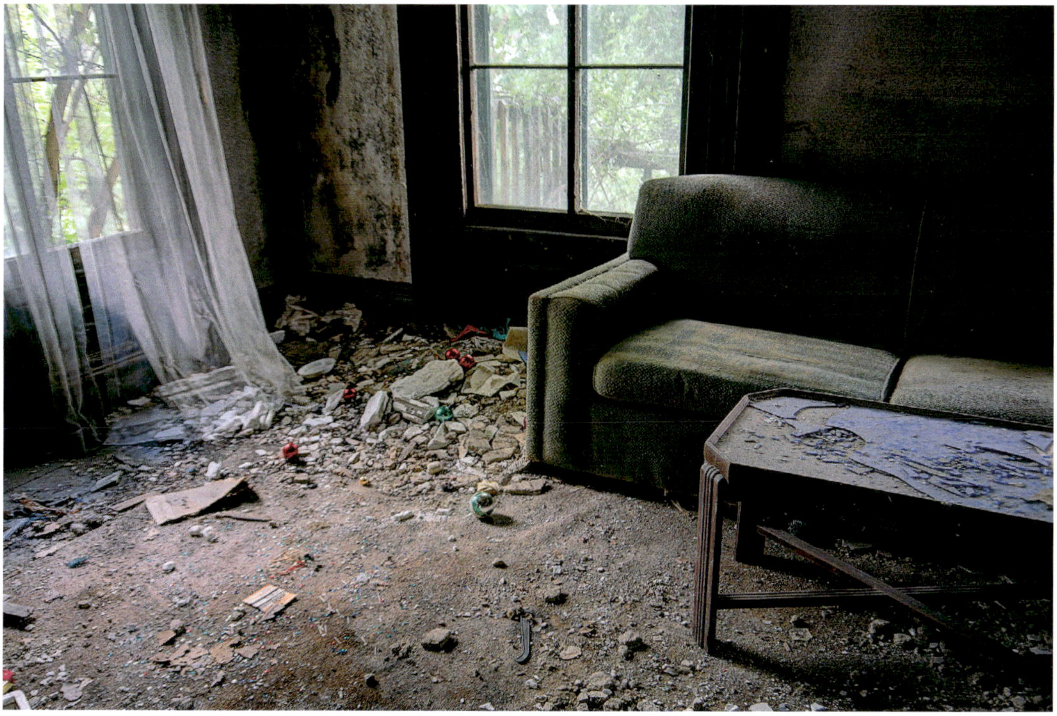

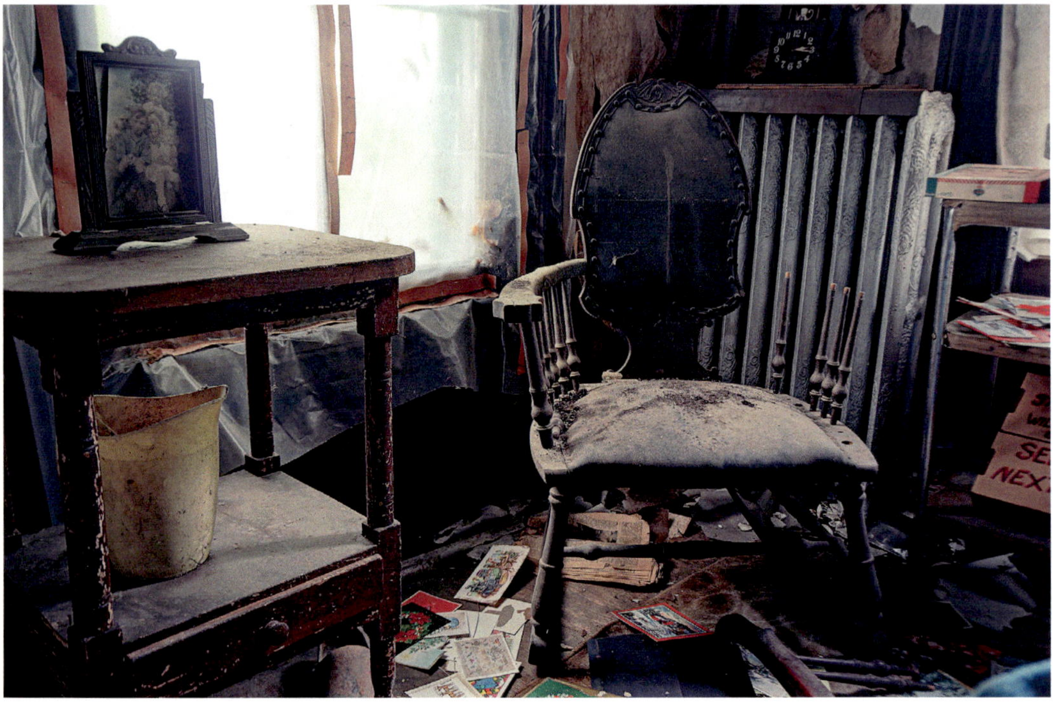

Old homes like this one, so full of relics and personal belongings, are often depicted as haunted. In truth, though, it is the house itself which has become a ghost.

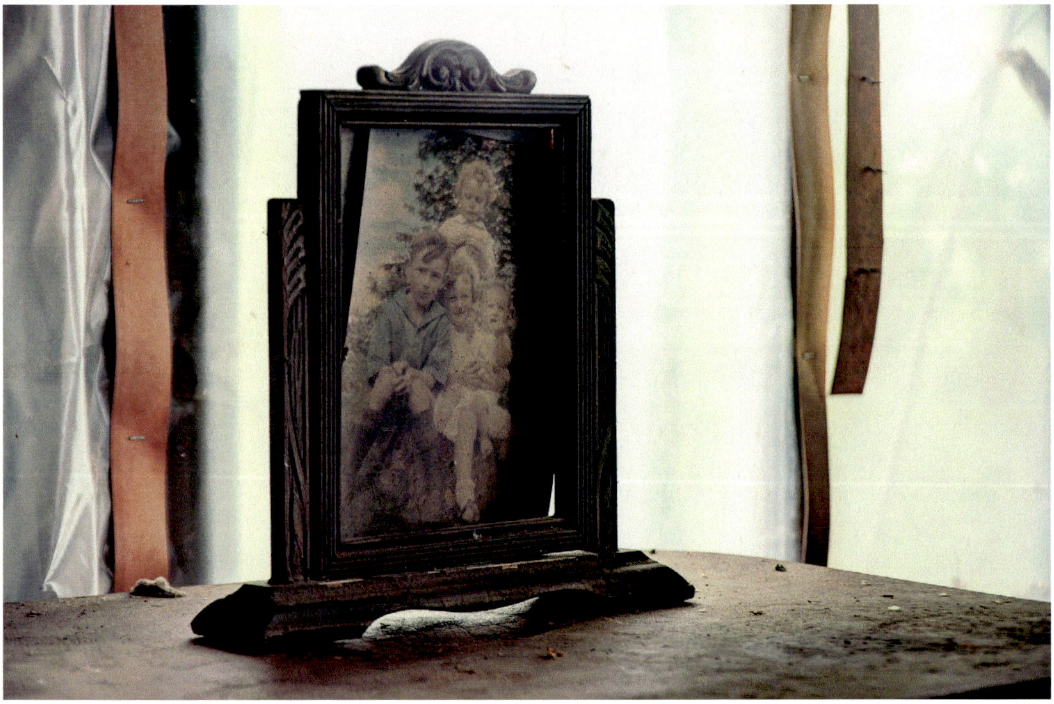

The cycle of life through these walls was stunning, but at some point that cycle had broken, and with it so too did the house.

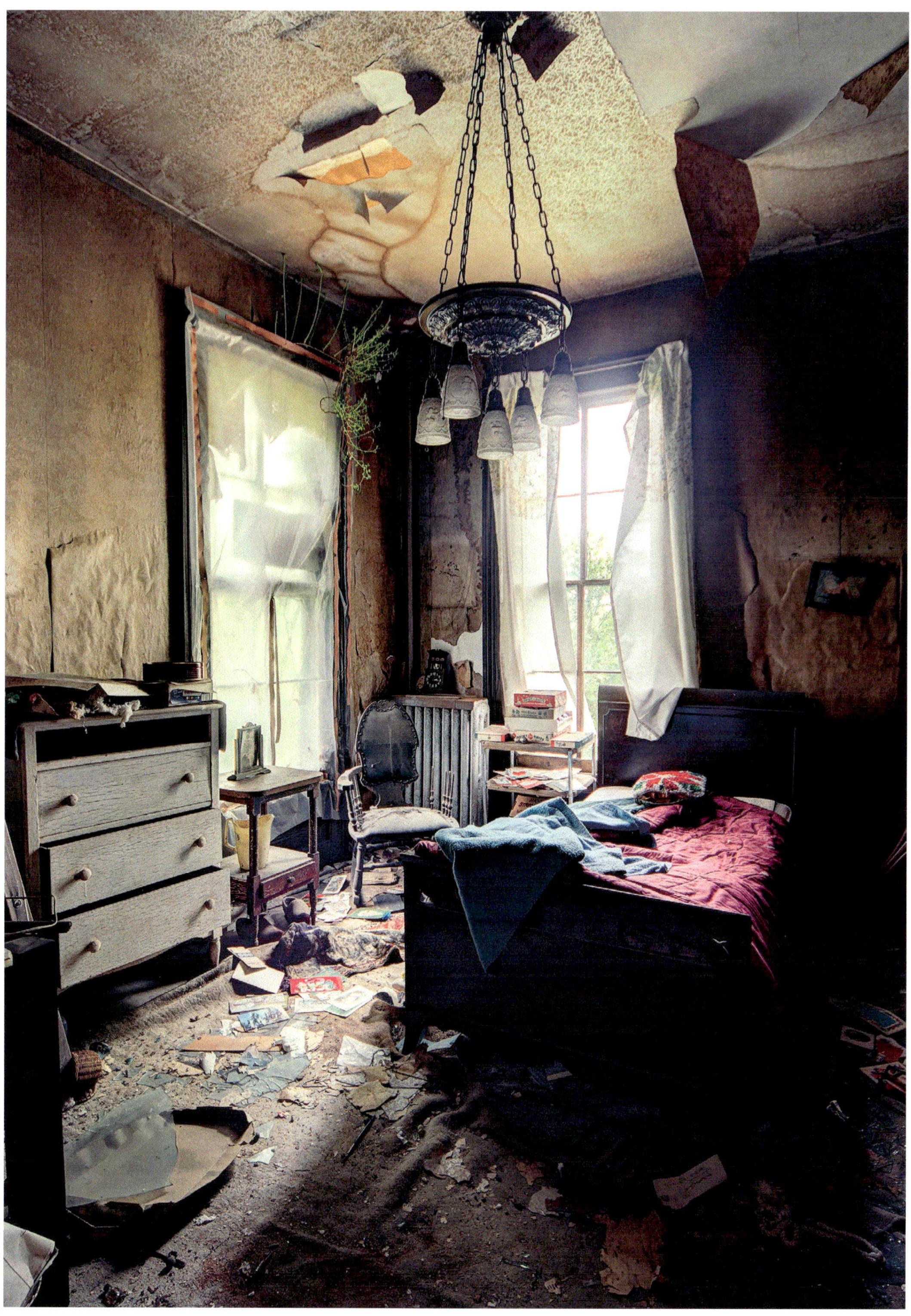

Spiderwebs hang and billow from chandeliers and the corners of furniture. Tiny paw prints track across the dusty floors, beginning and ending at broken windowpanes. How differently time flows in a place like this.

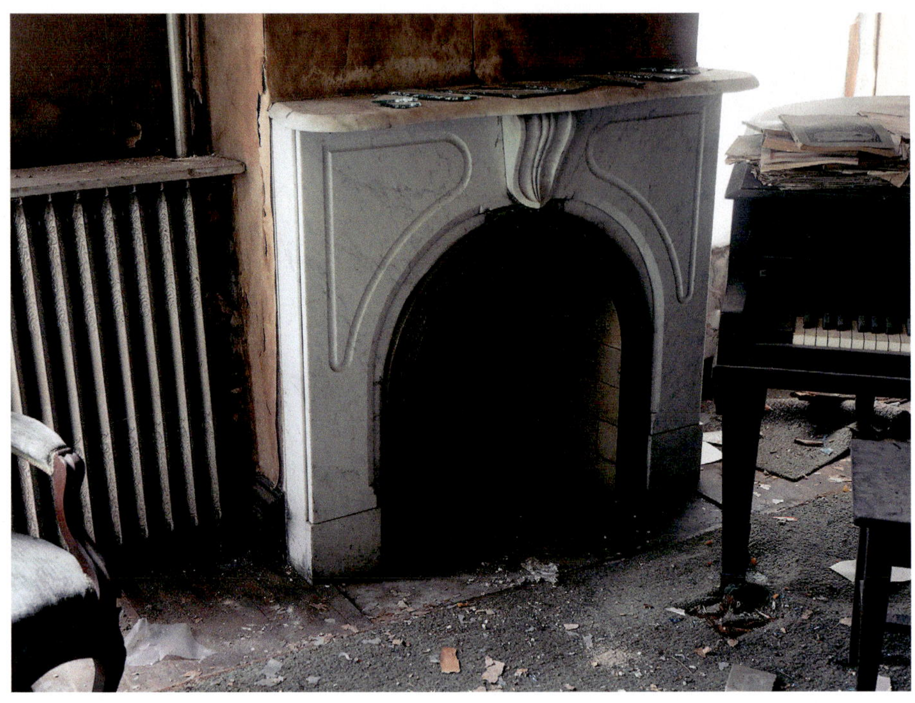

These walls fester and peel themselves apart. Purposeless. Forgotten. Spiraling toward an undeniable conclusion.

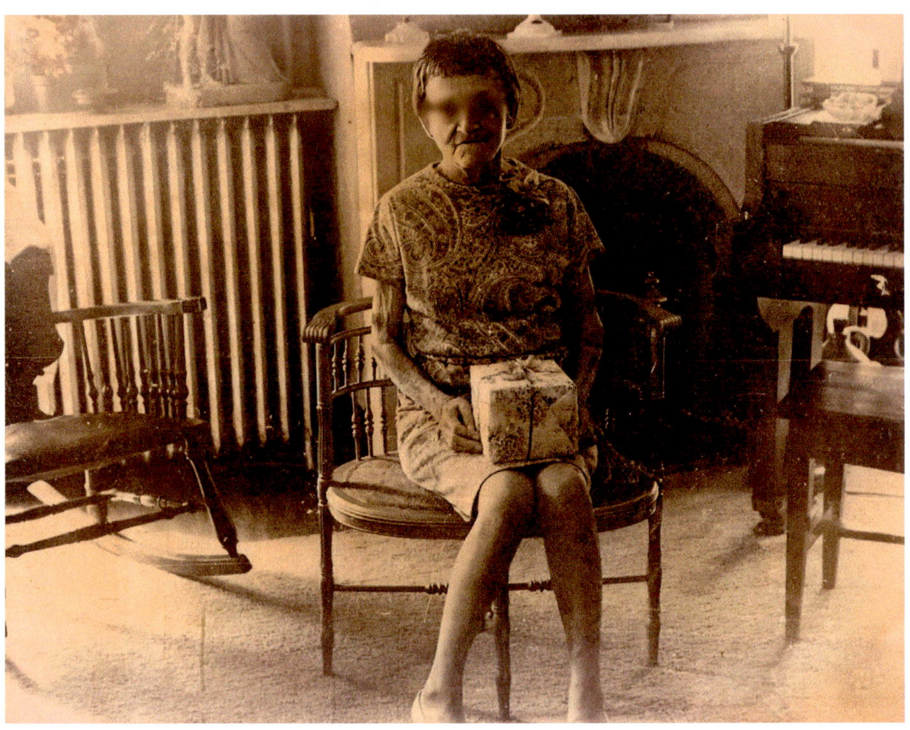

Yet, even as the structure slips away over the years, crumbling to dirt and timber, it remembers what it once was. (*Photograph found on floor—Face blurred to protect identity*)

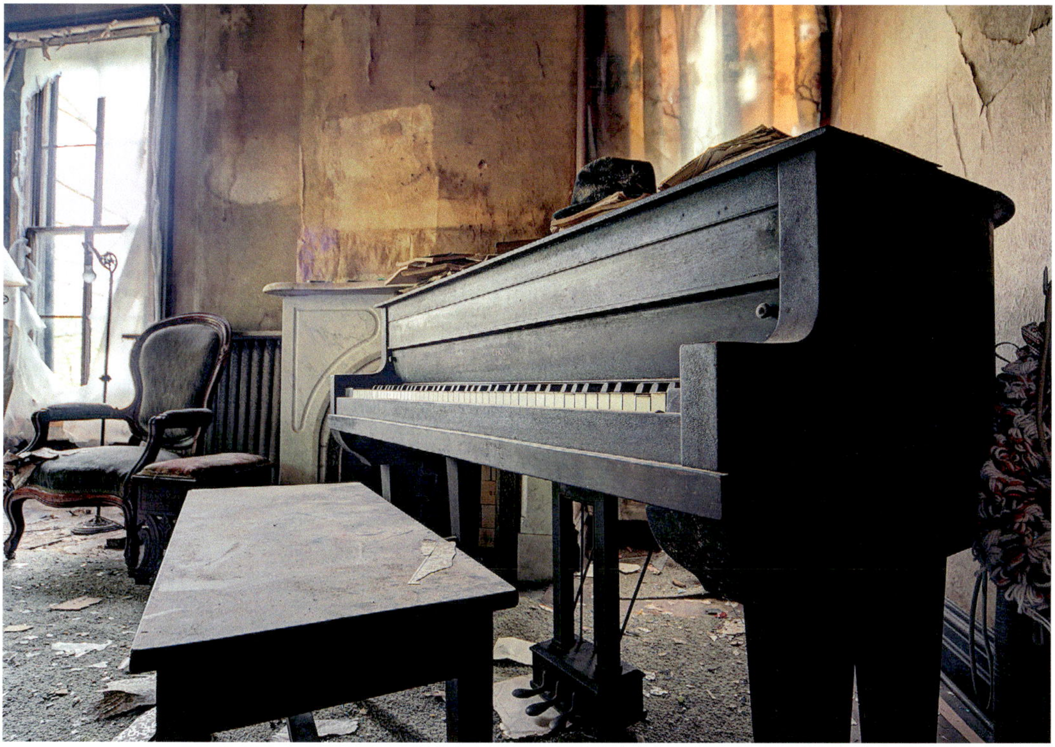

Above and below: What a beautiful manor this must have been, obvious even without the adornments and photographs that surrounded us, telling their tales of holidays past, birthdays and family gatherings, children growing up and leaving, only to return with children of their own.

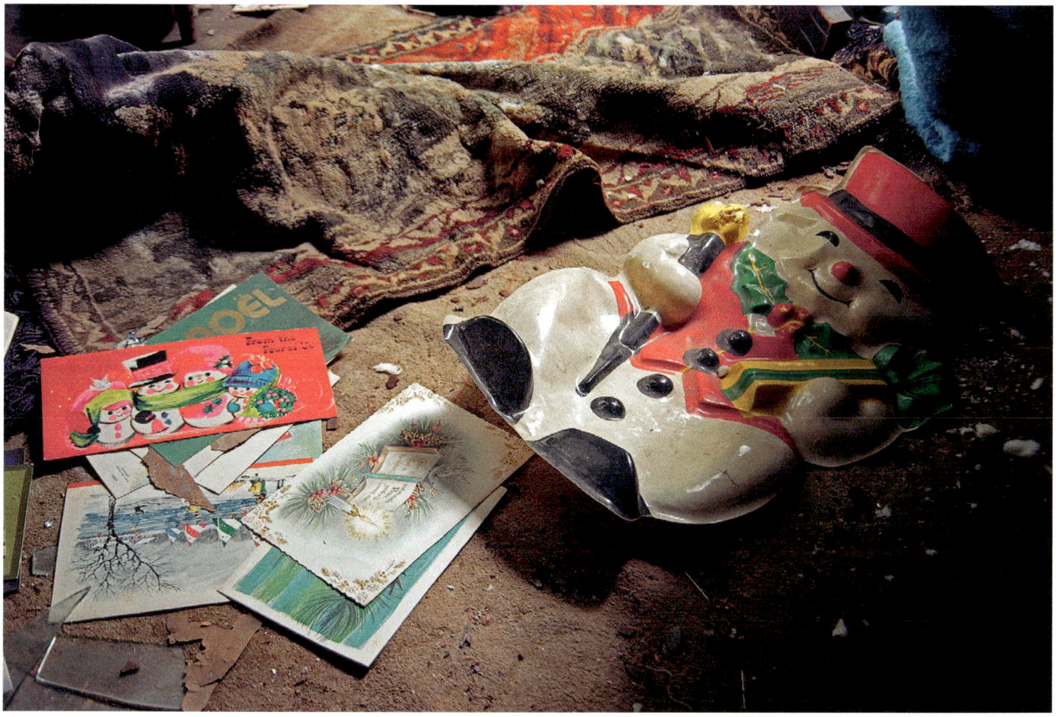

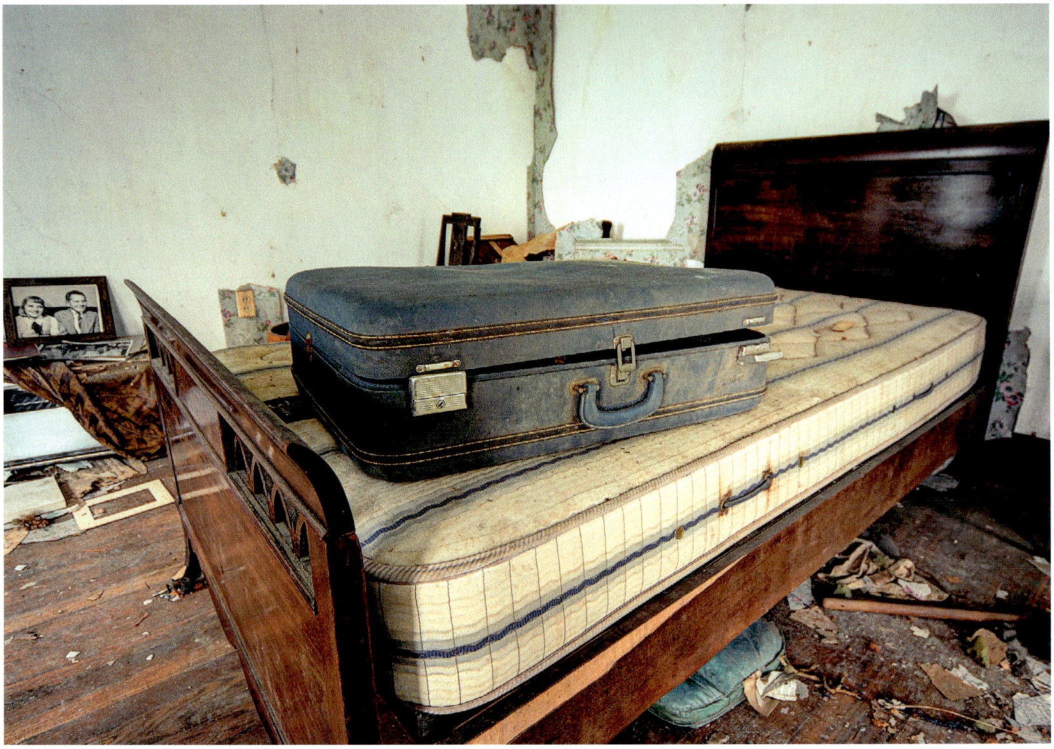

Above and below: Now, this once-grand estate slowly disappears, just as its cherished photographs fade from their paper backings.

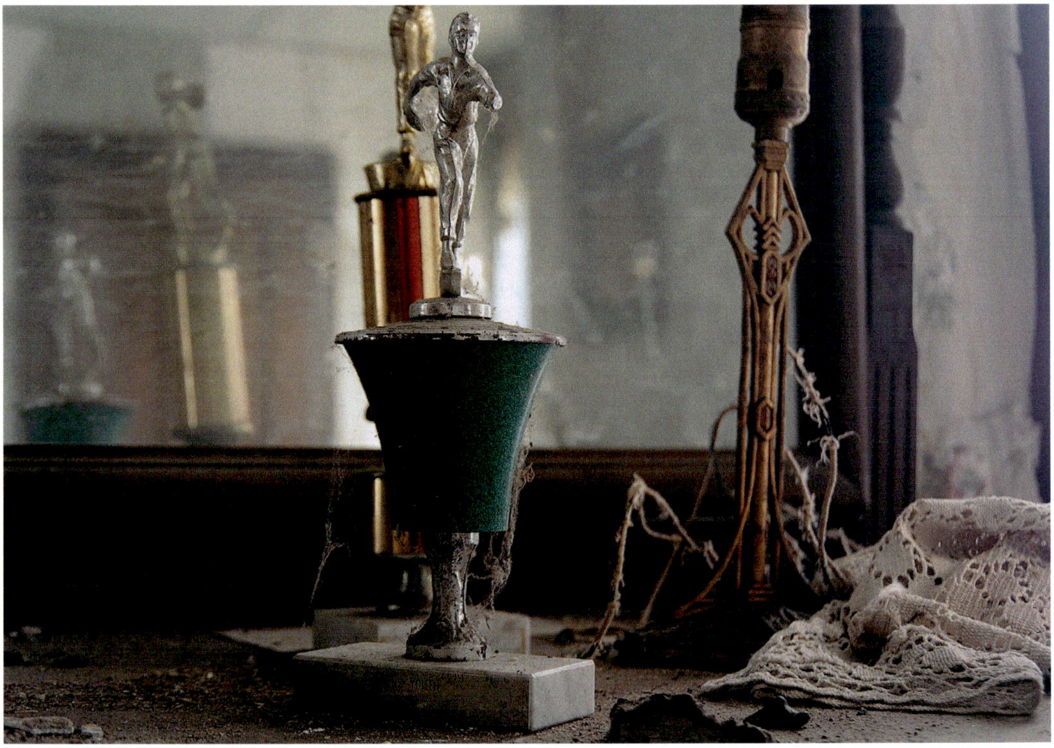

5

GREED

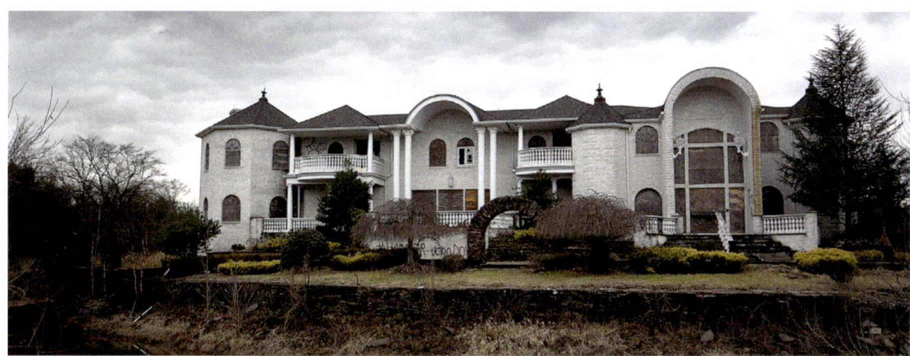

Above: All the world was a depressing grey. The air was bitter cold, the kind that gnawed at any exposed skin. The mansion too was cold, desaturated, as was the sky and the winter forest that lay beyond it. Massive and broken, it stood tall over a stagnant brown pit that was once a beautiful, landscaped pond and brook.

Below: Nearly every one of its windows were sealed shut with weathered plywood, all that remained of the few that were not sealed were bits of shattered glass. It was an incredible sight, and one that conjured up many questions, the most obvious being: Just how on earth does a sprawling estate (last listed for sale at an astounding $8 million) come to be forgotten and neglected in a patch of NJ woods? As it would happen, this home is the sad end to a sordid tale that involves the federal government and an alleged $11 million mortgage scheme.

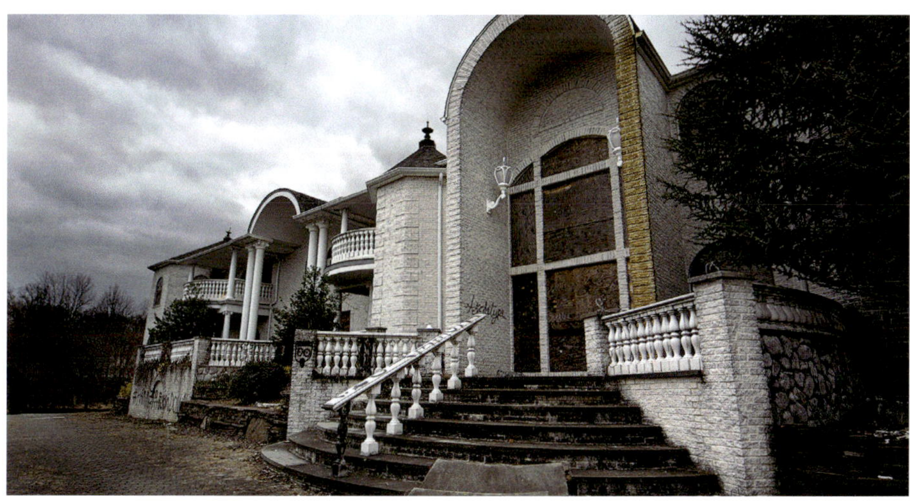

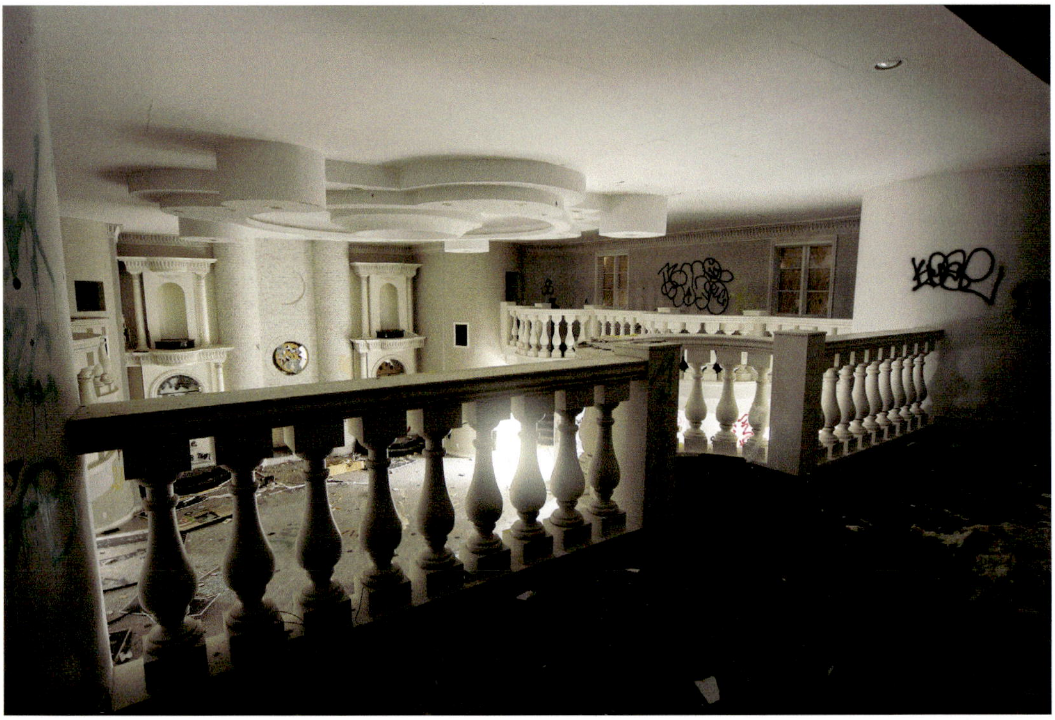

Venturing inside one experiences that uncomfortable temporary blindness one does when entering into a dark and shadowy interior from the bright daylight outside.

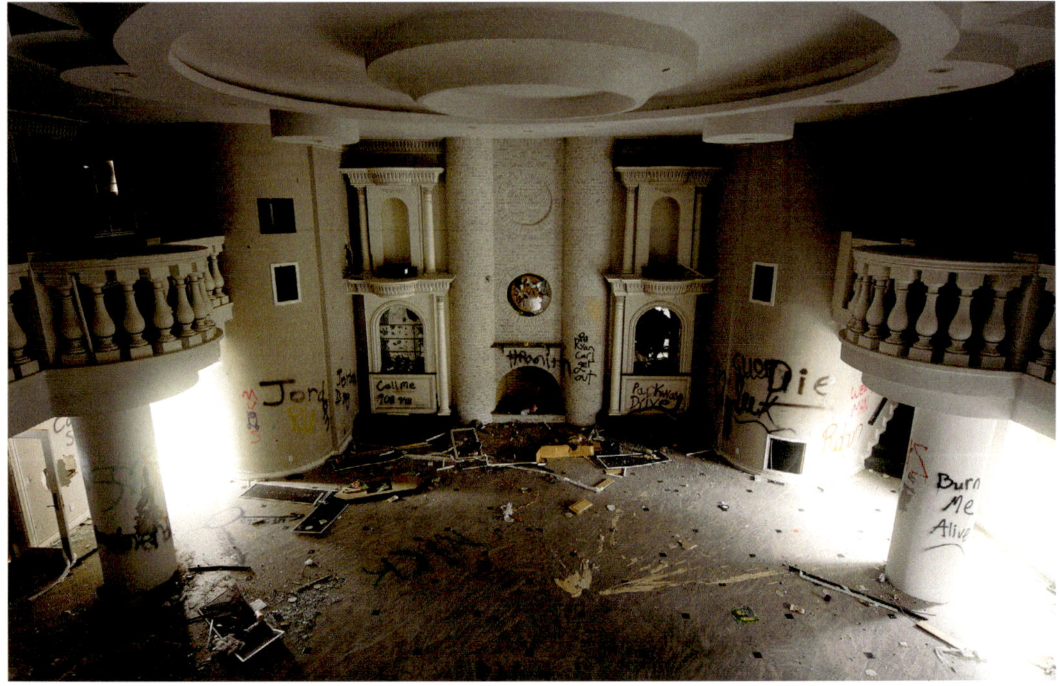

The ballroom, or at least that's what it used to be. A cavernous space which remained impressive even in a state of ransacked abandonment.

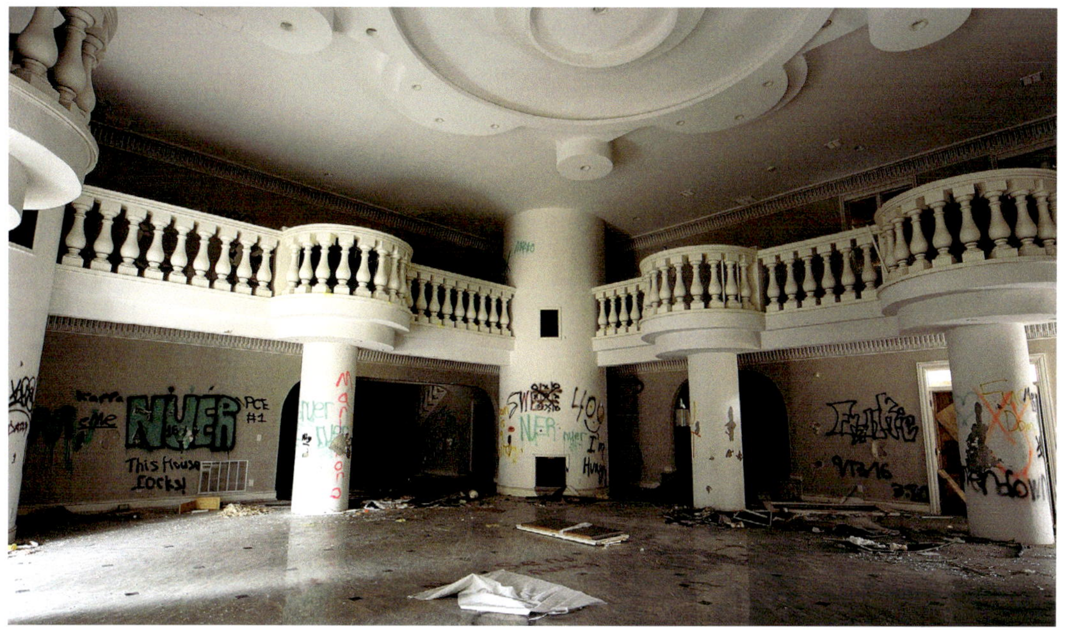

As we moved, the glass cracking under our feet echoed out into the emptiness, resonating back off the marble repeatedly before dispersing in a whisper. All was silent, save for the wind in the trees which could be heard through the broken windows. It was immediately evident that this vacant property had not gone unnoticed by the local kids, as graffiti covered most surfaces, punctuated by the occasional hole kicked through sheet rock. This unfortunate house has already seen so much during its relatively short lifetime.

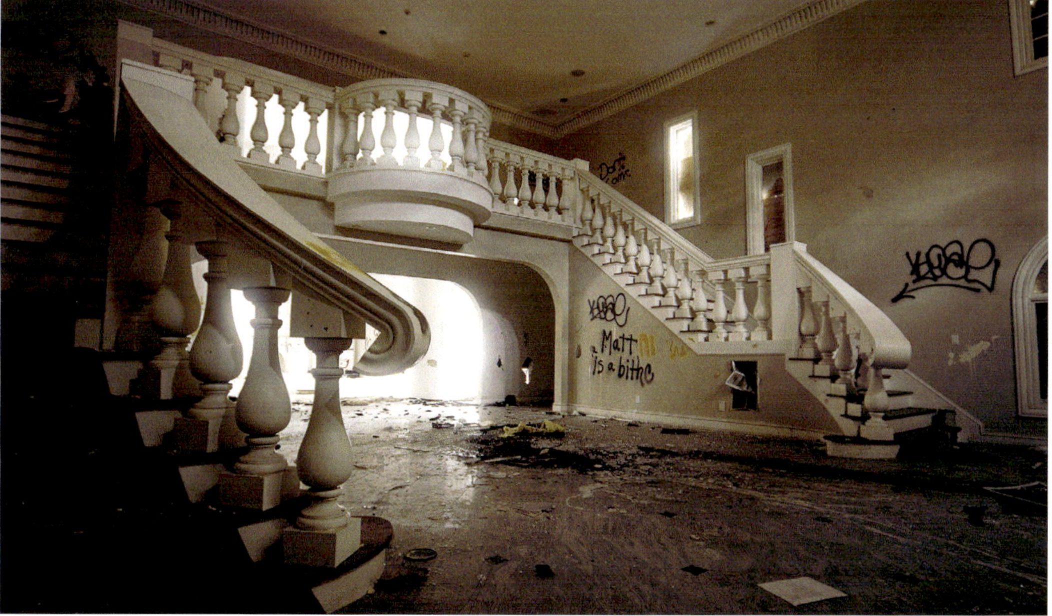

The estate was more a castle than a home. Beyond the massive ballroom stood a grand staircase that could very well be the physical definition of "grand staircase." Its railings were so wide that they seemed better suited as shelves than as a guide for your hands. The over-sized rails outlined two sets of curved stairs, each acceding to a landing and meeting at a balcony which overlooked both the main entrance and the ballroom.

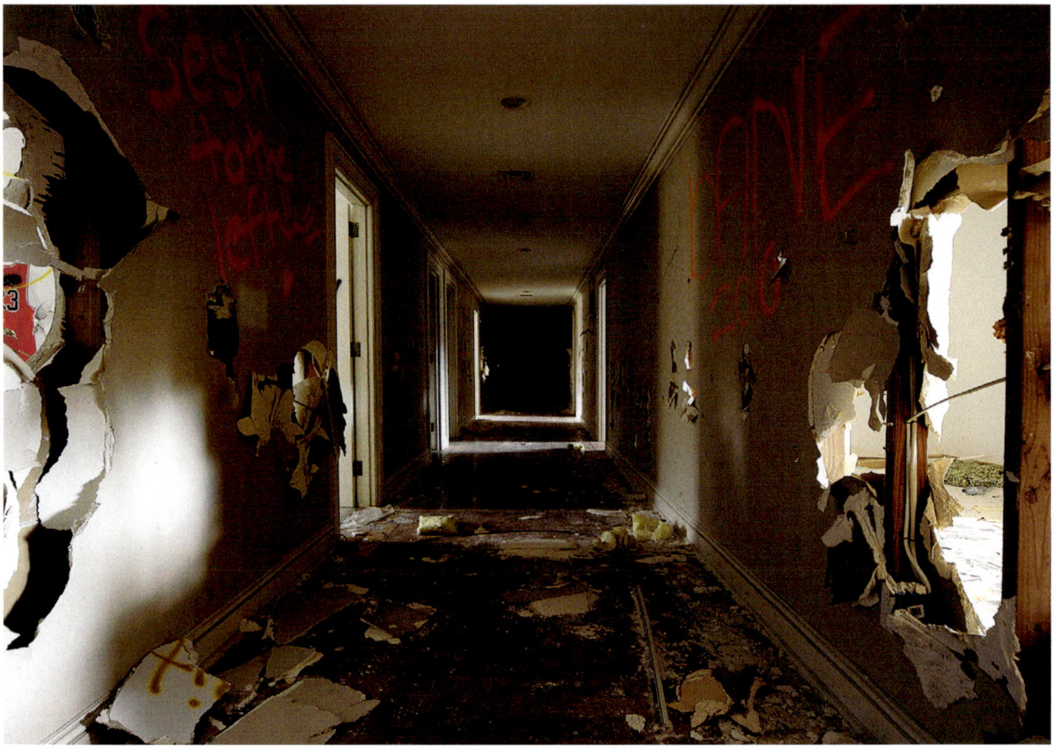

Above and below: On the upper floor was found the hallway that led to the bedrooms, with the master found beyond a double door at the far end, while the personal rooms of other family members line the walls.

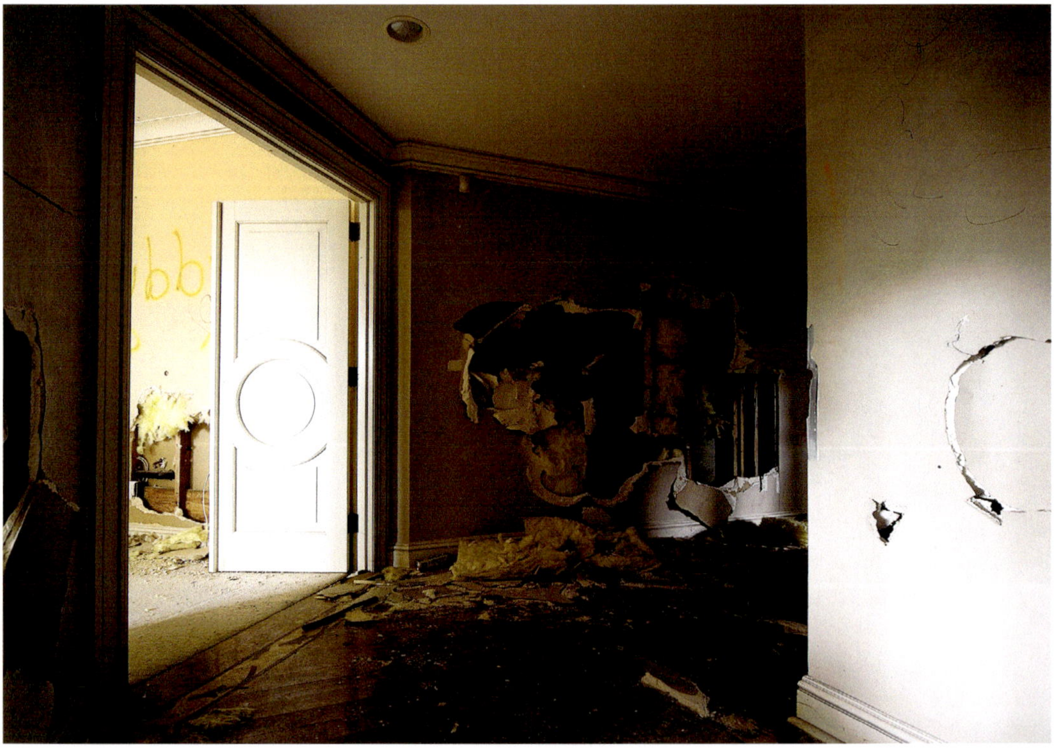

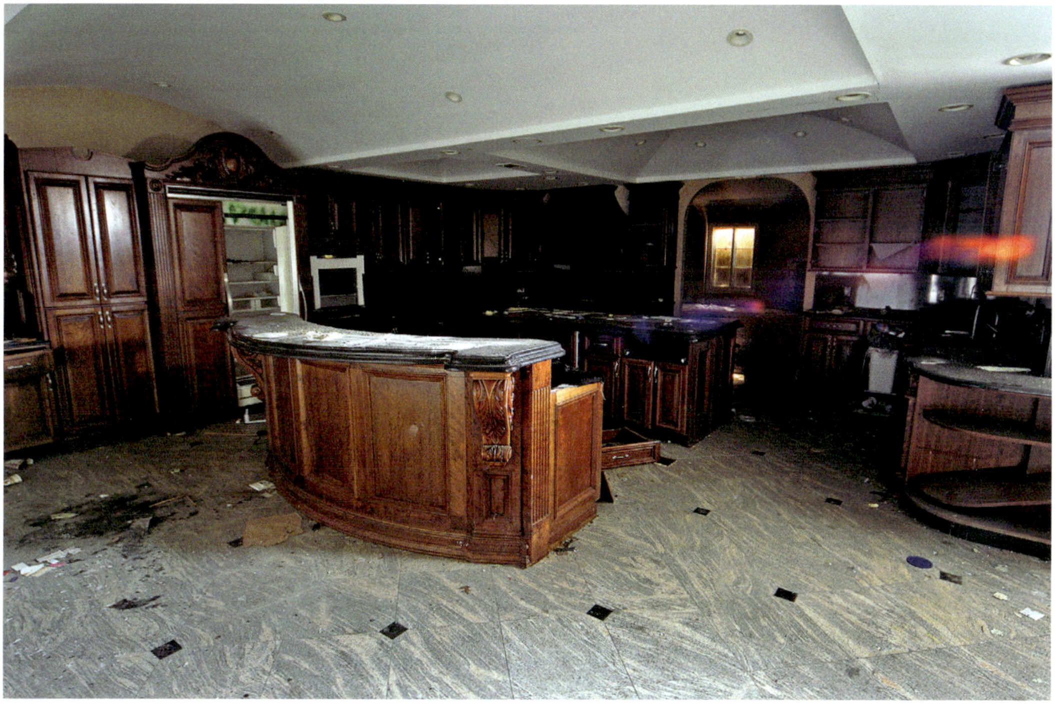

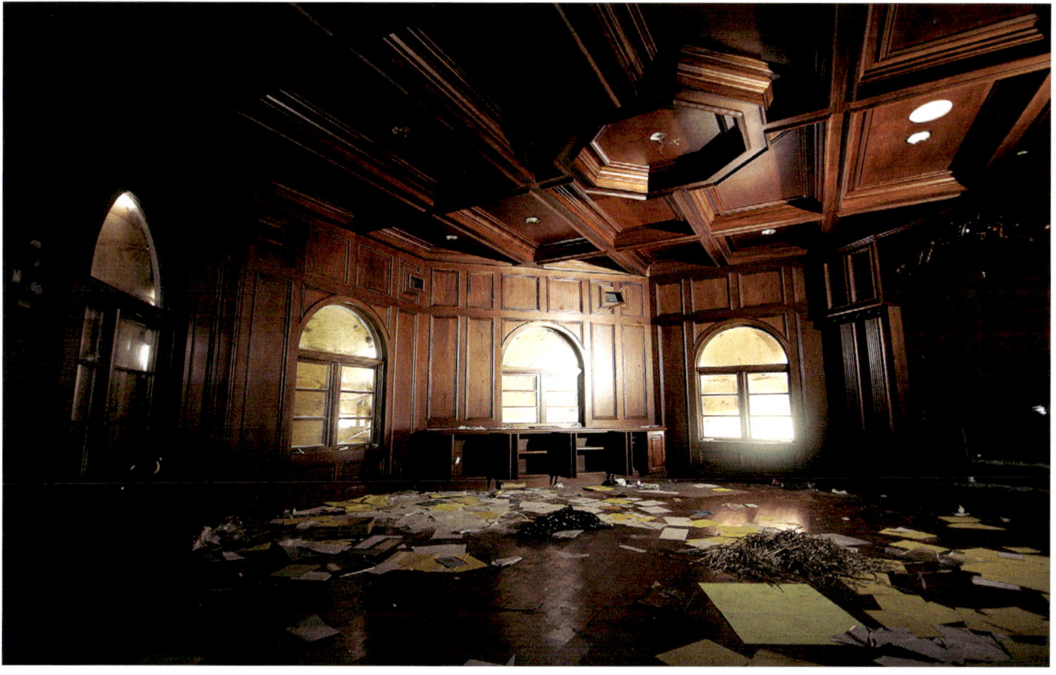

On the ground floor could be found the kitchen, a cooking space large enough to properly cook for a platoon let alone a single family. There were also numerous common rooms, a dining room, and a large living room.

Considering the design and imposing scale of the mansion, many of the rooms felt sterile and exceedingly empty, factors that were amplified by the sparse sunlight. It was as if the entirety of the house had been drained of its life and unceremoniously discarded.

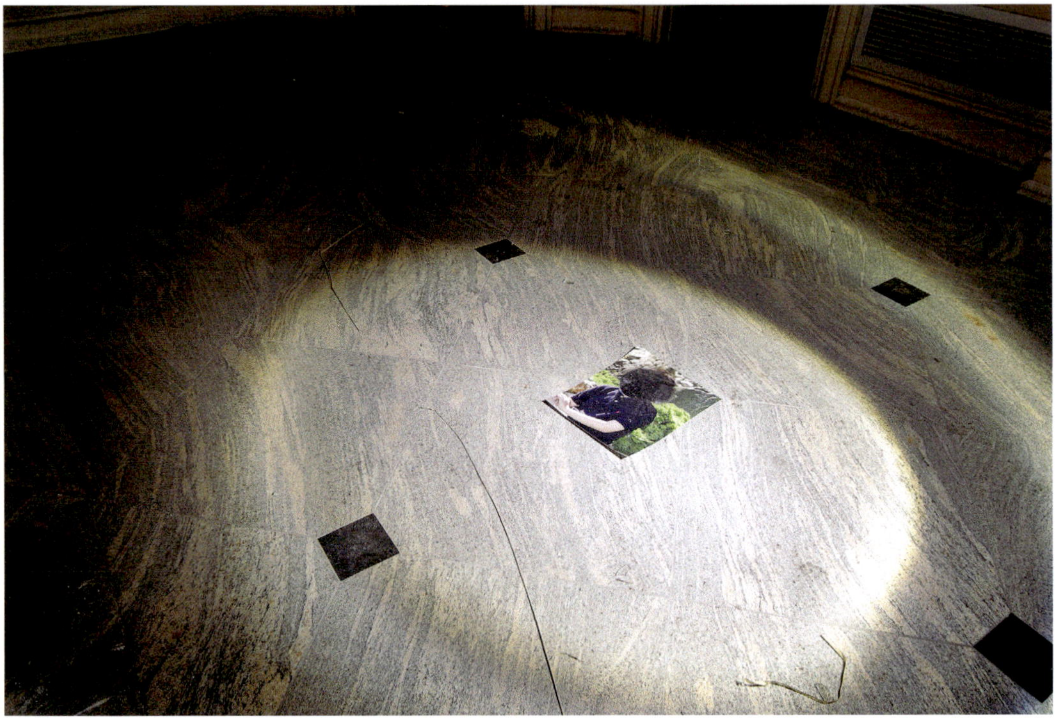

Above and below: One of the lone remainders from this house's days as a home was a single 8 by 10-inch portrait of a young boy. The face was burnt away, leaving the child in the photograph unrecognizable. It lay on the marble floor, the only item in a pitch-black corridor. A cryptic harbinger of things yet to come.

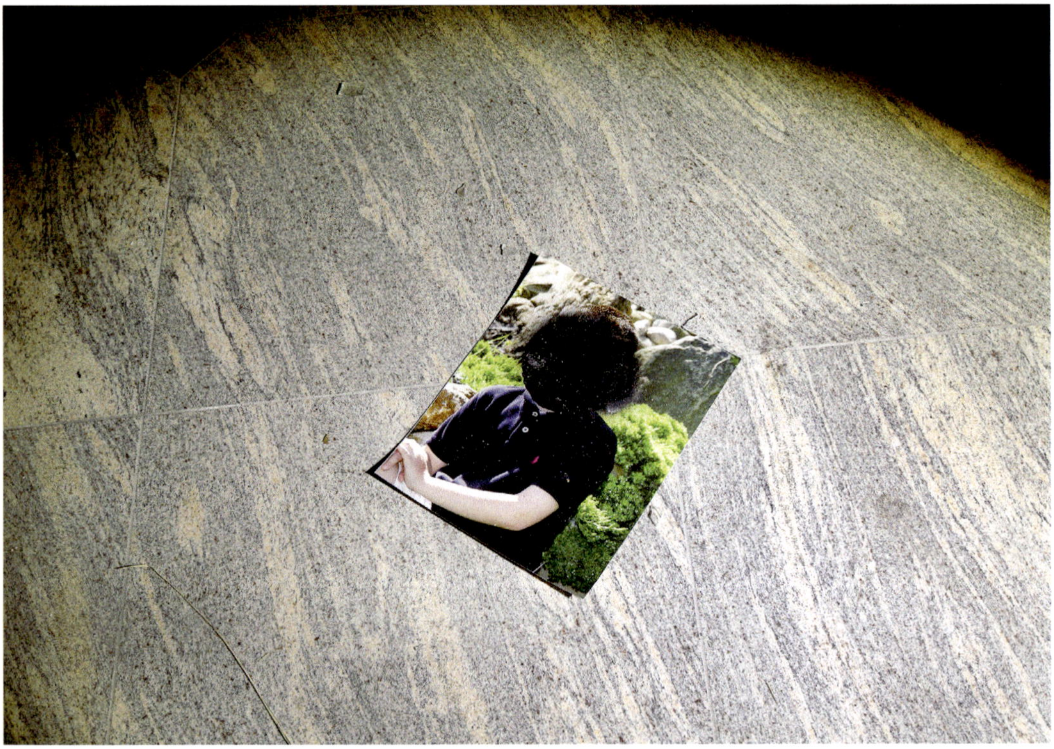

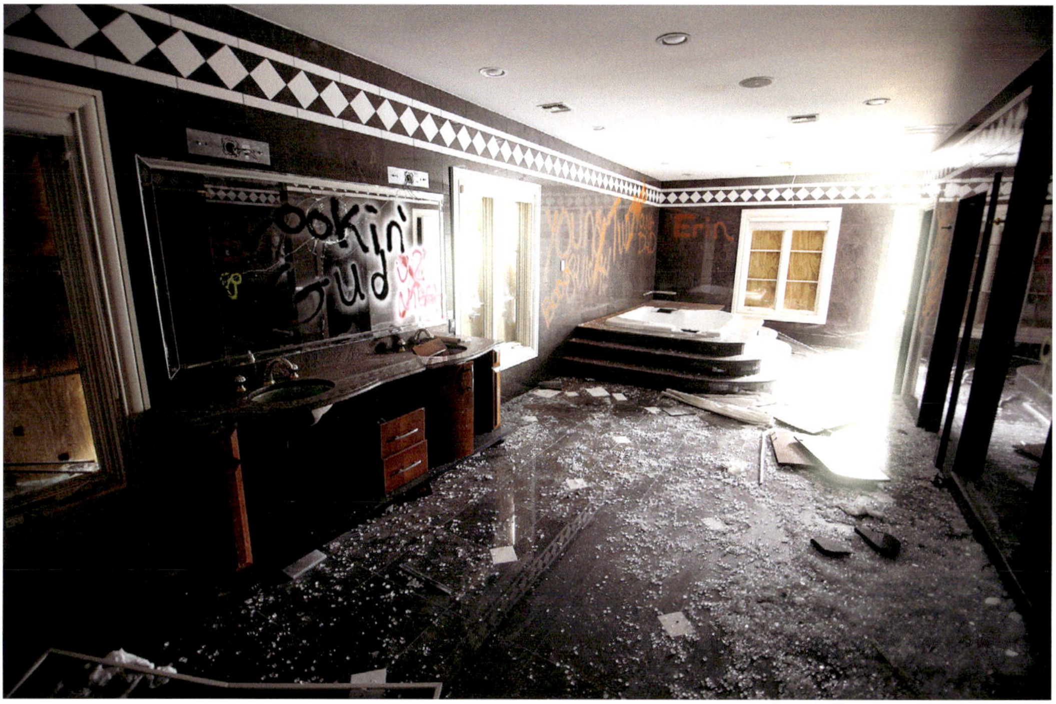

For years the home existed in a kind of limbo, vacant but caught in the middle of a legal battle between multiple mortgage lenders, each claiming to be the rightful owner of the sprawling estate.

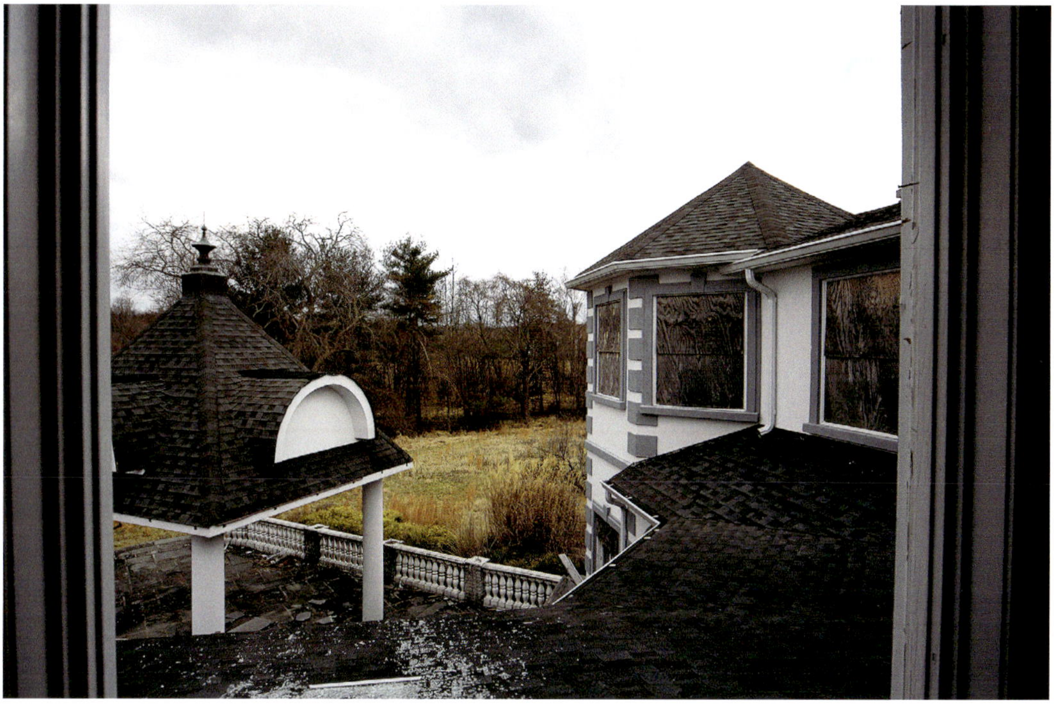

It simply sat in silence, a depressing sight that greeted anyone who wandered up its long, overgrown drive. Or so it did until just after midnight on February 2, 2017.

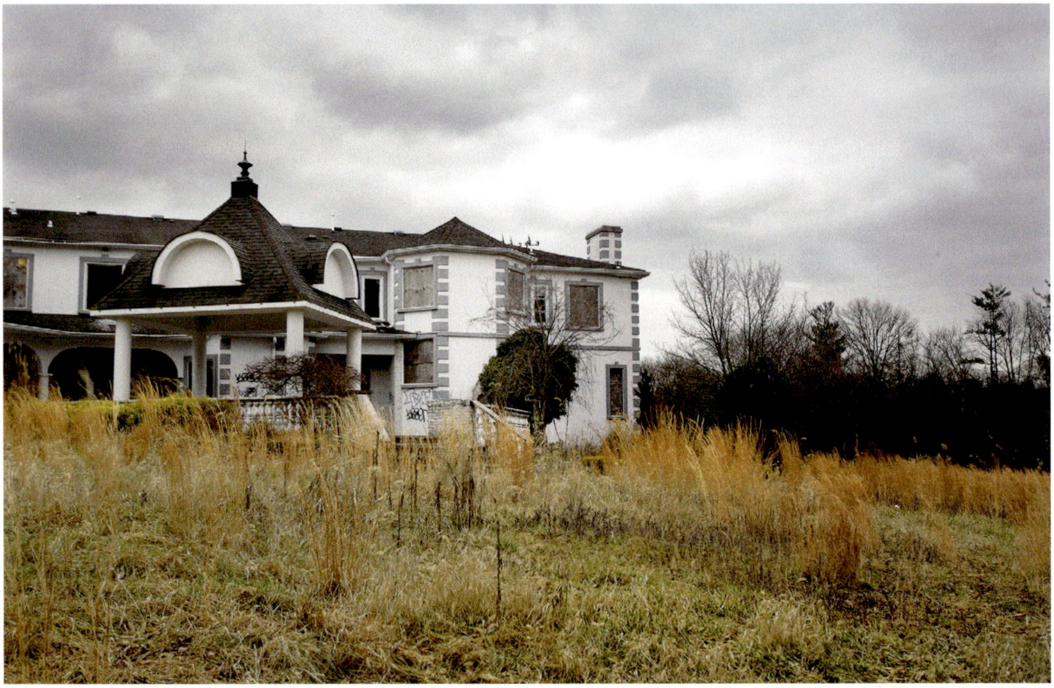

Reports of a fire on the property reached the police just before 12:30 a.m., and by the time fire crews arrived at the scene, the entirety of the mansion was in flames. Come afternoon of that same day, all that remained of the estate amounted to little more than smoldering ashes.

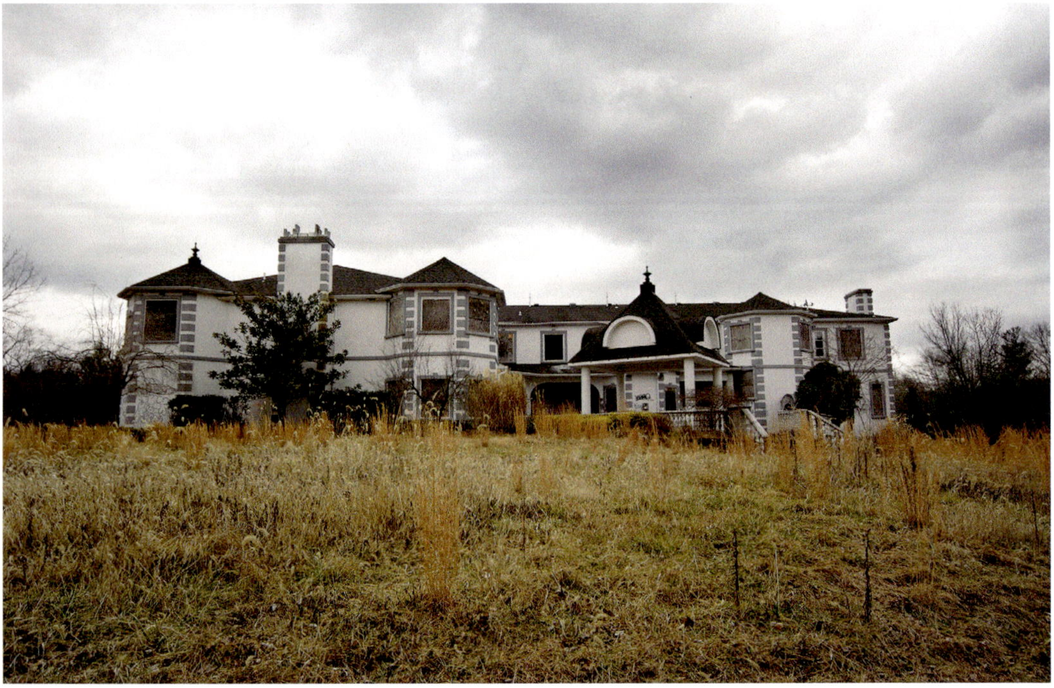

A fiery end to a building that will never get a chance at redemption, to be forever remembered in infamy as a home destroyed by greed, many years before flames finally took it away.

6

ELDA CASTLE

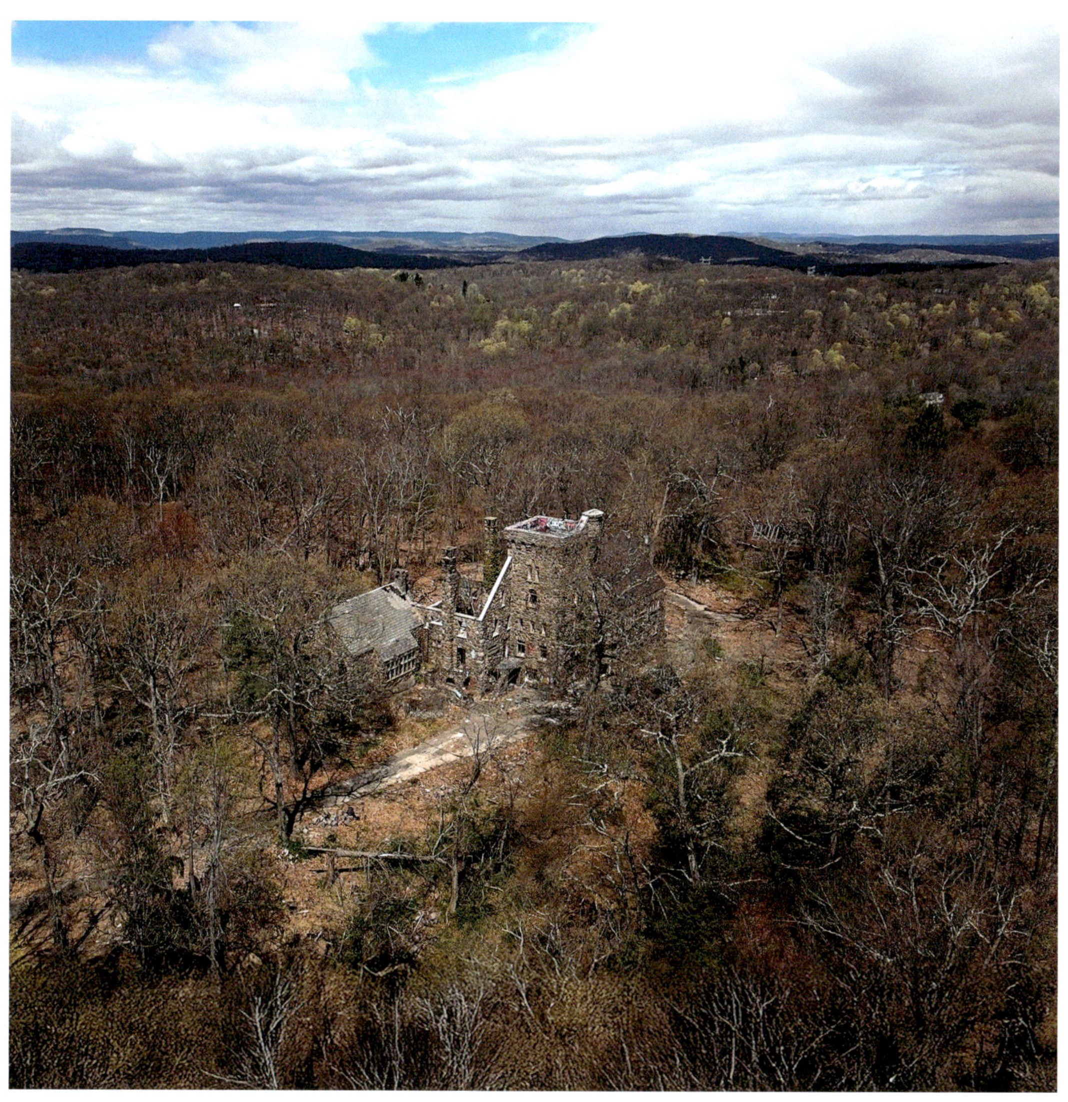

In the midst of a sprawling forest in New Castle, New York, can (perhaps unsurprisingly) be found a castle. Its beautiful stone construction, originally built to complement the woods, now seems utterly lost to it.

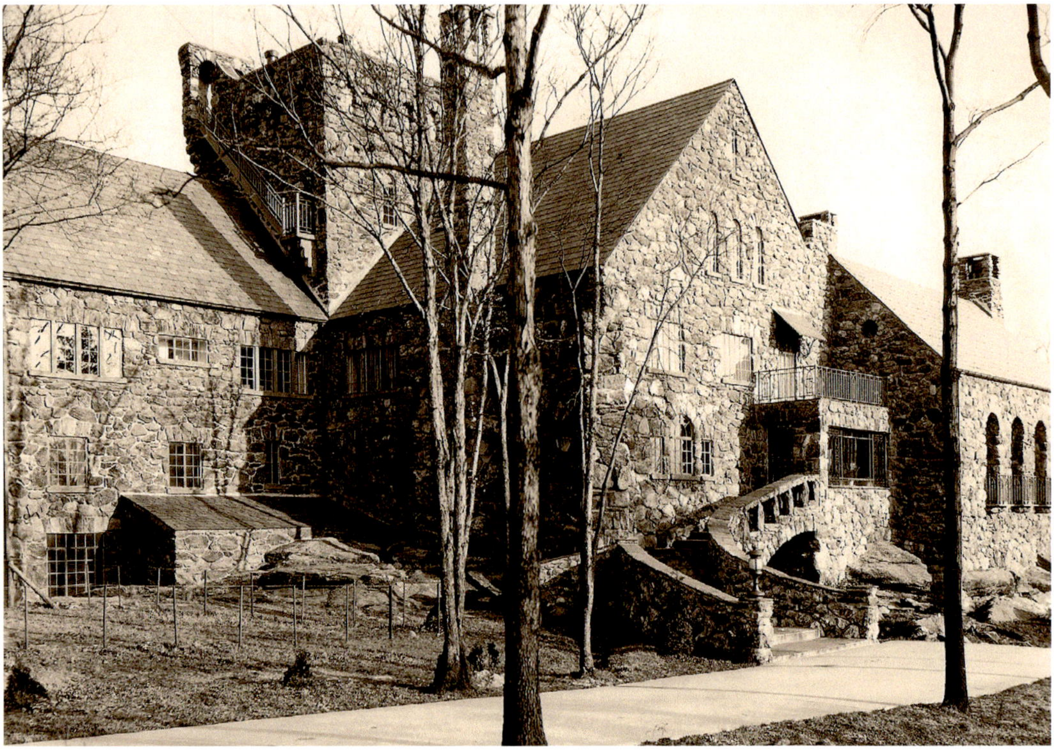

Above and below: Today the old manor has been reduced to a ruinous state, one which seems lifted straight from the pages of a fantasy. The fallen kingdom of a noble family. The family in this case being that of David Thomas Abercrombie. A name many know from his hand in the foundation of the brand Abercrombie & Fitch. (*Historical photograph courtesy of Doug Leen*)

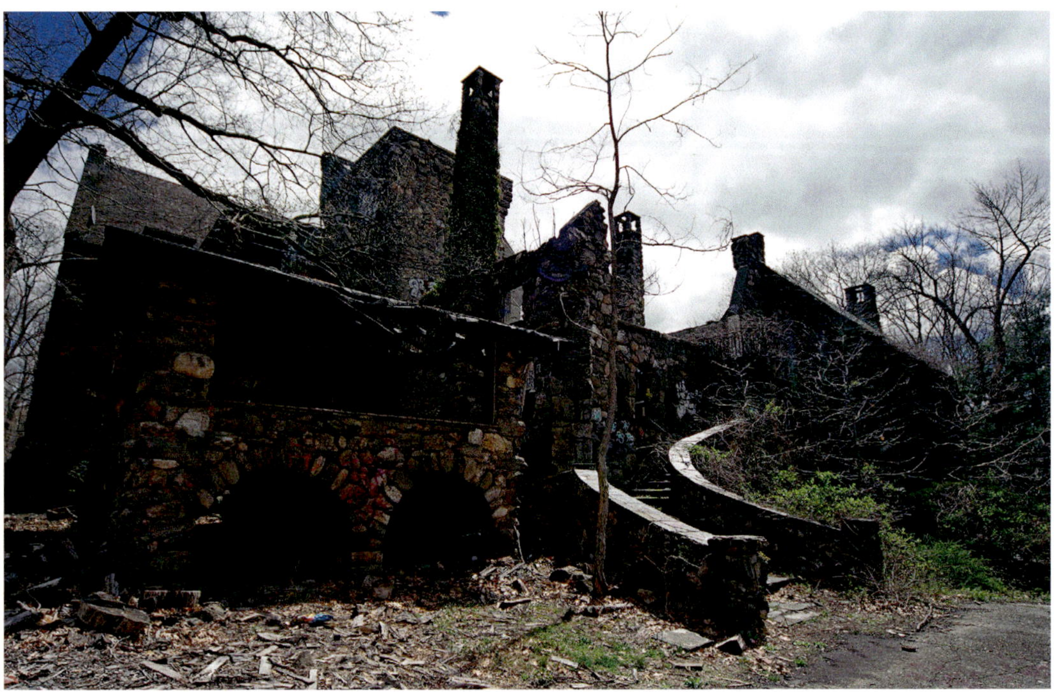

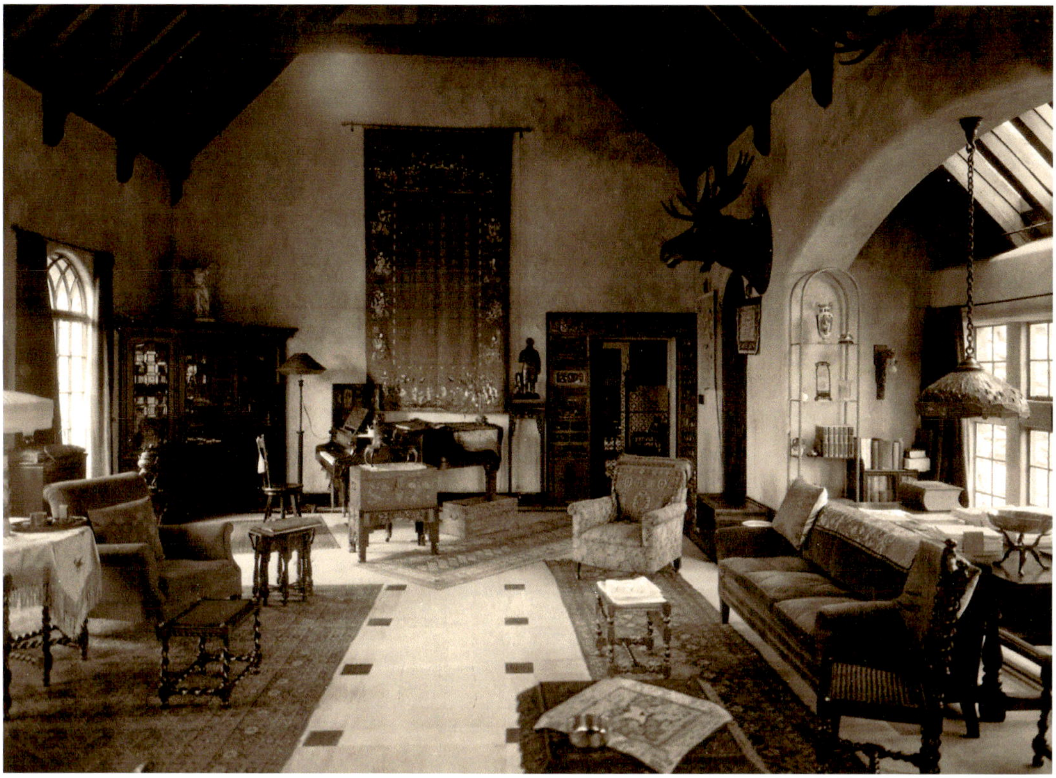

Above and below: Completed in 1927, the mansion was known as Elda, though properly written as ELDA, the combination of the first initials of their four children from oldest to youngest (Elizabeth, Lucy, David, and Abbott). (*Historical photograph courtesy of Doug Leen*)

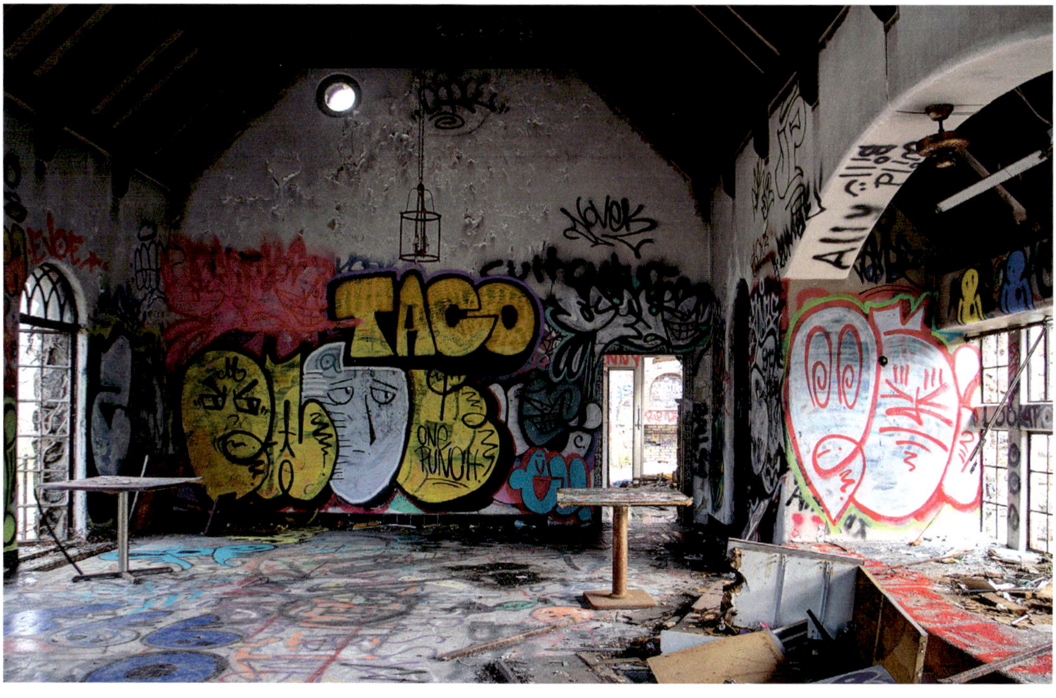

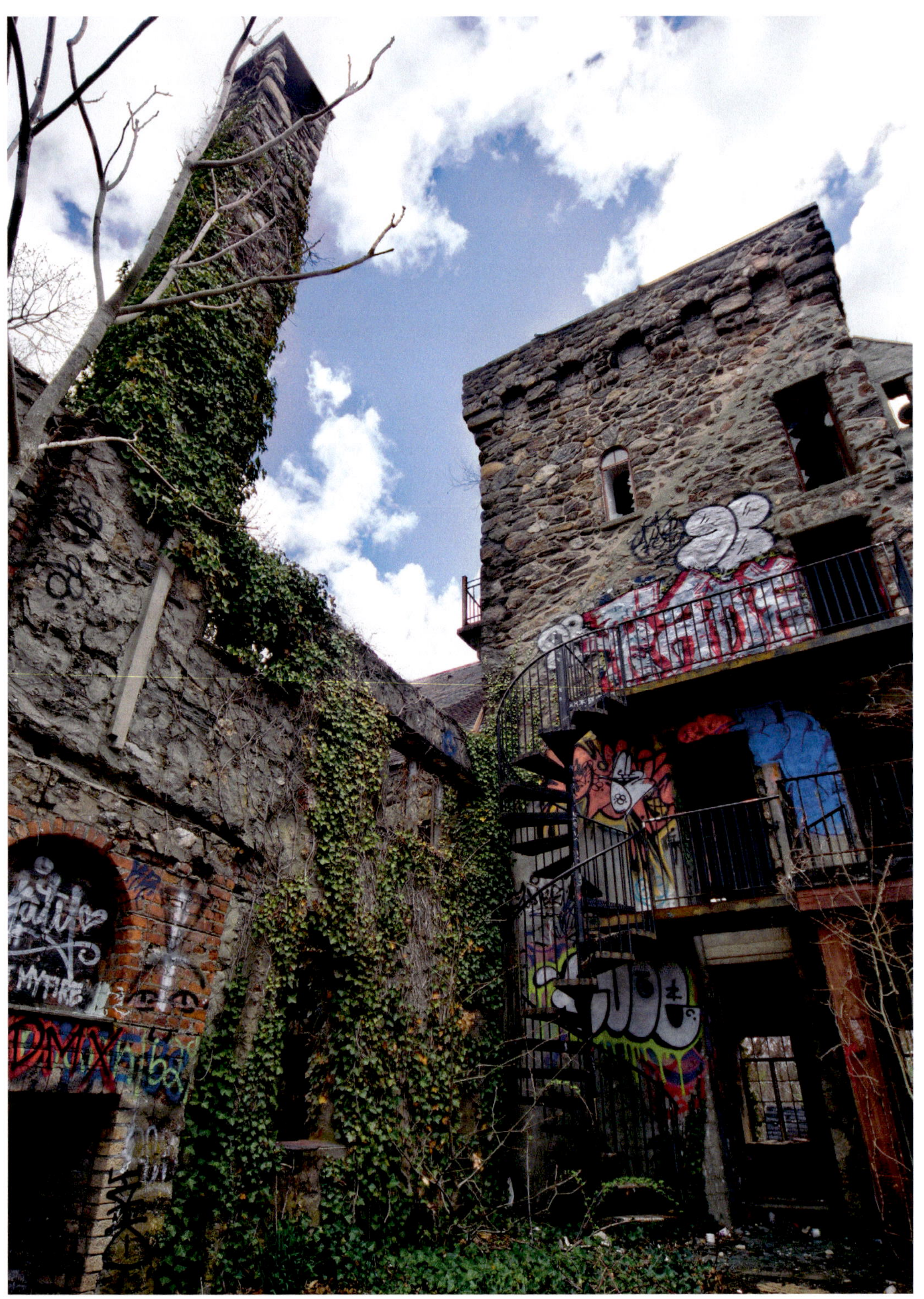

Time has not been kind to ELDA Castle, but neither have people. The structure has suffered a multitude of fires over the years, and vandals have smashed nearly every one of the mansion's windows, as well as cover much of the natural stone with rainbow-hued graffiti.

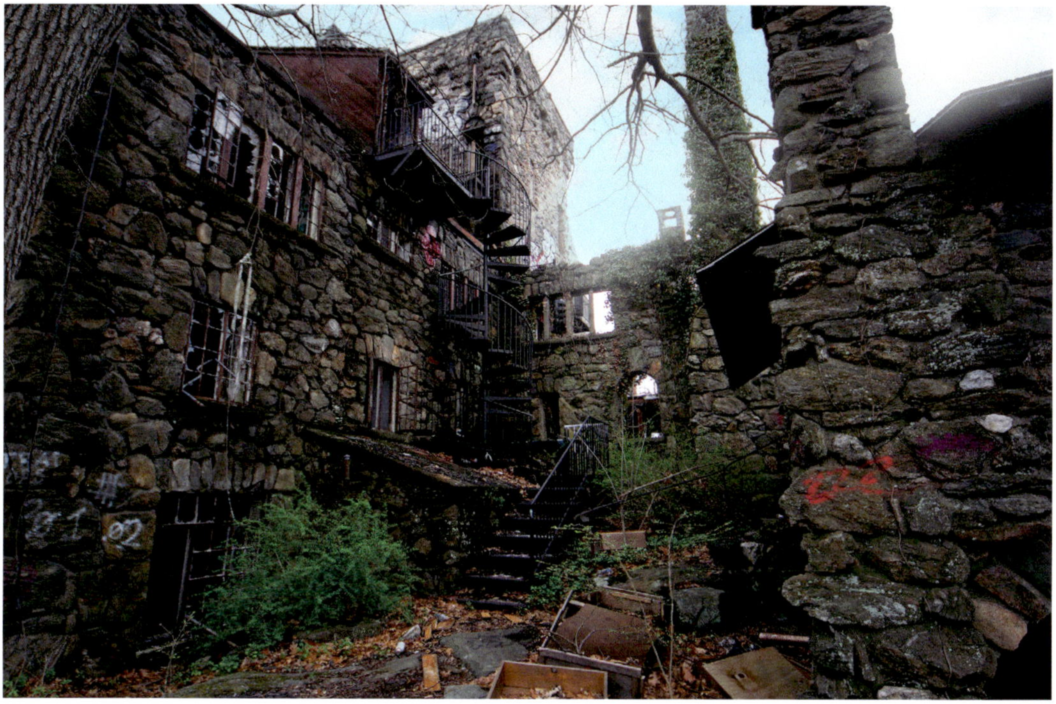

After the death of David Abercrombie on August 29, 1937, his widowed wife, Lucy, moved away to New Jersey to live with her daughter, Elizabeth. The castle sat vacant for years afterwards.

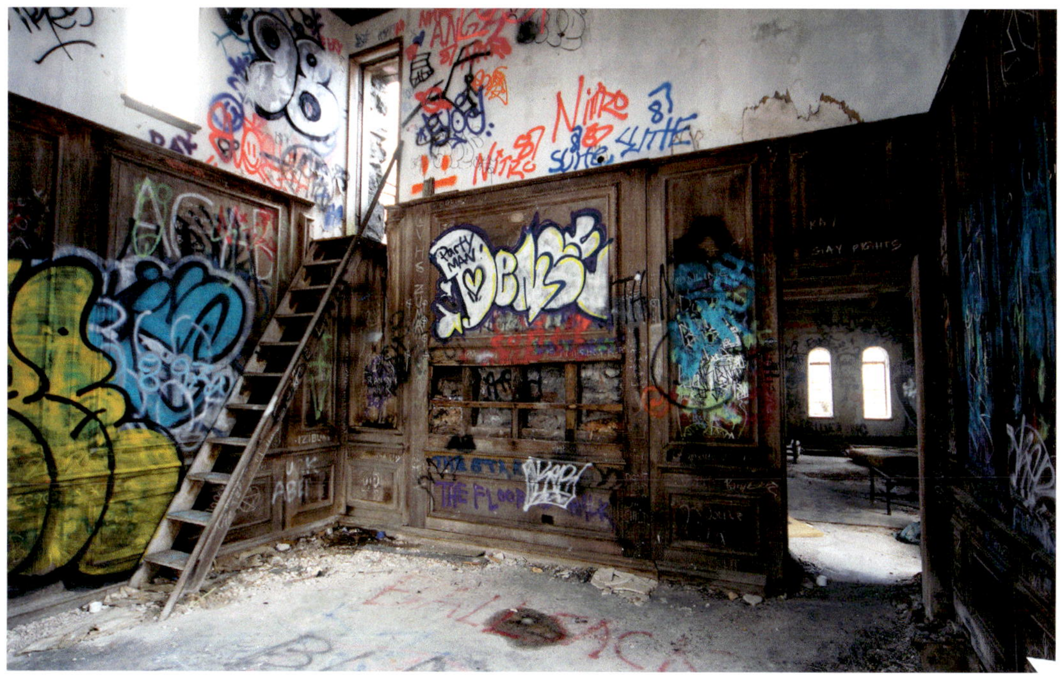

Throughout the decades that followed David's death, more than a half-dozen owners attempted to revitalize the property, none proving a success. Eventually the castle was abandoned in 2012, left to tend to itself in a forest that was ever-encroaching upon its walls.

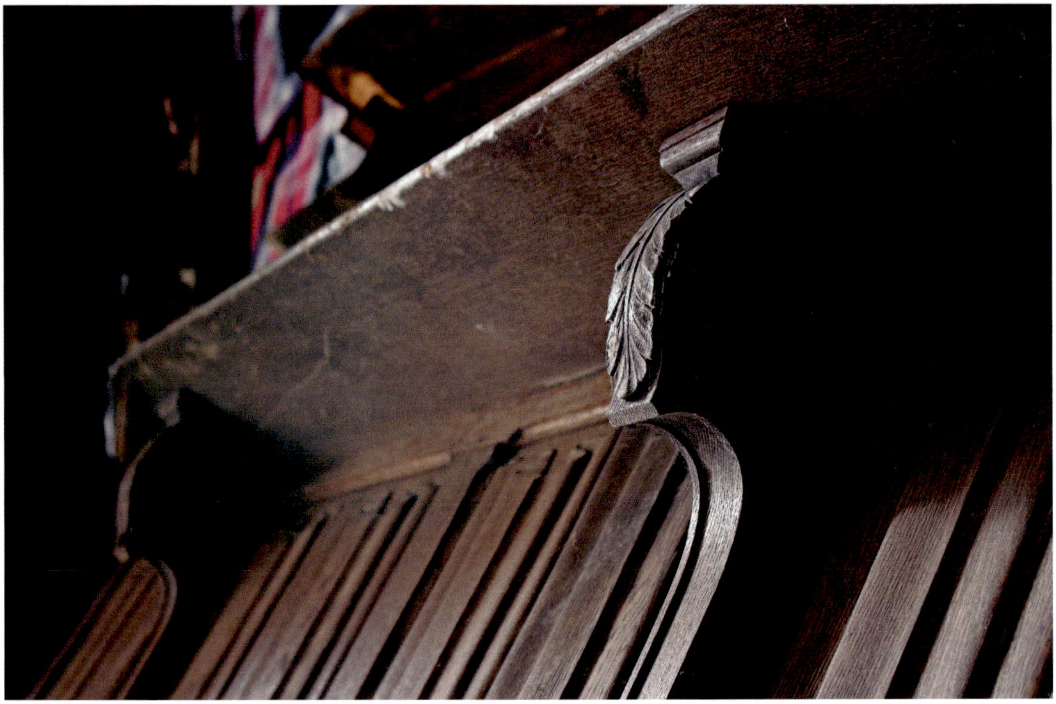

As ransacked and destroyed as the castle is today, tiny glimmers of what was are still present if one takes a moment to look.

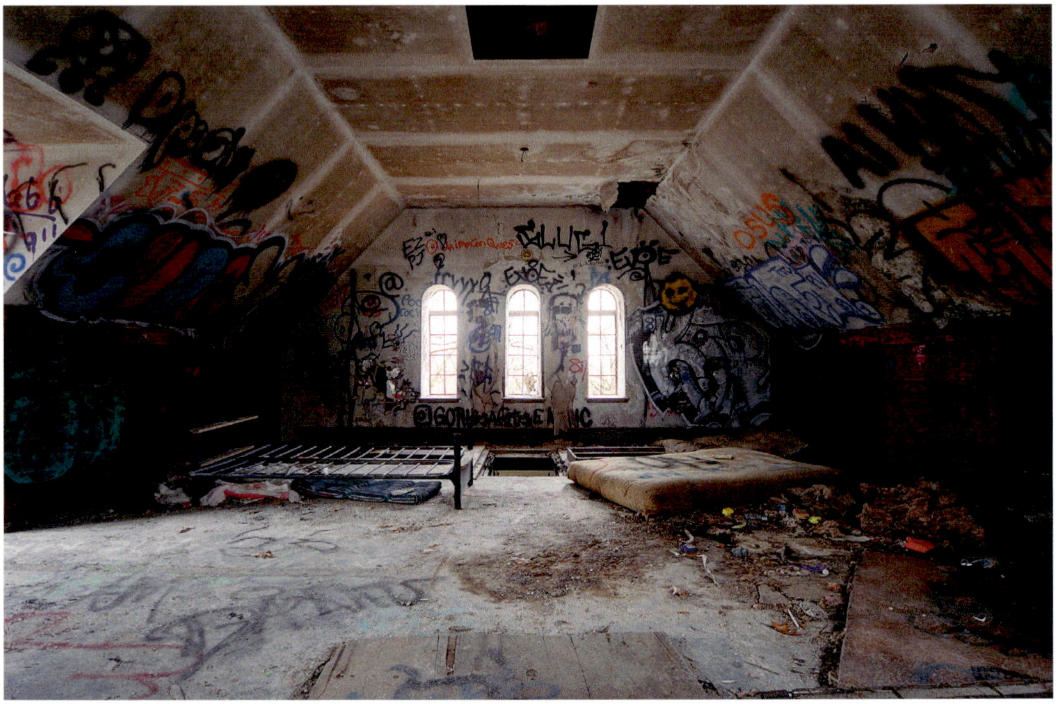

Unfinished walls and ceilings from a failed restoration project decades ago, now painted with layers of graffiti from an untold number of explorers.

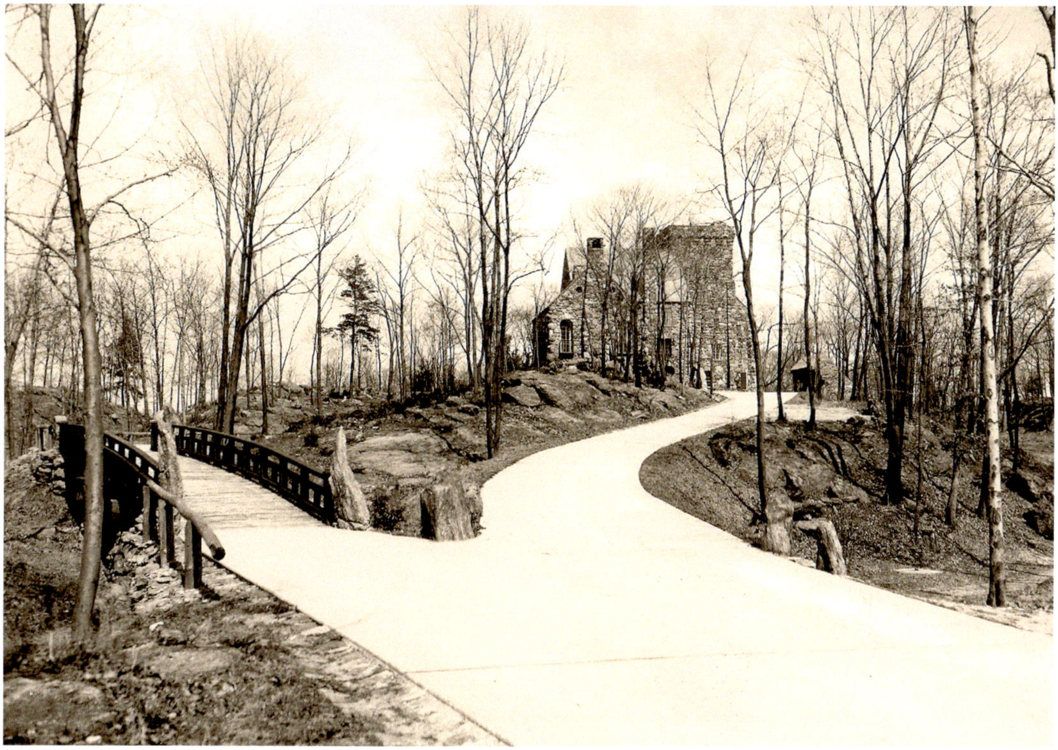

Above and below: The entry drive with ELDA in the distance, as it was nearly a century ago and as it exists today. The forest has all but swallowed the grounds, embracing the castle as it slowly weathers away. (*Historical photograph courtesy of Doug Leen*)

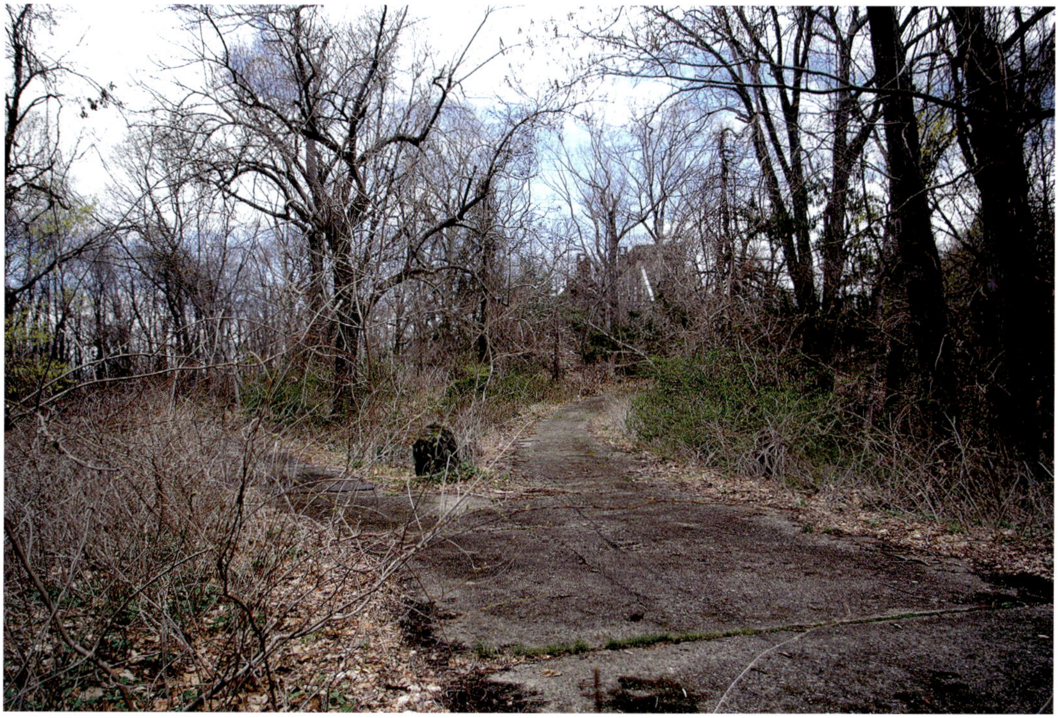

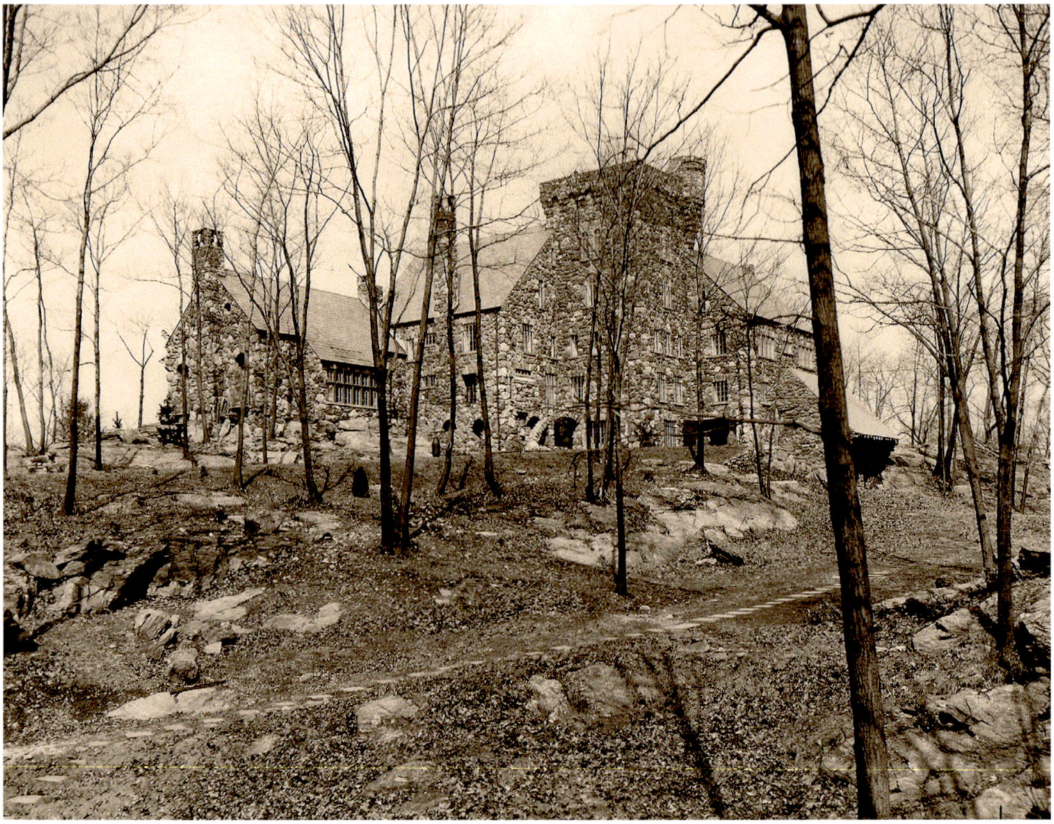

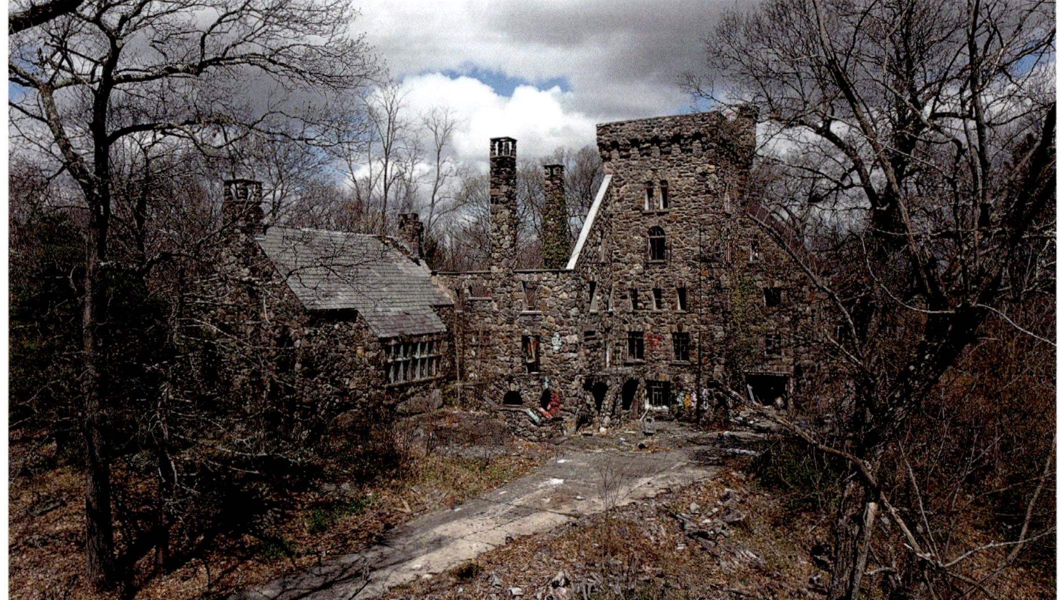

Above and below: When ELDA was first constructed it would be difficult to imagine its creators as seeing anything but an edifice that was built to stand the test of time, something rugged, strong, perpetual. In reality, however, the property is an illustration of everything but those concepts. In a sense, that's where the allure of a place like ELDA stems from—nothing is certain except uncertainty.

7

SELMA PLANTATION MANOR

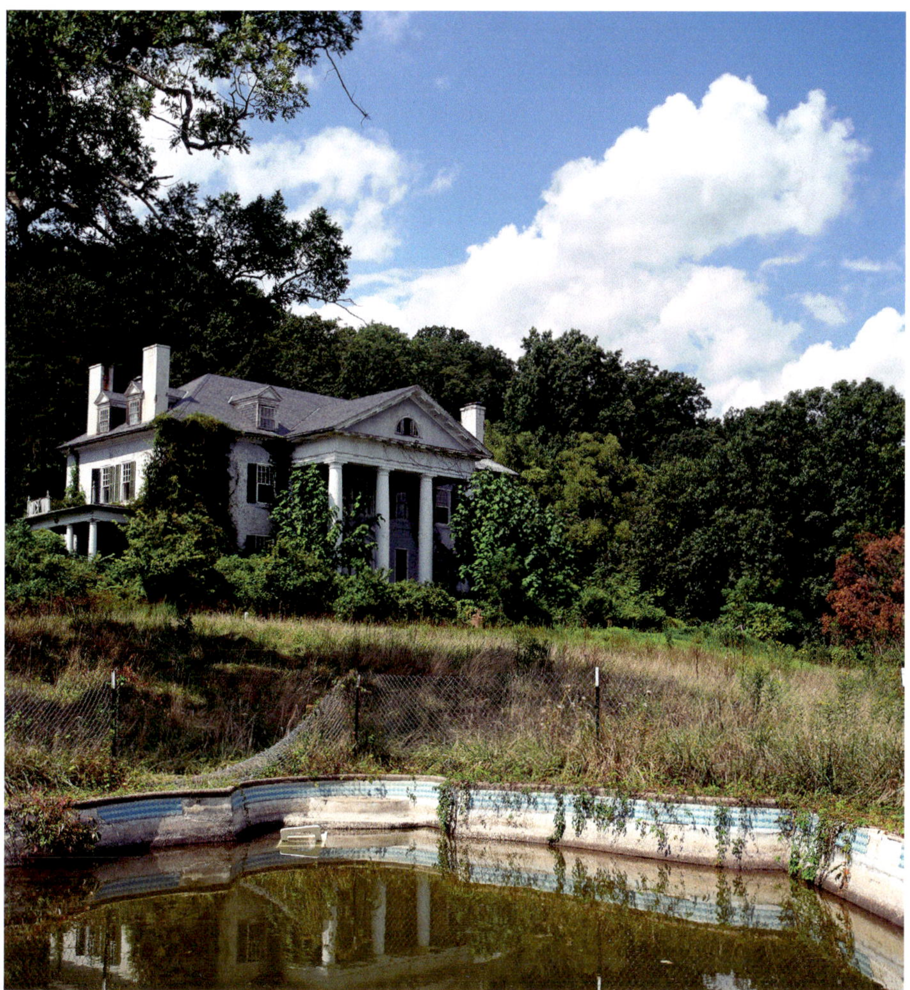

Far off, at the crest of a wild-grown field, stood a faded, weathered facade. Ivy-wrapped and ashy white, it lingered like a ghost over the housing development which had come to nest in valley below. Even from a great distance, you could recognize that the old mansion was a storied one, and from out across the meadow of tall grass and brier, it invites you to come closer, to listen to its tale of life and death, and life again—to know the story of the Selma Plantation Manor.

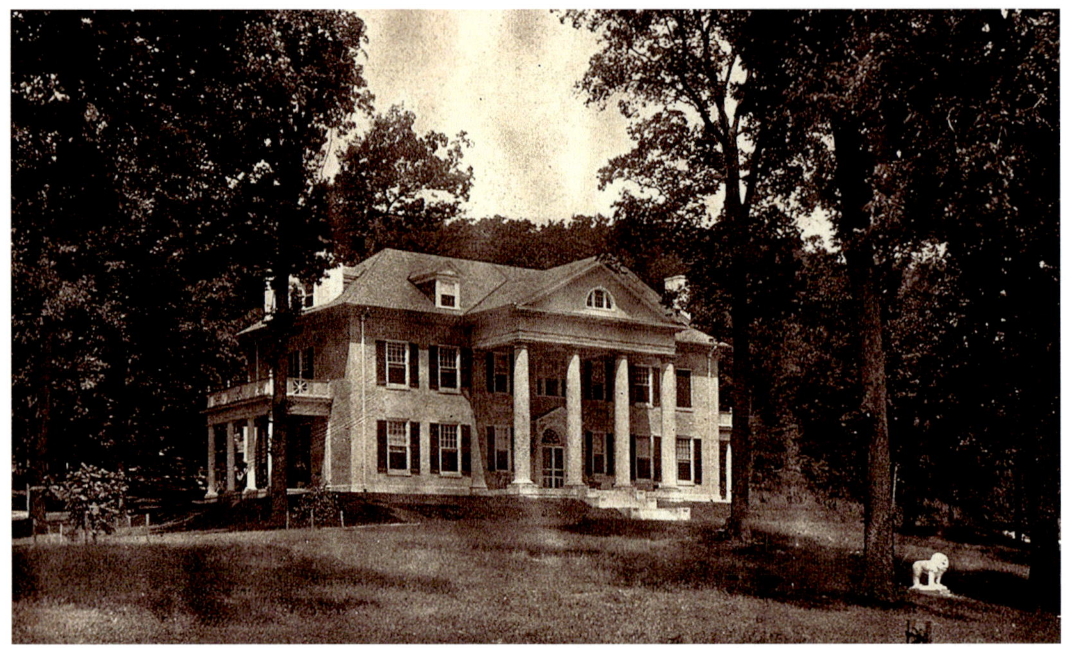

Above and below: As we made our slow approach, and as the old structure became increasingly clear, and more minute details came better into view, the ambiance of the property began to turn. No longer did this old manor seem a looming phantom, it was in fact much more humble, much more melancholy, like an elderly person left without a family. Abandoned with only their thoughts and no one to share them with. (*Historic newspaper image depicts the Selma manor as it was in 1906*)

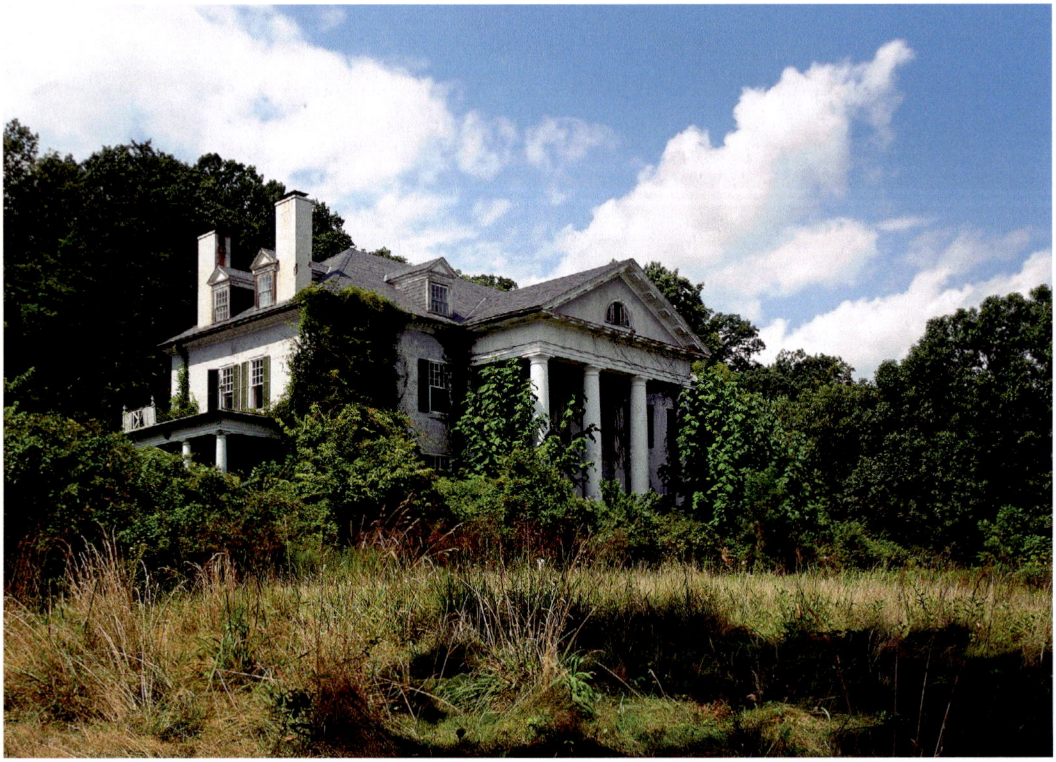

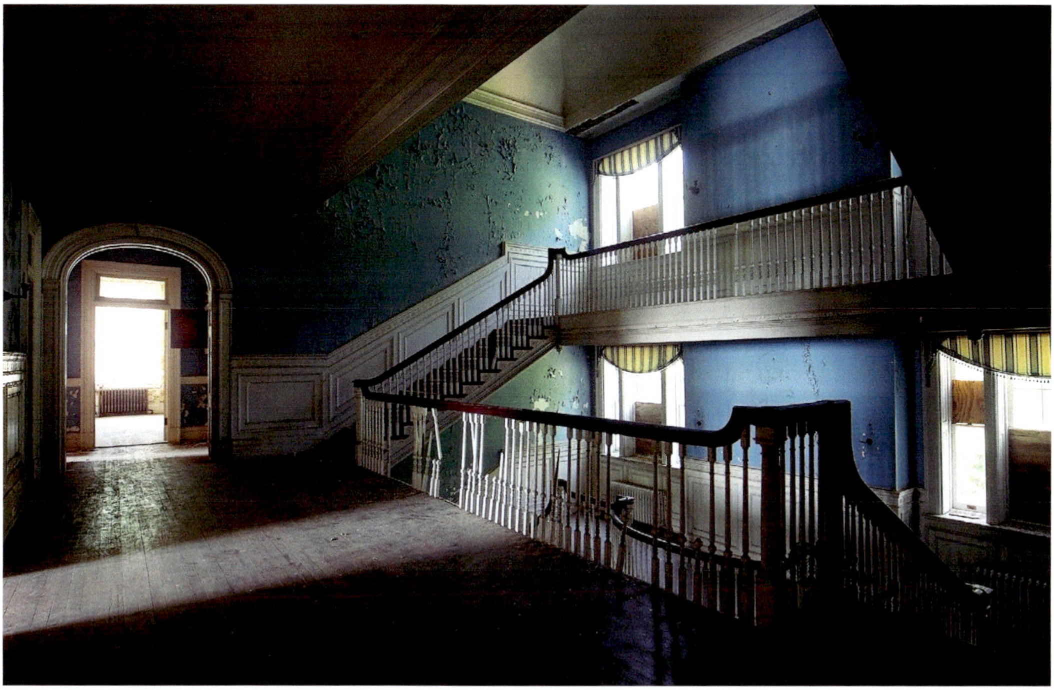

Within, the air was dense. Not with dust or debris, but the atmospheric weight of a house that had witnessed countless generations of people pass through its halls, and recalled each one with clarity.

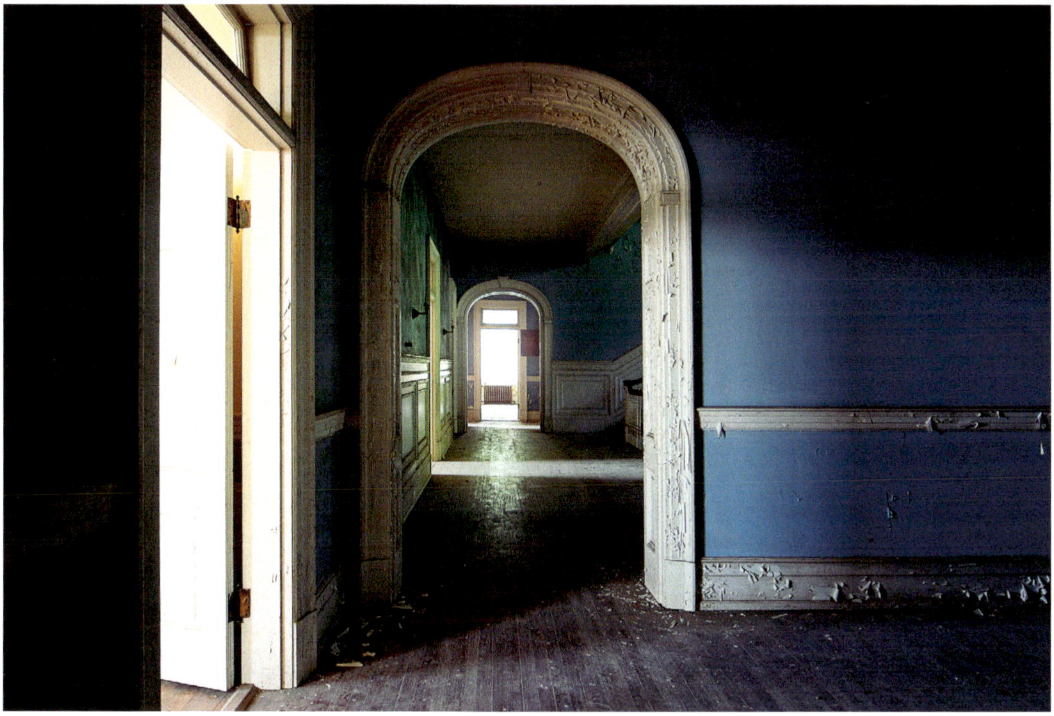

The history was held there, still, palpable, coursing through the fibers of the lath beyond the plaster. A lifeblood which served to sustain a house which many may have viewed as long-dead.

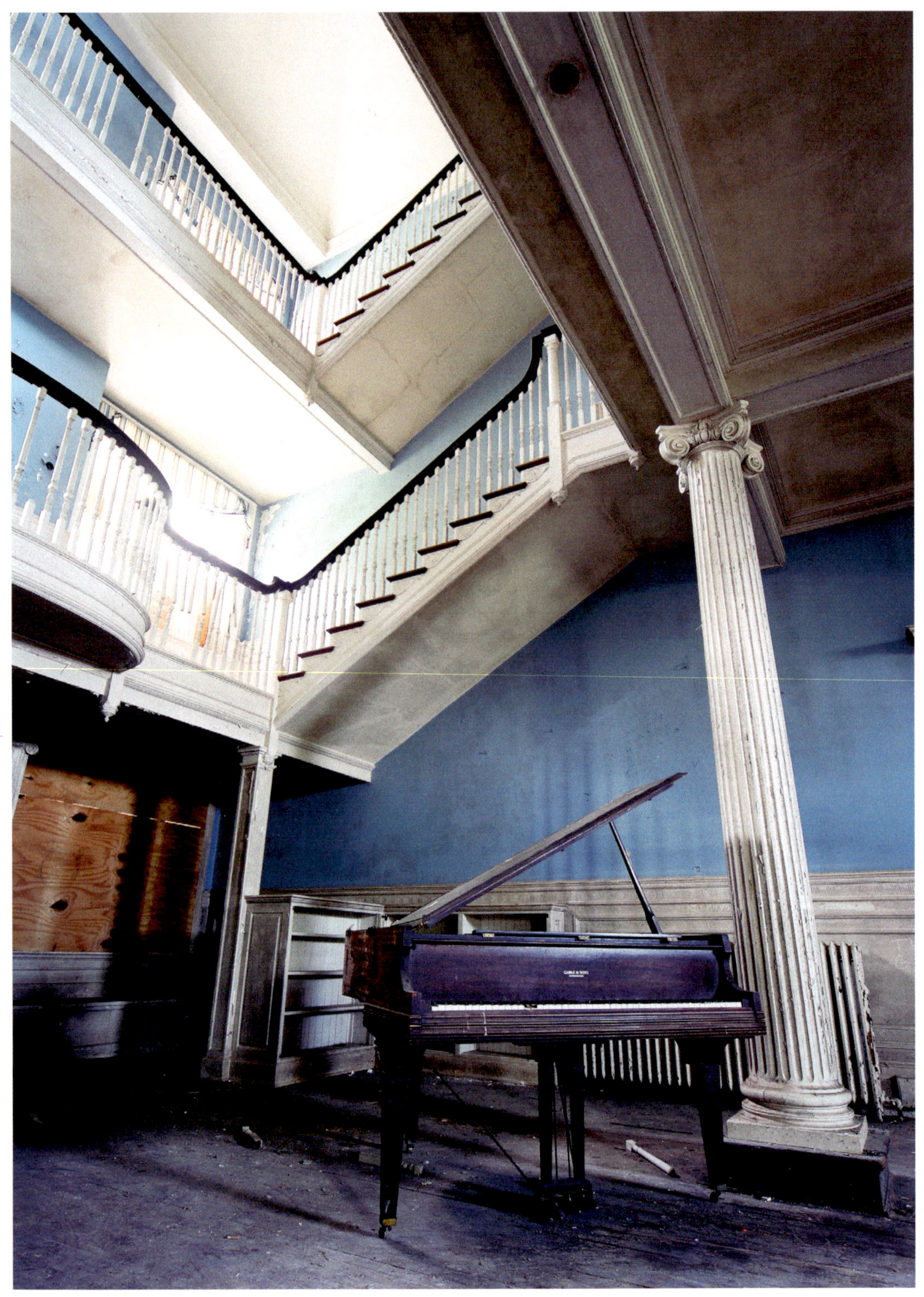

An immense main hall was, by any metric, the backbone of the mansion. Three stories of balconies formed the master staircase that spiraled around the perimeter of the pillared hall. At the center stood a deteriorating grand piano, crooked and out-of-tune, a reflection of the manor which it called home.

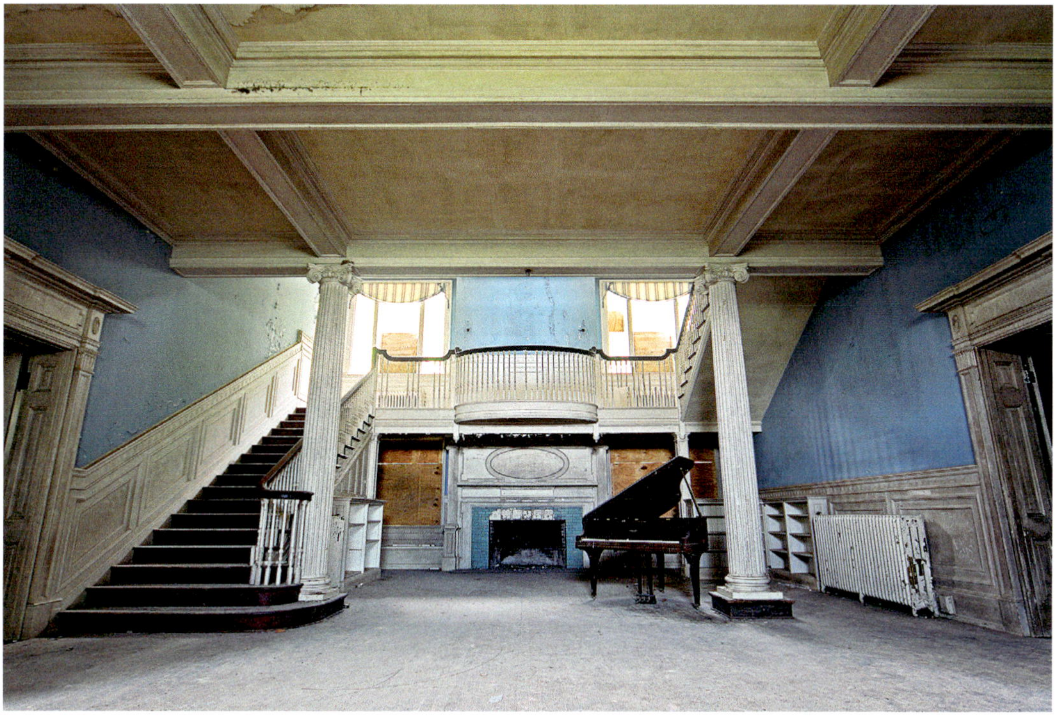

The view one had immediately upon entering through the front doors.

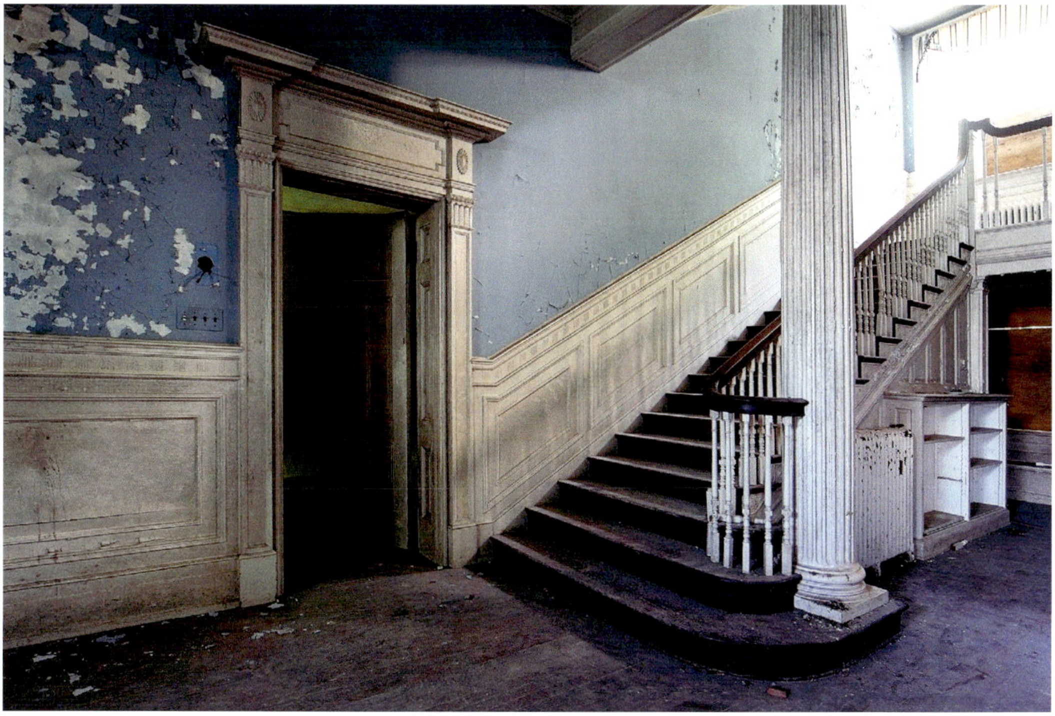

The base of the master staircase. The surrounding space was so large and empty that every step echoed countless times off towering ceilings and through arched doorways.

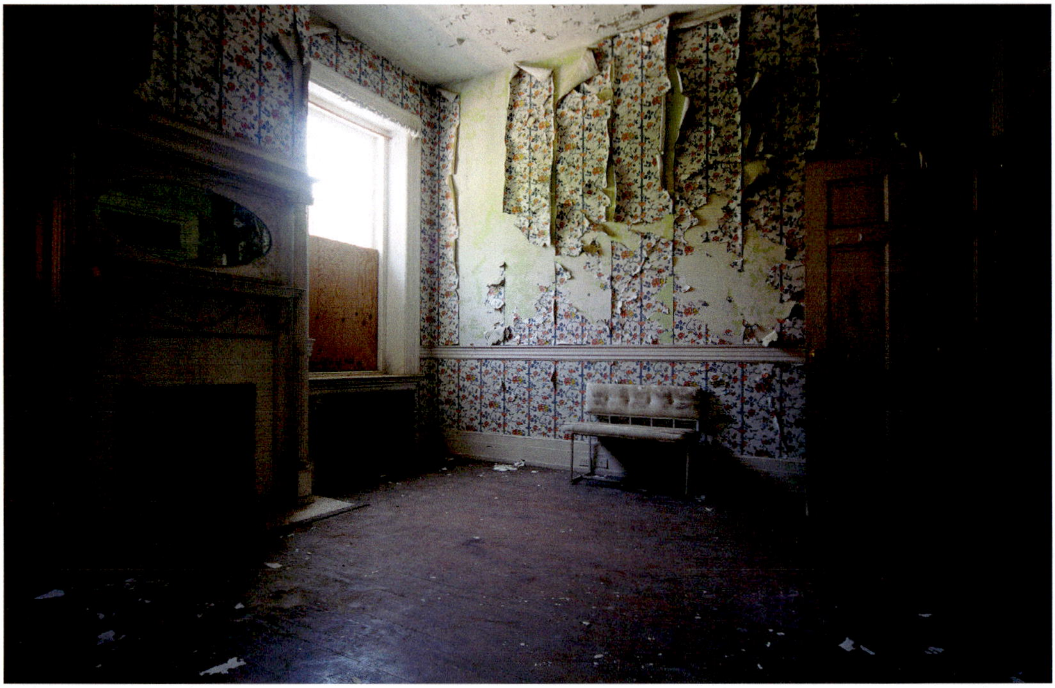

Wallpaper hung in strips from cracked and tired walls, decorative woodwork adorned doorways to dark chambers of grime and murk.

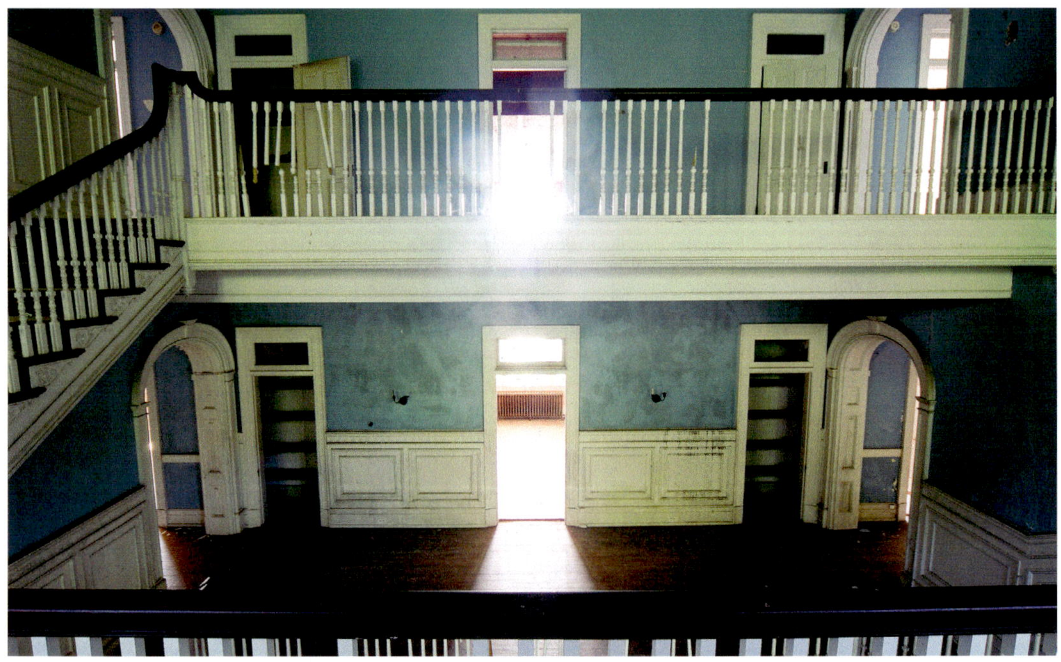

The oldest of these walls date from the nineteenth century. In a past existence, they formed a beautiful home which endured upon this Virginian hilltop for nearly a century before surrendering to a terrible fire. For years thereafter, a burned-out ruin at the crest of a field was all that remained of the former home. The walls that survived the blaze stood resolute, though, as nature began to reclaim the property.

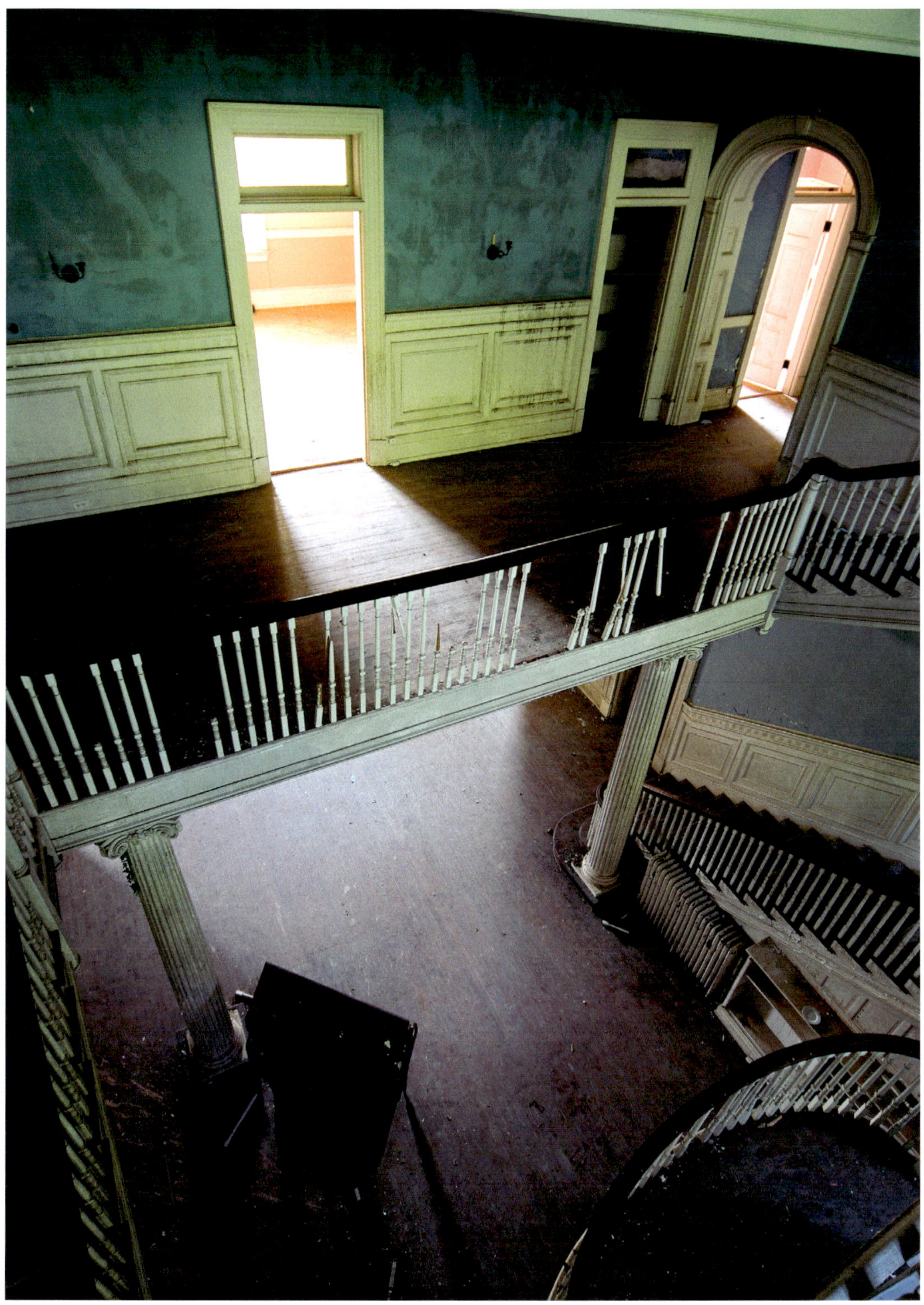

After the passing of some years a grand new mansion began construction upon that same hilltop, with the surviving walls of the original home incorporated into the design. This final form, completed in 1902, is what stands to this day.

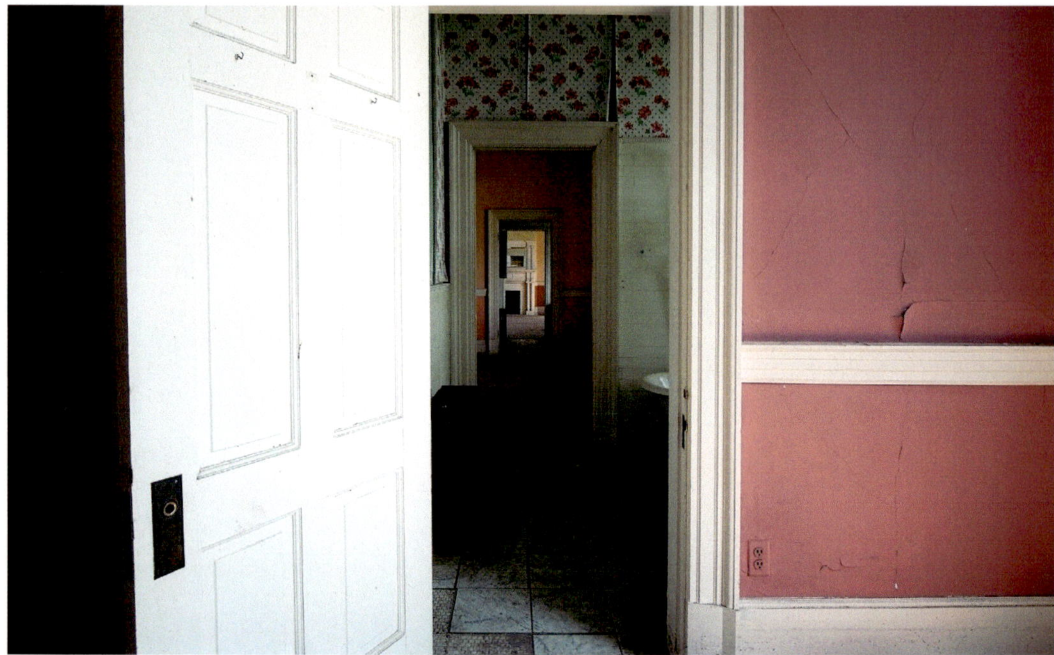

This estate, and the surrounding 200-plus acres, existed as a private residence until the mid-1970s when it was sold off and converted into an impressive wedding and event venue. This endeavor lasted until the early 2000s when the property was sold yet again. This time the land surrounding the mansion was sub-divided off for new construction, and the mansion was left deserted.

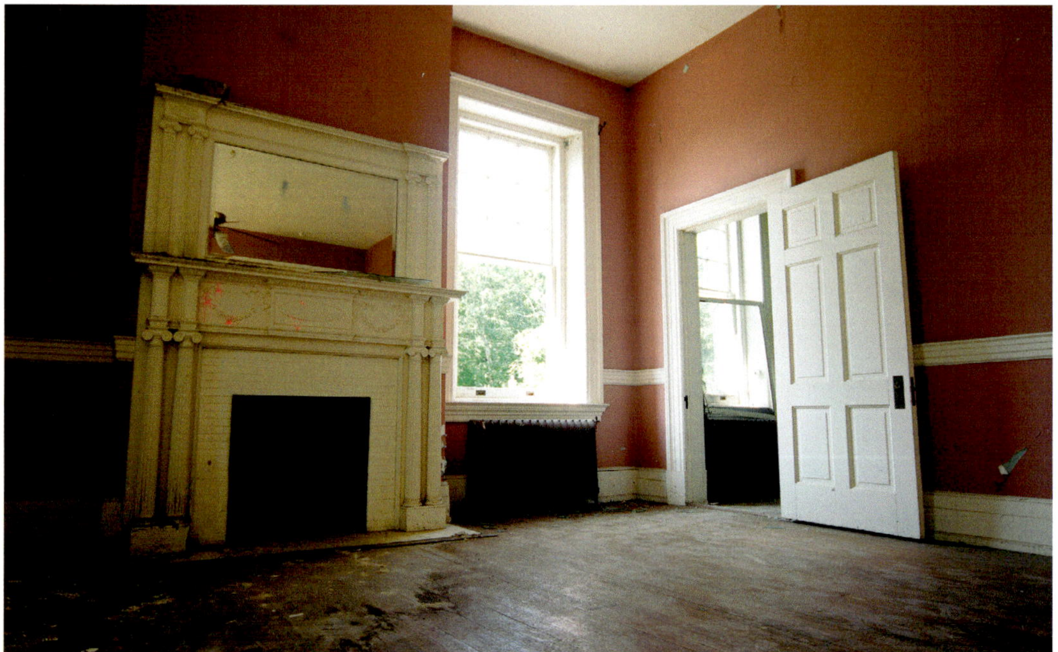

As the years progressed, new homes began to appear on the landscape, and the mansion watched on, every year slipping further and further into decay and the ever-encroaching wood-line. A once-proud estate is now home to the few buzzards who have taken up roost in the attic rafters.

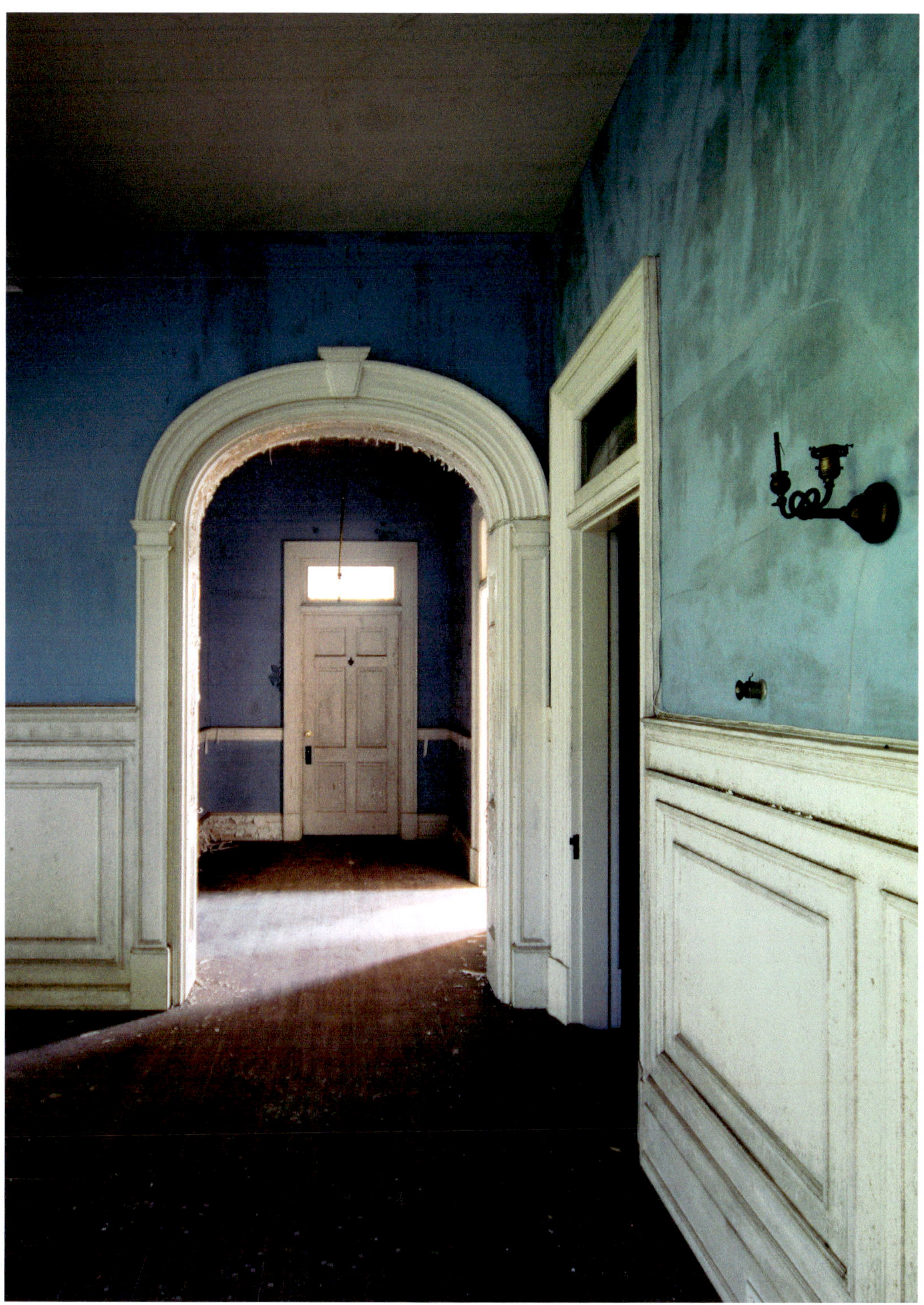

How could a place so steeped in history be thrown away? What does it say for us as a culture when we can build dozens of new homes a stone's throw from a historic mansion, on the very land that was once its property, yet take no effort toward its preservation?

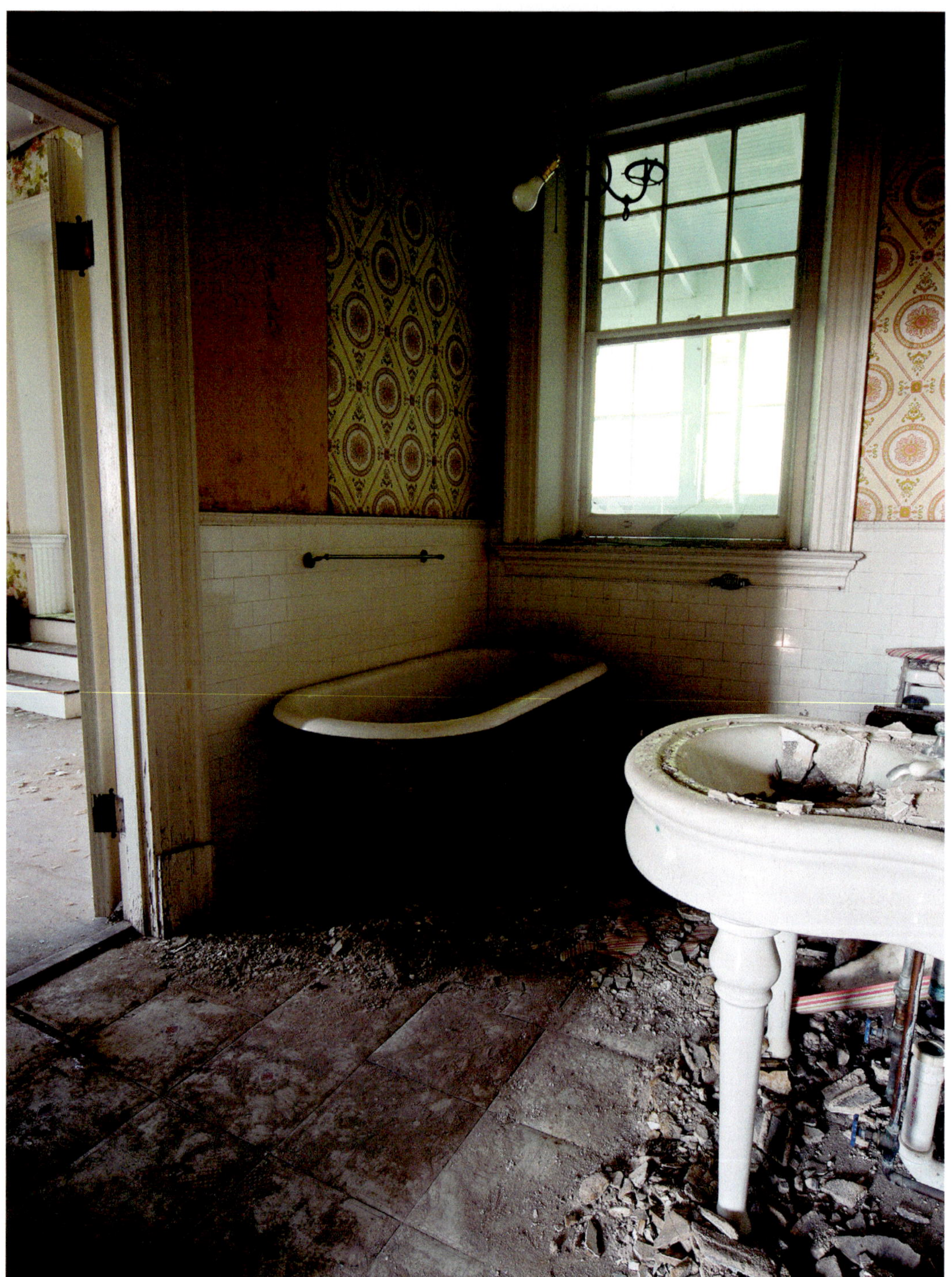

Luckily, some time after our visit to the Selma Manor, it was saved by an impassioned couple who saw through the grime at the gem that lie just beneath. Their endeavor was called the "Selma Mansion Rebirth," and it proved to be exactly what the name implies: the ardent rehabilitation of the old Selma Plantation. To see the neglect scraped away, and the home once again cherished, was uplifting in a way that is terribly difficult to articulate. We strongly urge readers to look into the project for themselves, it will leave you not only impressed but inspired.

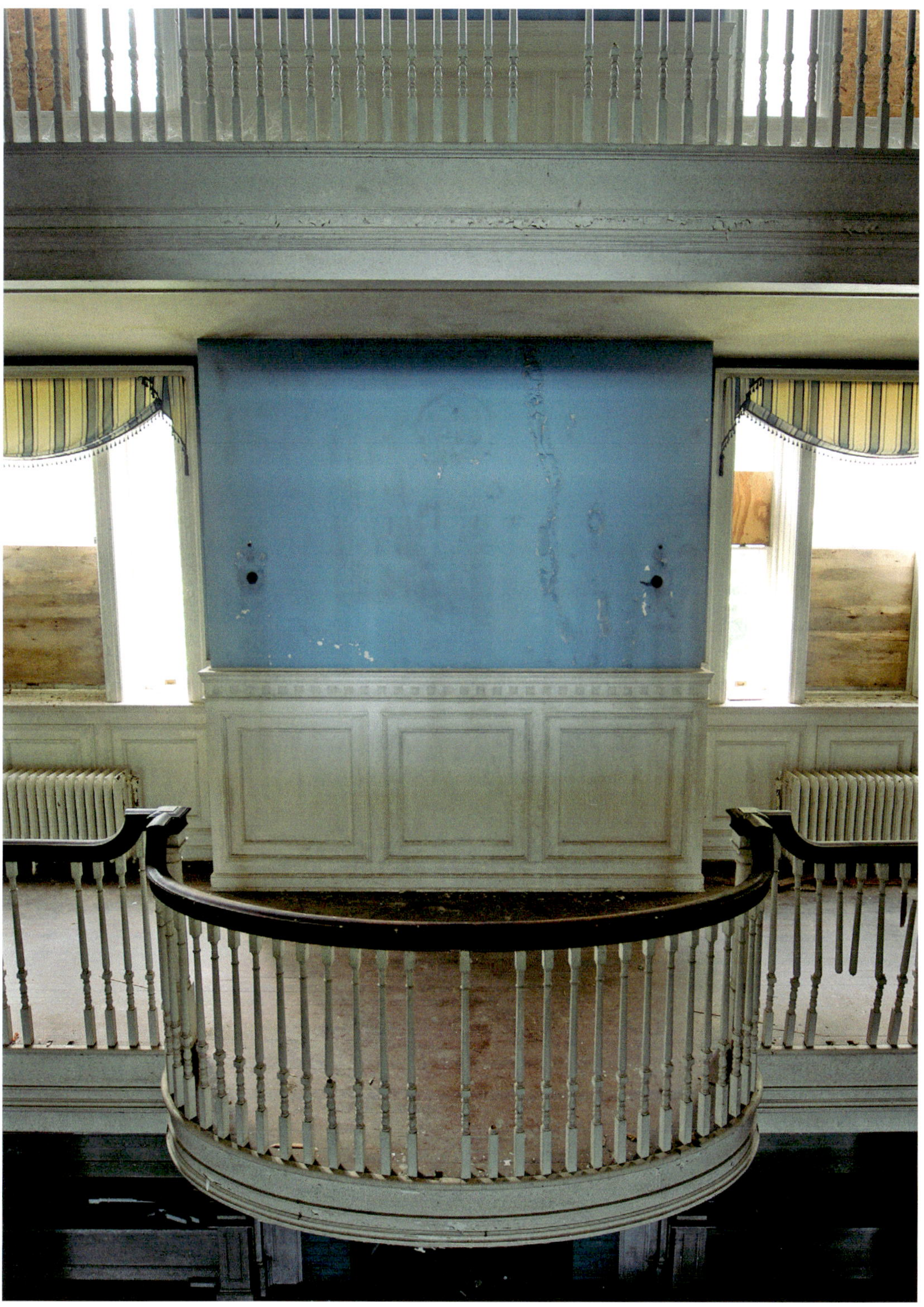

To watch as a building seemingly written off to rot in the forest is carefully brought back from the brink, to now serve as a wonderful home, is genuinely moving. It also serves as a strong example of architectural conservation that other properties may point to as a preservation tool in the future.

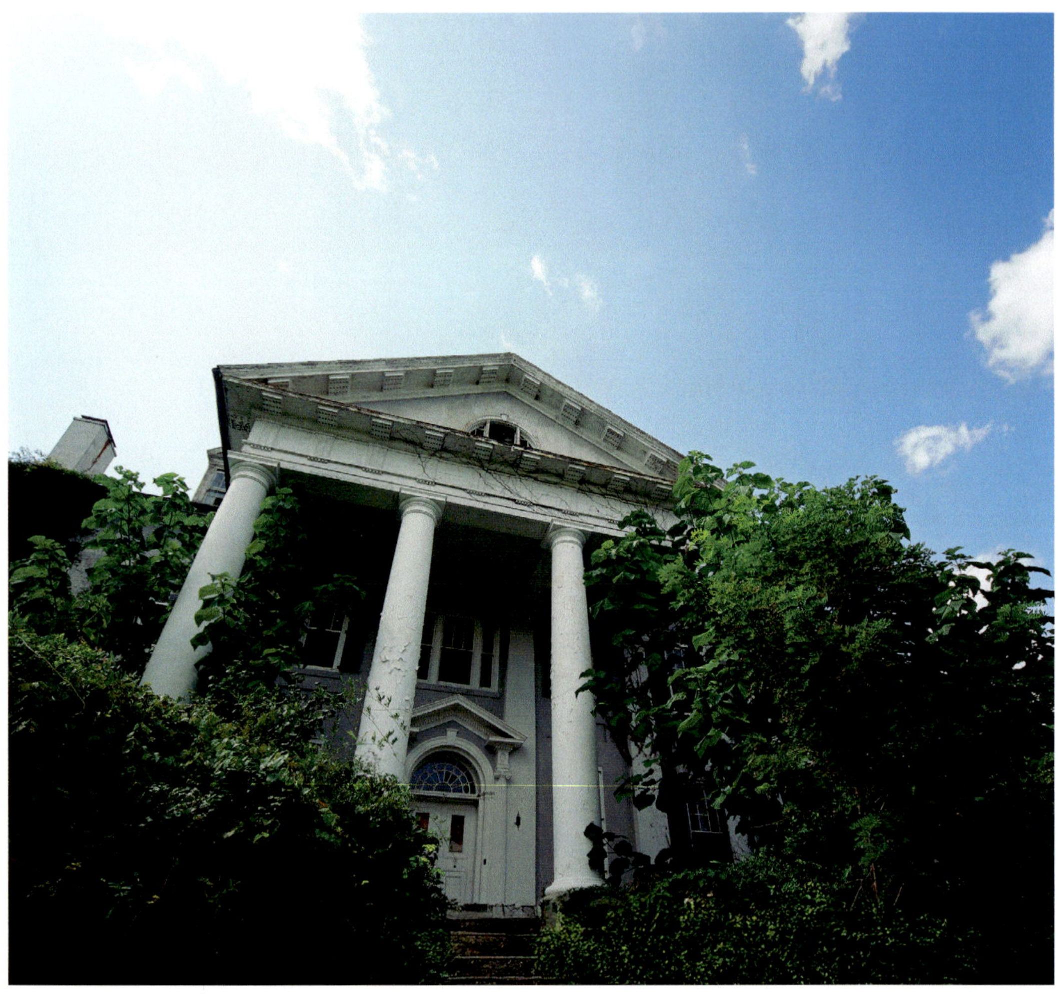

There is an expression which goes "if walls could talk." When looking back upon the Selma grounds from the vantage point of today, what was it that those walls were saying as they slowly moldered on that hilltop for all those years? We would like to think they were quietly repeating, "We are not dead, simply waiting."

8

MODERN RUINS

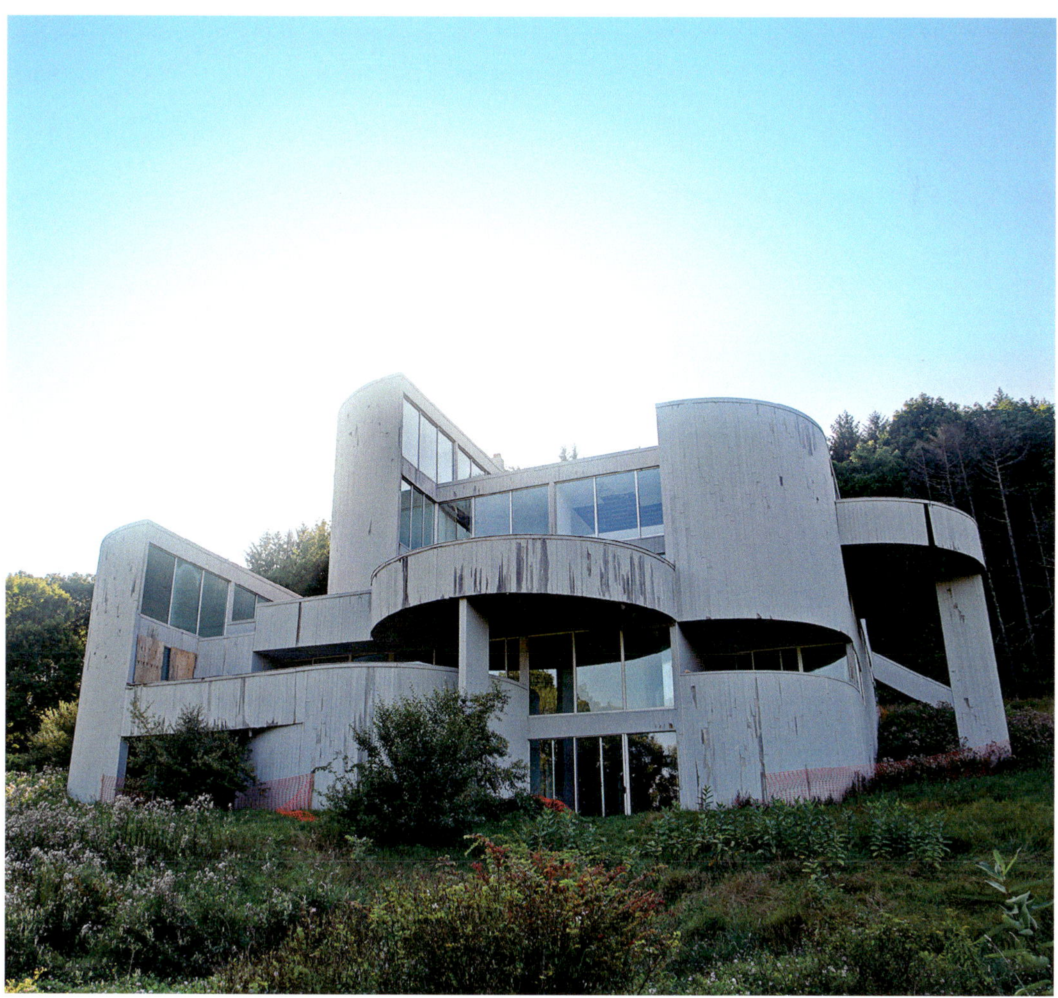

There exists an old proverb that conveys a timeless truth: "Pride goeth before destruction." Over time, this saying became the contemporary expression "pride before fall." A caution against becoming so engrossed with one's own self-importance and accomplishments that you lose sight of all else, which leads inevitably to a downfall. Perhaps this is partly the allure of abandoned mansions; these grand structures, left to decay, represent far more than just once-grand homes left to rot, they stand as haunting relics of collapsed empires, intimate as they may be.

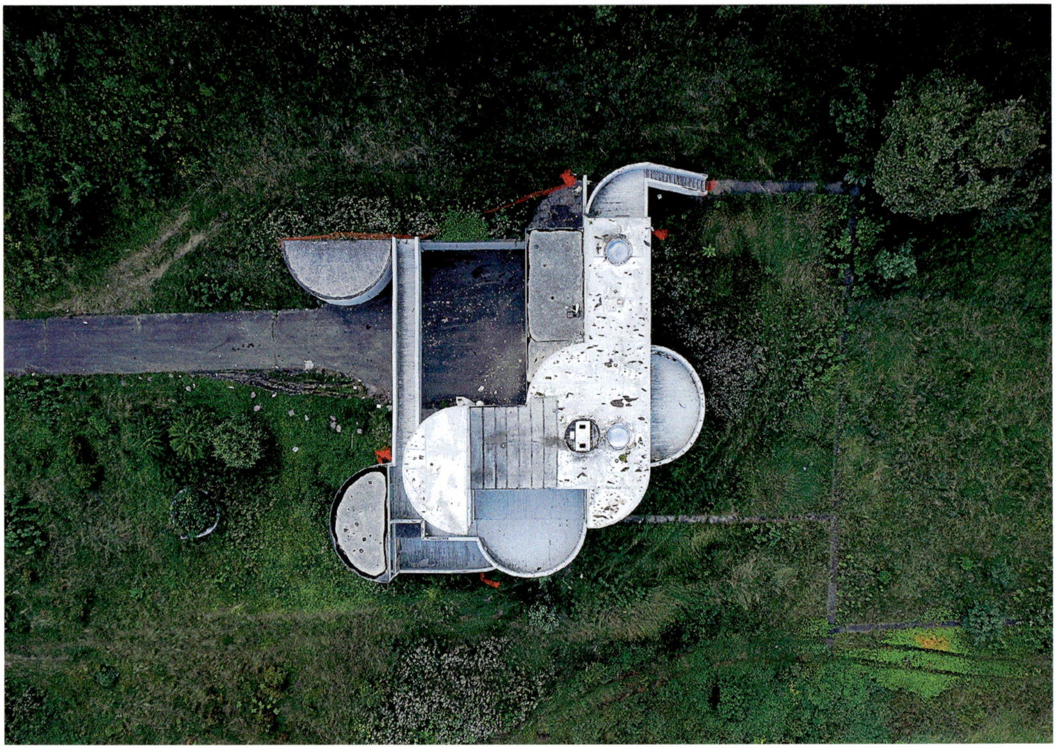

Above and below: In these ruins, some see the physical embodiment of pride's demise. These ravaged mansions remind us that neither individuals nor their creations are immune to failure, and that the steady workings of nature and time pay no mind to grandeur.

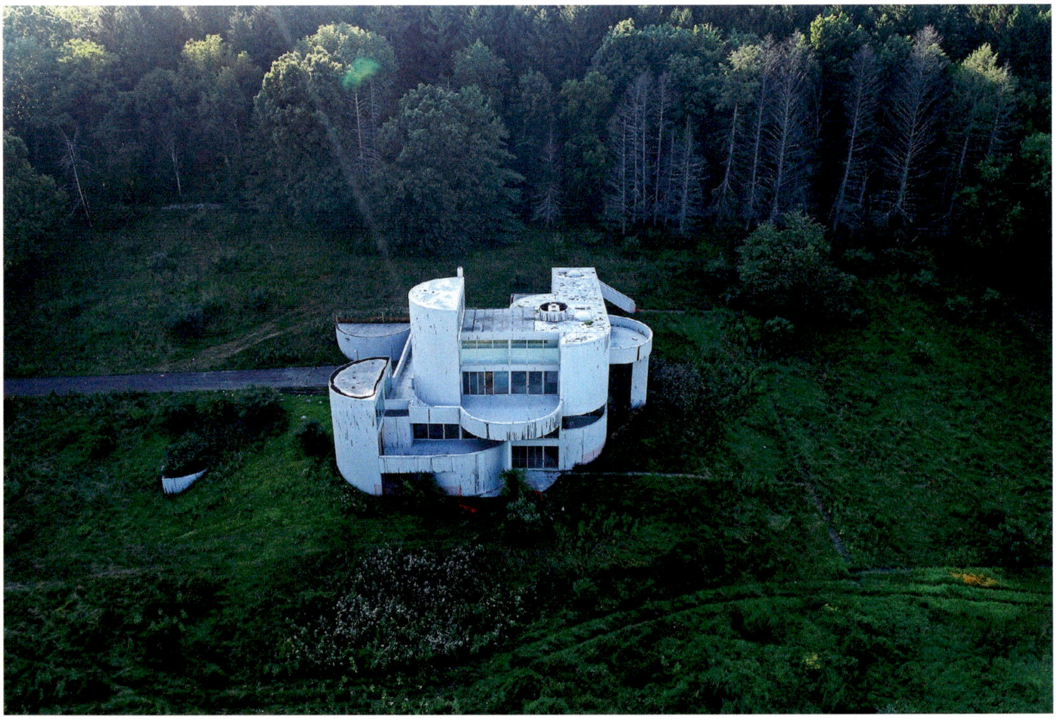

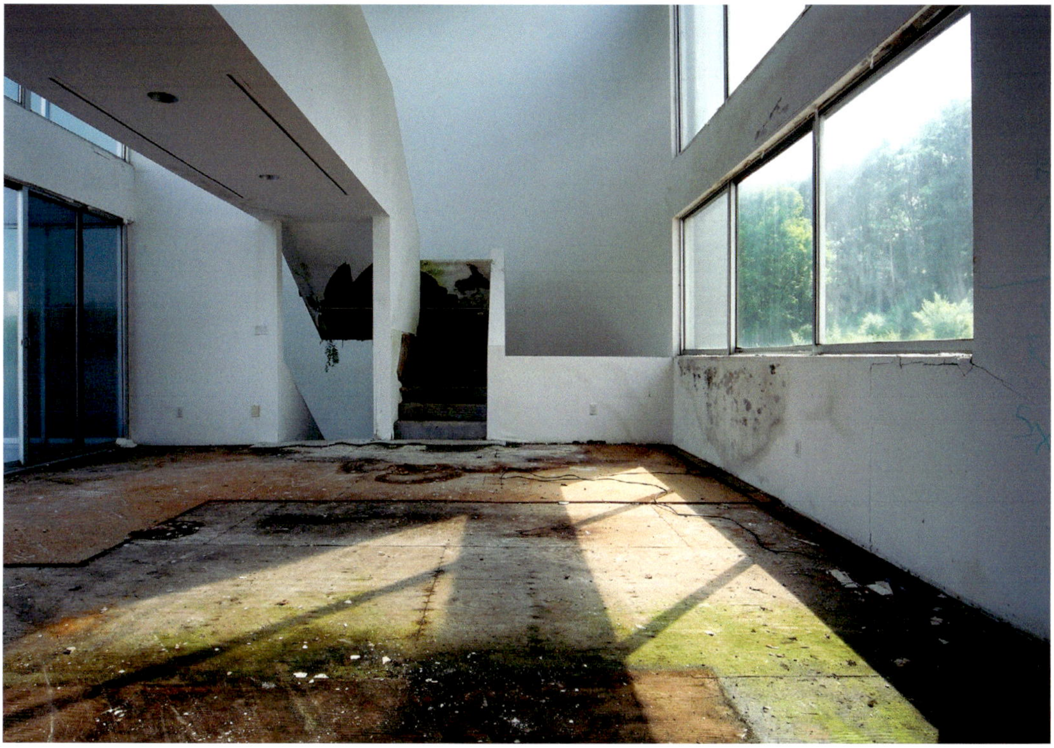

Above and below: A modern ruin presents this concept with even greater clarity. Stark and empty, they lack the veneer of historical significance or imagined nostalgia that shroud older, historic ruins. Instead, they stand in plain view, stripped of any romanticized past.

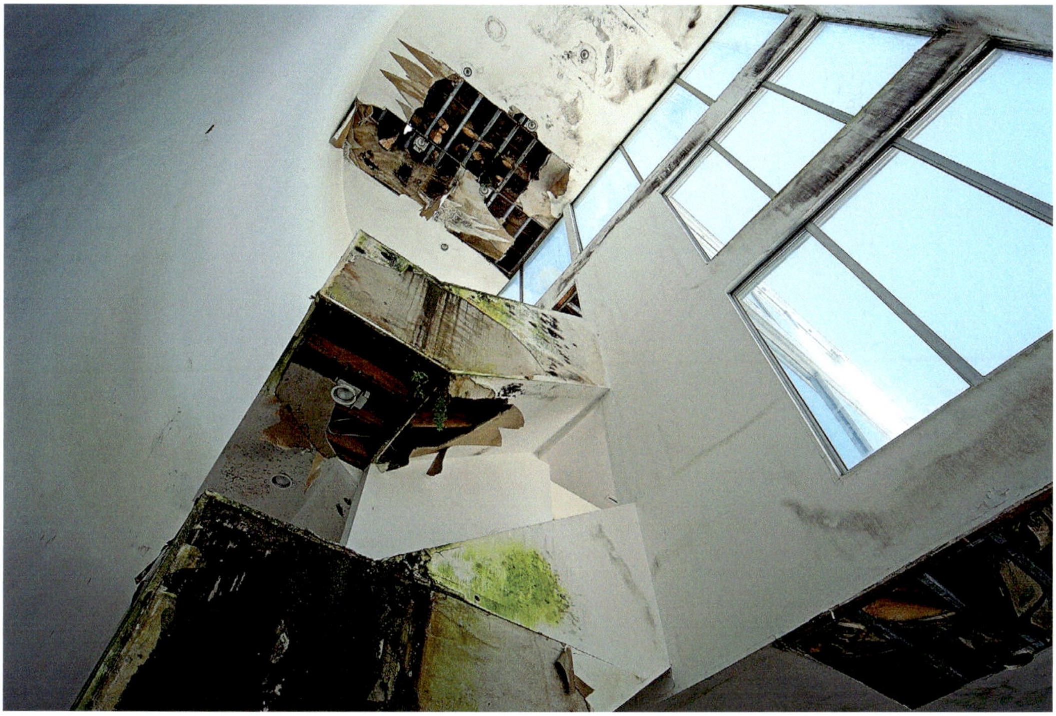

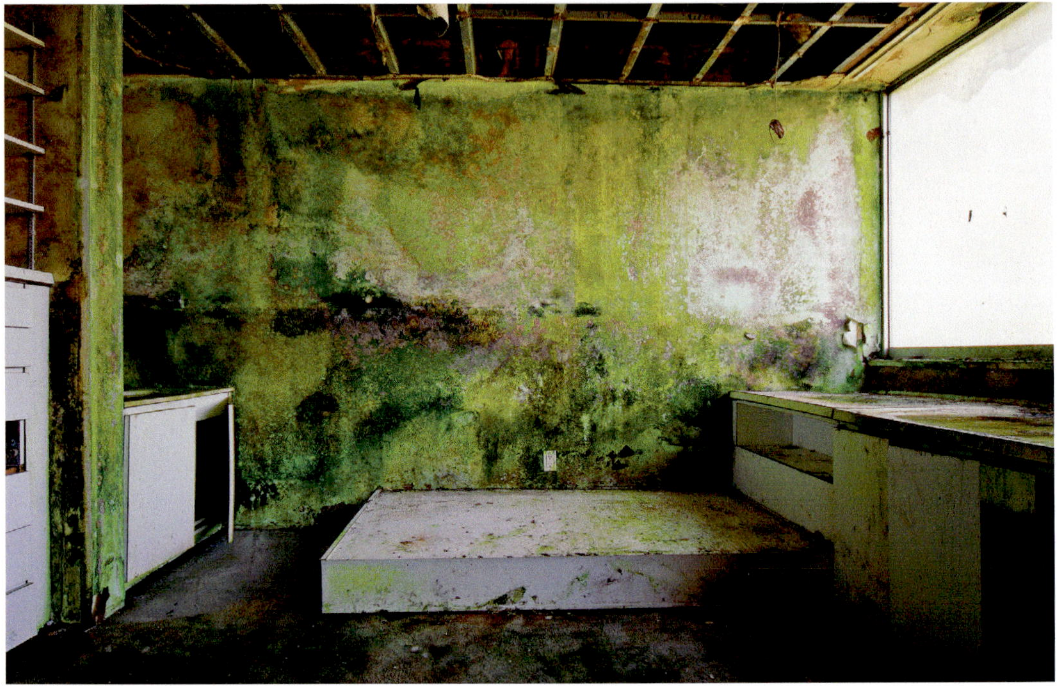

Above and below: Inside, rather than the sweeping curves and ornate craftsmanship one may imagine when thinking of an "abandoned mansion," we were greeted with sharp angles, bare sheet-rock, and austere square windowpanes. The absence of intricate detailing created an atmosphere of desolation within the building. However, the feeling of solitude was, to a degree, an illusion. A thick, spreading mold had laid claim over the upper floors, nourished by the leaking roofs, spreading its tendrils across the floors, walls, and ceilings.

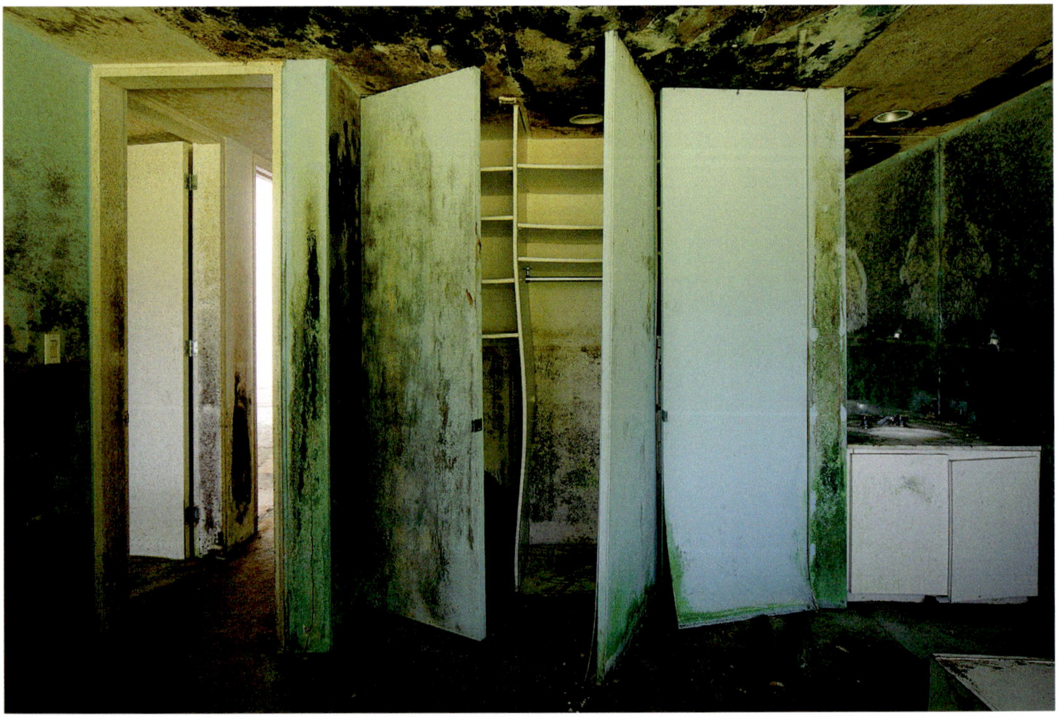

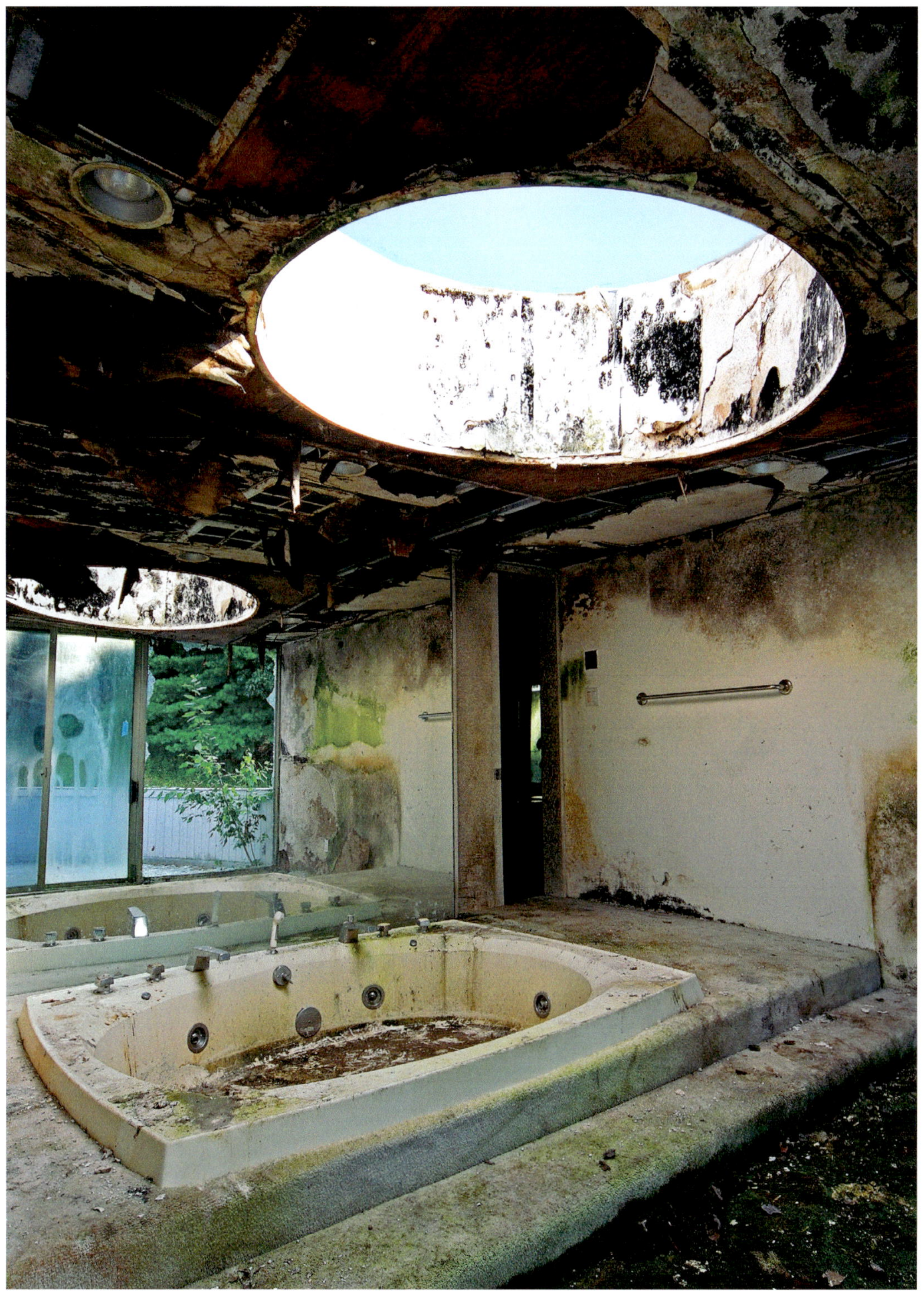

The former master bath, where a tub watches on as the room and house crumble around it. Mold and the pungent stench of decay clung to the air, thick and unyielding. Yet above, through the skylight, serene white clouds drifted across the expanse of the blue sky.

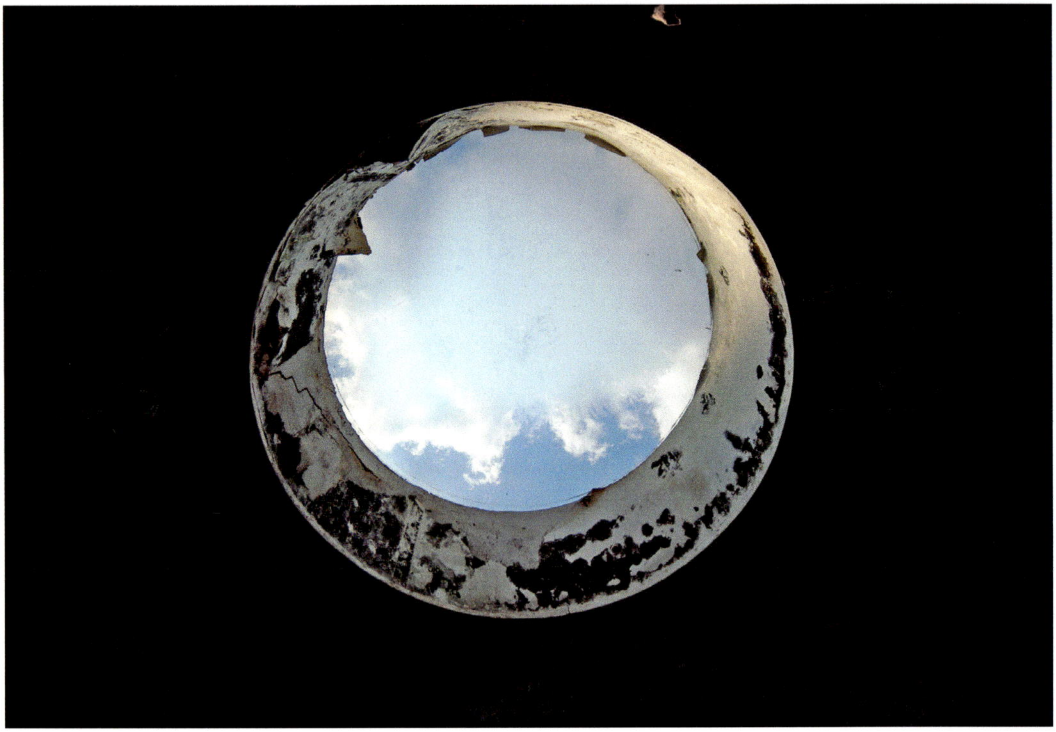

Fresh air and sunlight, just out of reach.

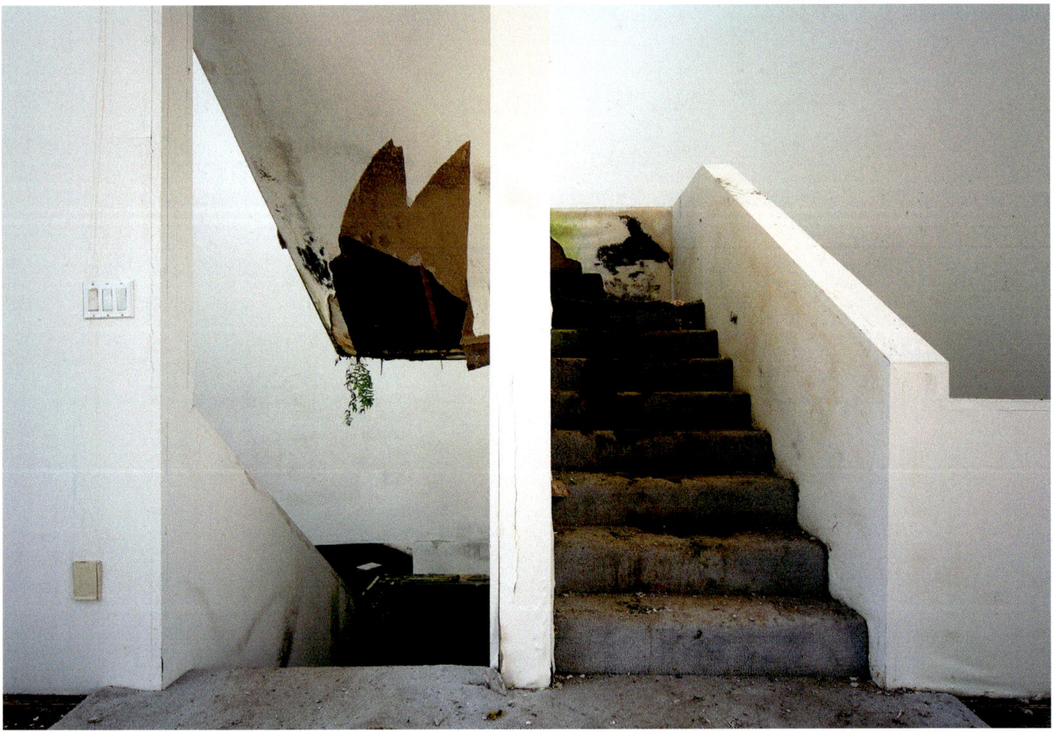

The house was slowly being digested by nature. Inch by inch turning to dirt.

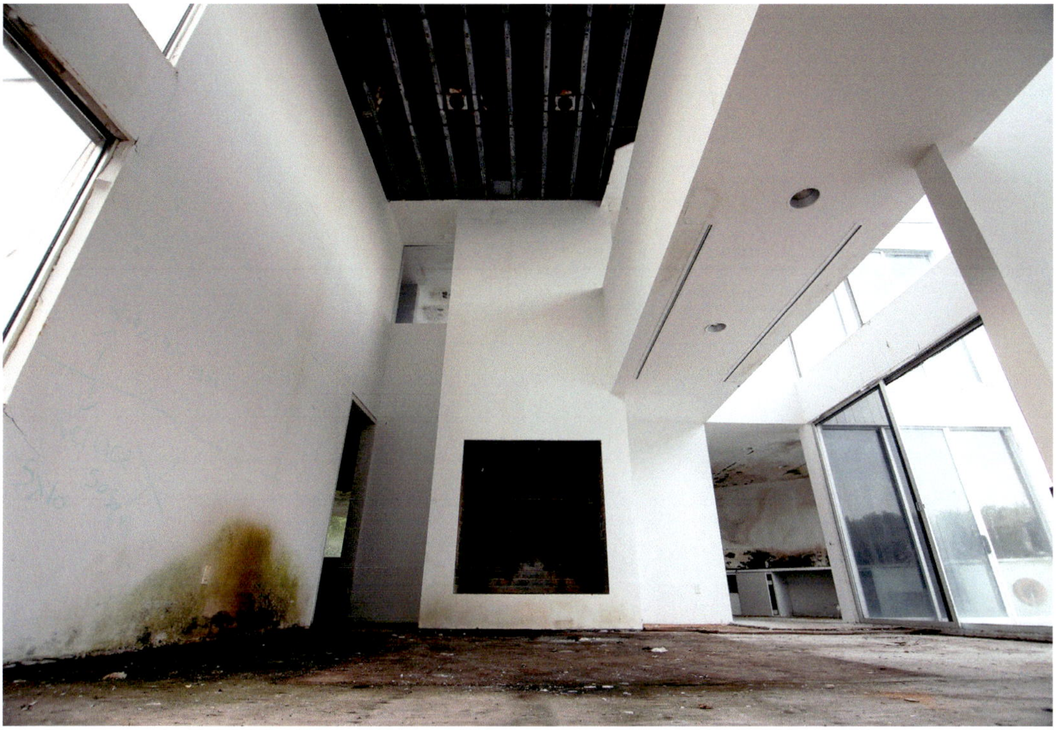

Above and below: This home was surely cherished by its former inhabitants; they undoubtedly created fond memories here within its walls. However, in its current state of abandonment, the house exudes none of that. Instead, a heavy emptiness persists that offers no glimpse of that past life. A cold void.

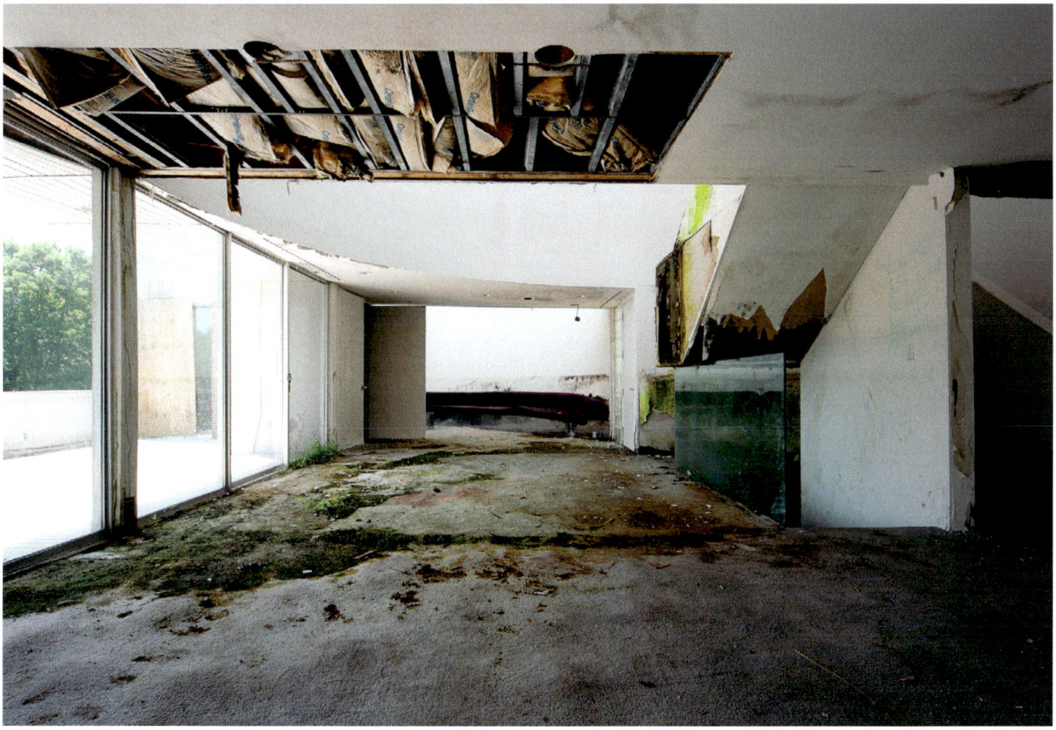

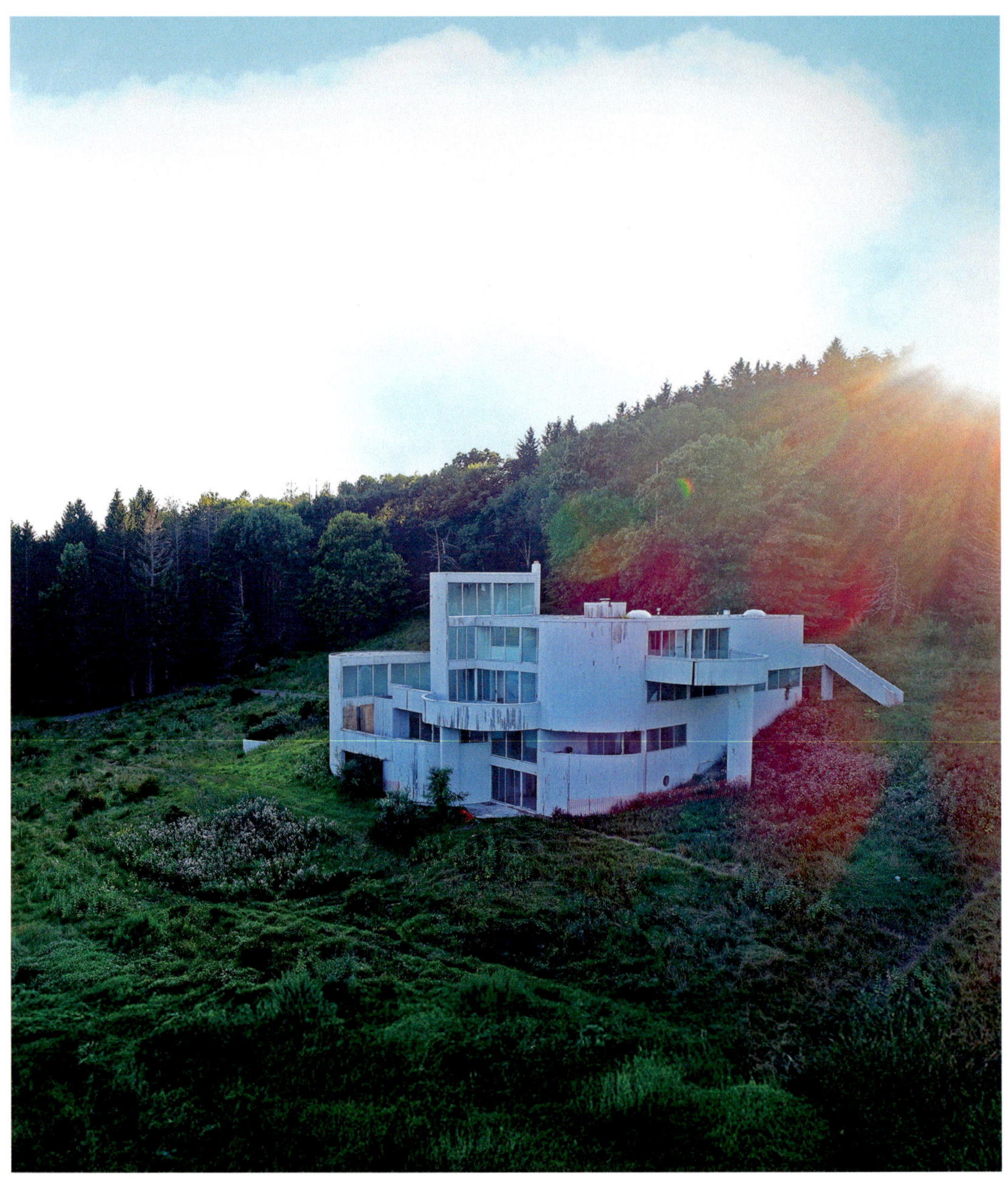

For now the house stands, watching from its wooded knoll as the sun rises, sets, and rises again. Each passing season an unyielding cycle, one that gradually wears down the massive structure as mold, decay, wildlife, and vegetation consume its halls and chambers from within. This home has likely succumbed to a level of deterioration well beyond saving; yet, in this gradual demise can be found a poignant beauty—the tale of a home abruptly silenced, a narrative left unfinished right as it was beginning. And so the house endures the only way it can, while composing its own tragic ending in the absence of closure.

9

THE BURNED REMAINS

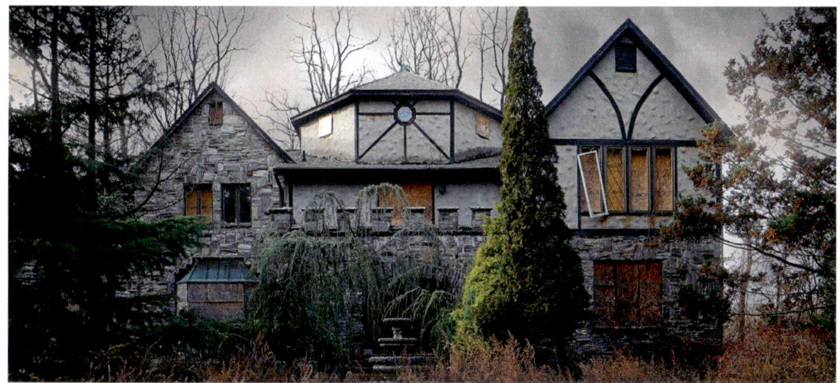

Above and below: Light creeps in through shaded and obstructed windows. Dim in places, but enough to see a family's life rent apart and scattered across every surface. A murky odor is suspended in the half-light, one of mildew and long-extinguished cinders. This house was once a home, but it now stands as the site of a family tragedy, one which we still feel ambivalent about, even years after visiting. There is a fuzzy line that divides trespassing from intruding, and it runs directly through the foundations of this house.

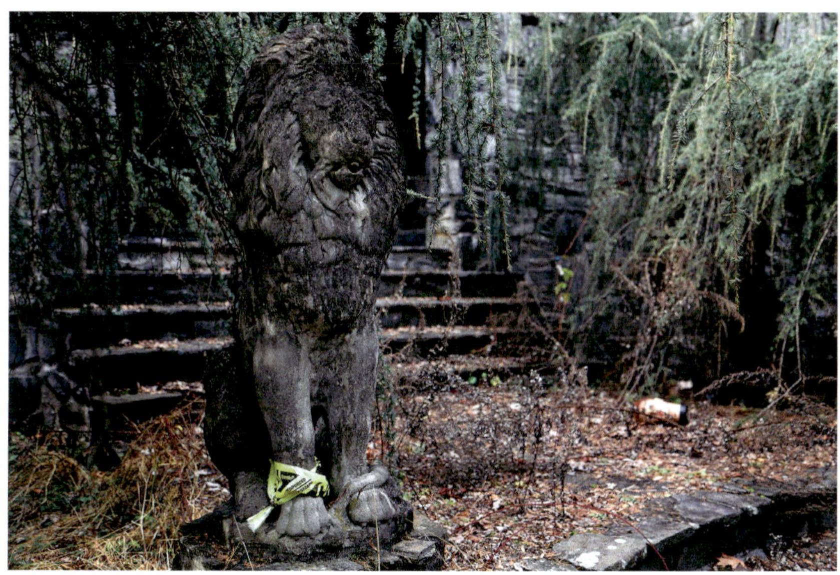

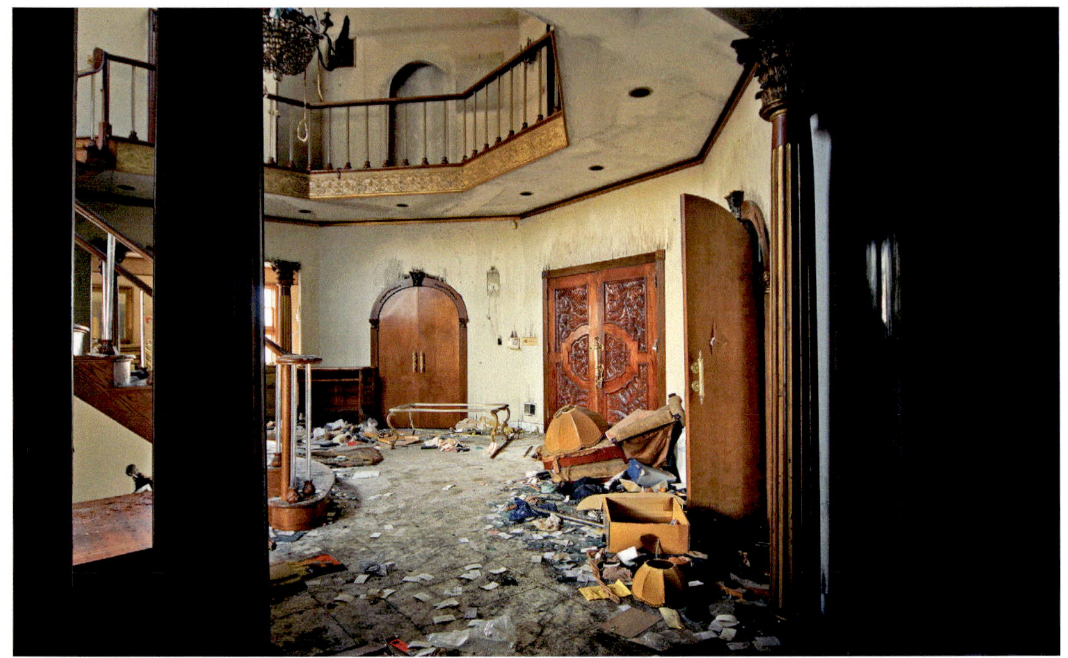

Almost immediately upon entering the former home, we were hit with an uneasy feeling of intrusiveness, of prying into the private matters of a family we had no business being involved with. This was entirely unlike any other home we have visited throughout the years.

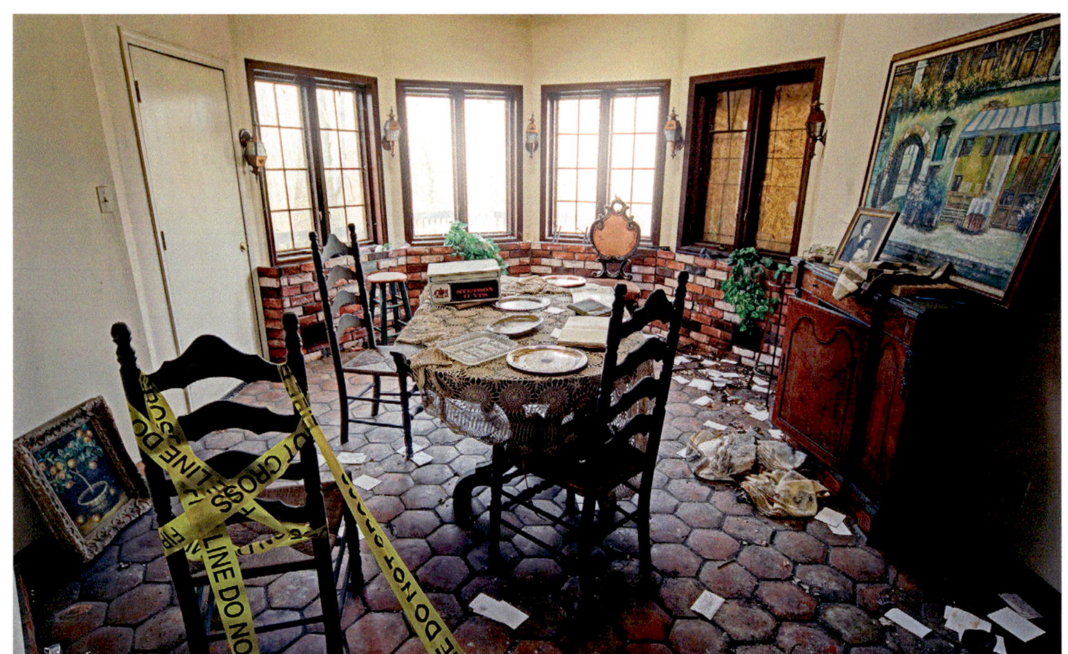

Yes, many old homes are filled with vestiges of past families: clothing, photographs, old letters, memorabilia of previous lives. These items, most often, are simply left behind when a family vacates a home. When that happens, these everyday items transform into poignant reminders of how fleeting existence can be. This was not the case here; the vacating of this house was both violent and tragic.

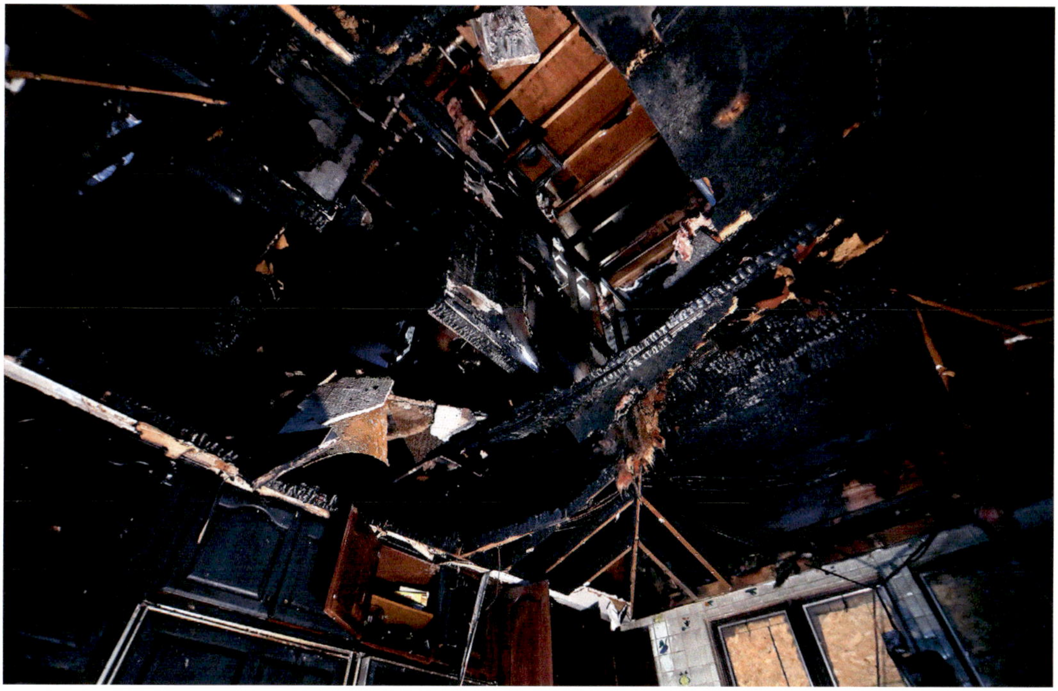

This house suffered a considerable fire, one which gouged a massive hole, upward, from the ground level up into the roofing over the kitchen area.

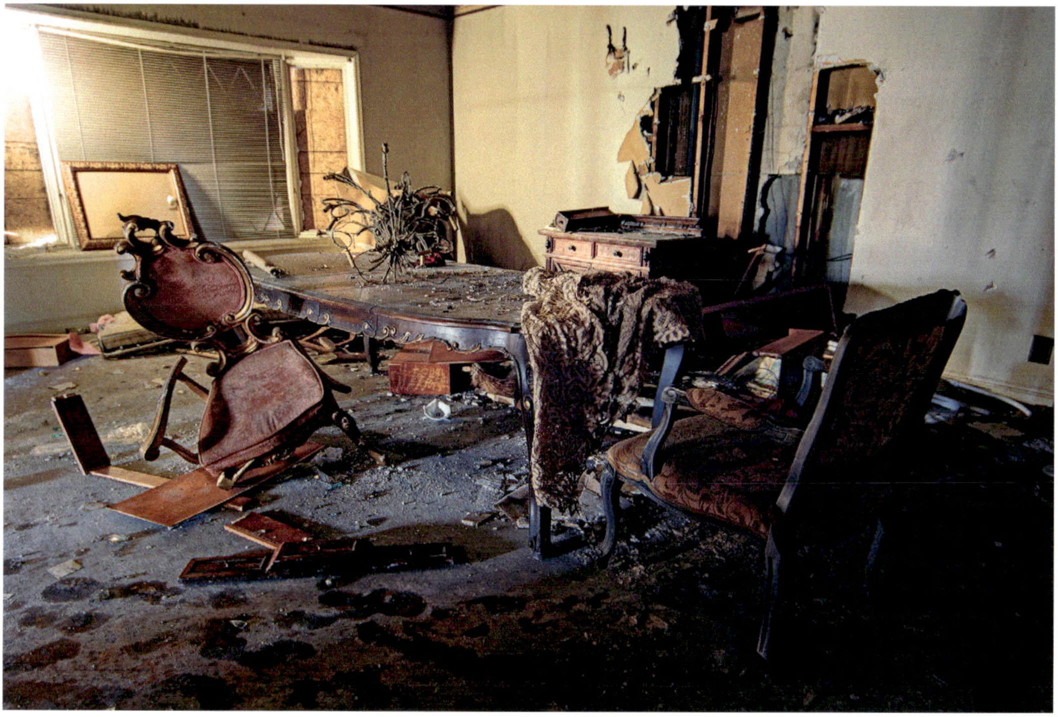

The family who once lived here was uprooted from their home overnight and unable to return for their belongings due to the danger the jeopardized building now presents.

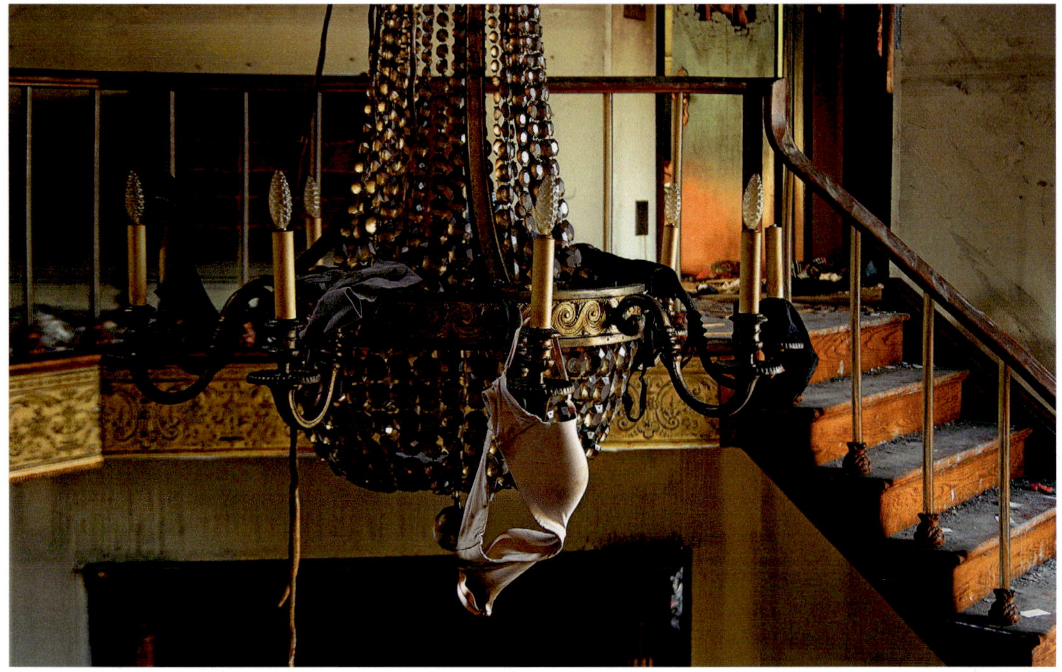

Most of their belongings remained, left to decay through the years, under a roof that fails more and more with each season. A sad ending, but also one with a poetic sense of peacefulness. Or it could have been, but any hope of a dignified end was lost once people discovered the vacant home and ransacked it.

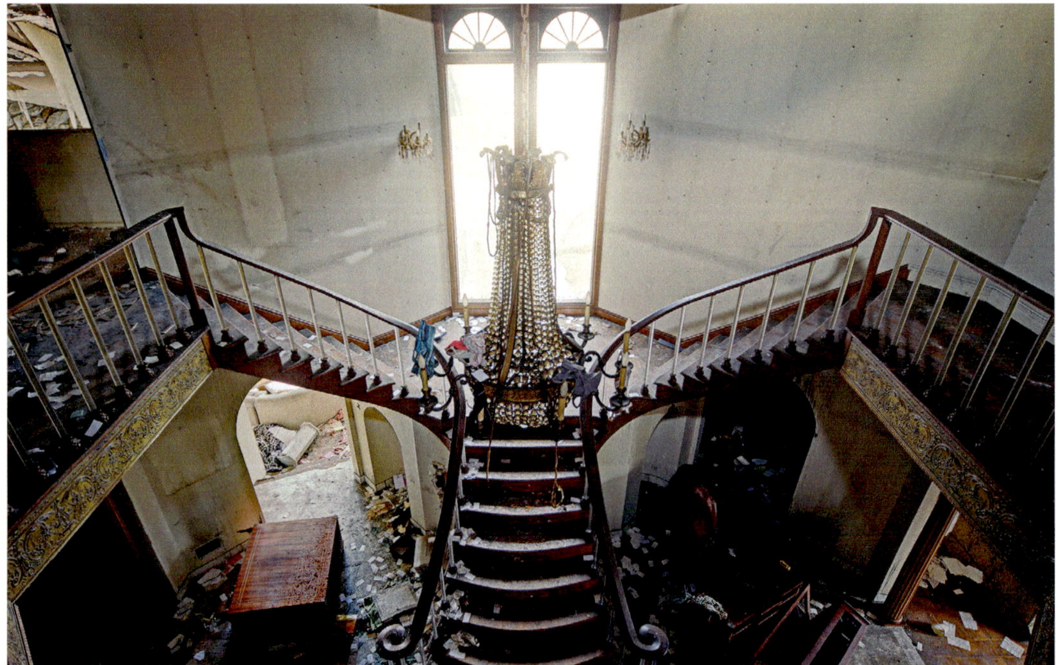

Our visit found the house in total disarray. Clothing and personal items obscured so much of the flooring in some areas that we were forced to walk upon them like an uneven and disjointed carpet. Brassieres dangled from the chandler over the master stairwell, the counter tops and floors covered with mail, photo albums, and personal journals.

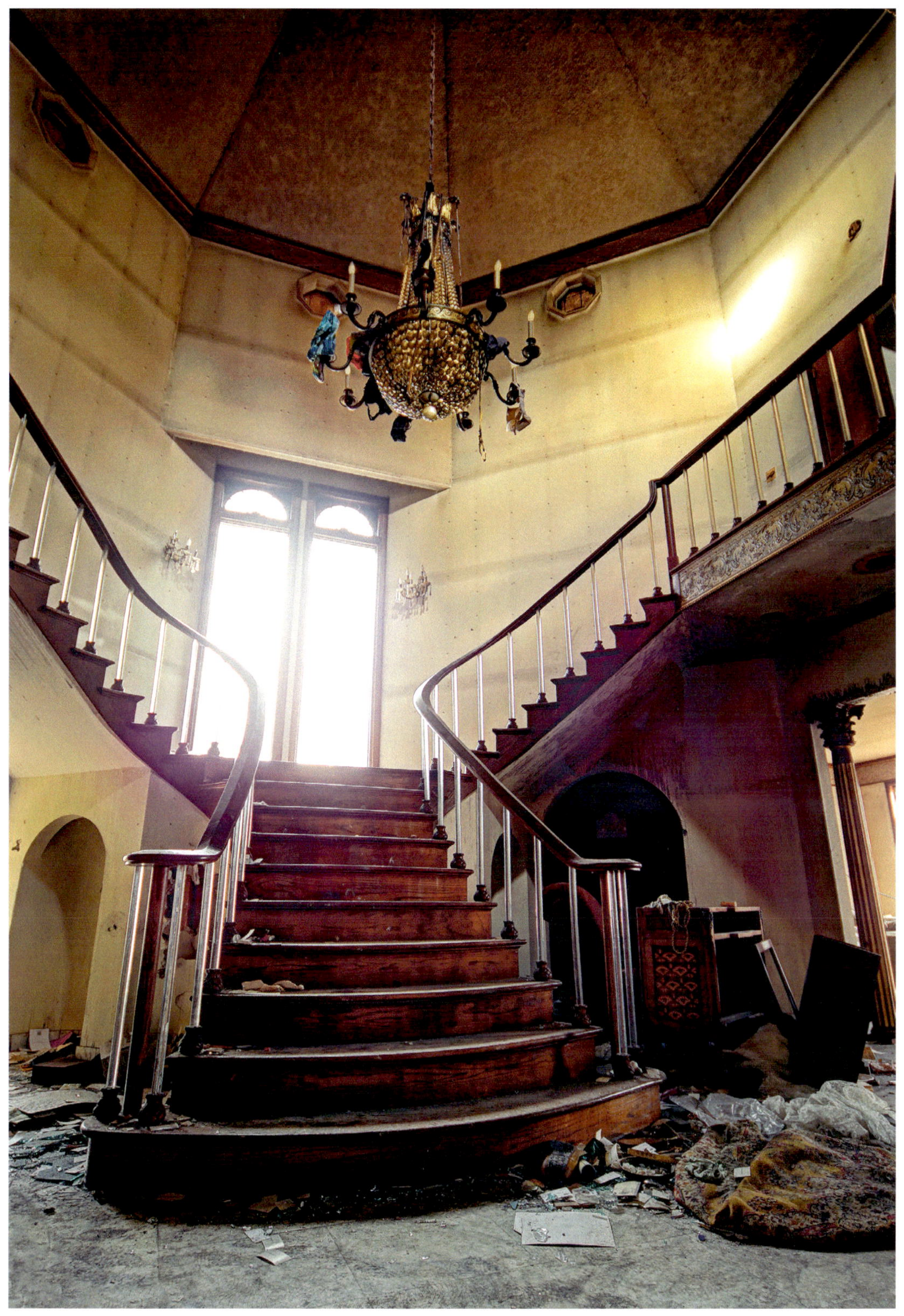

The central staircase cuts a beautiful curve through the chaos which surrounds it.

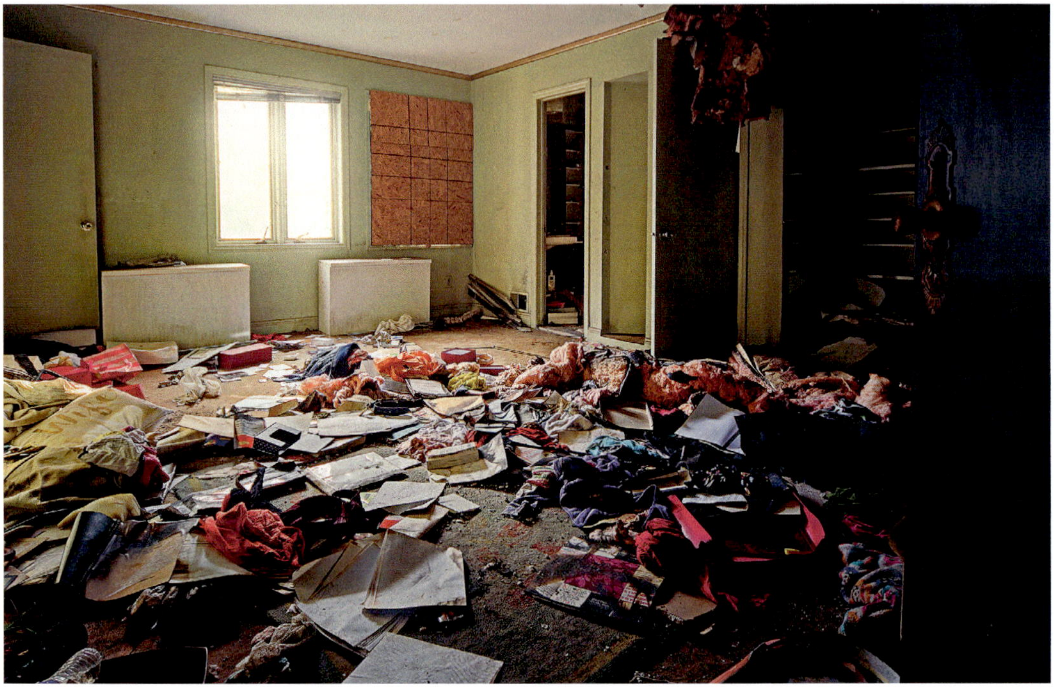

It was clear that the house had become a playground for people who held no consideration for the victims of this fire. More jarring to us than the scale of the mess was the level of disrespect that crafted it.

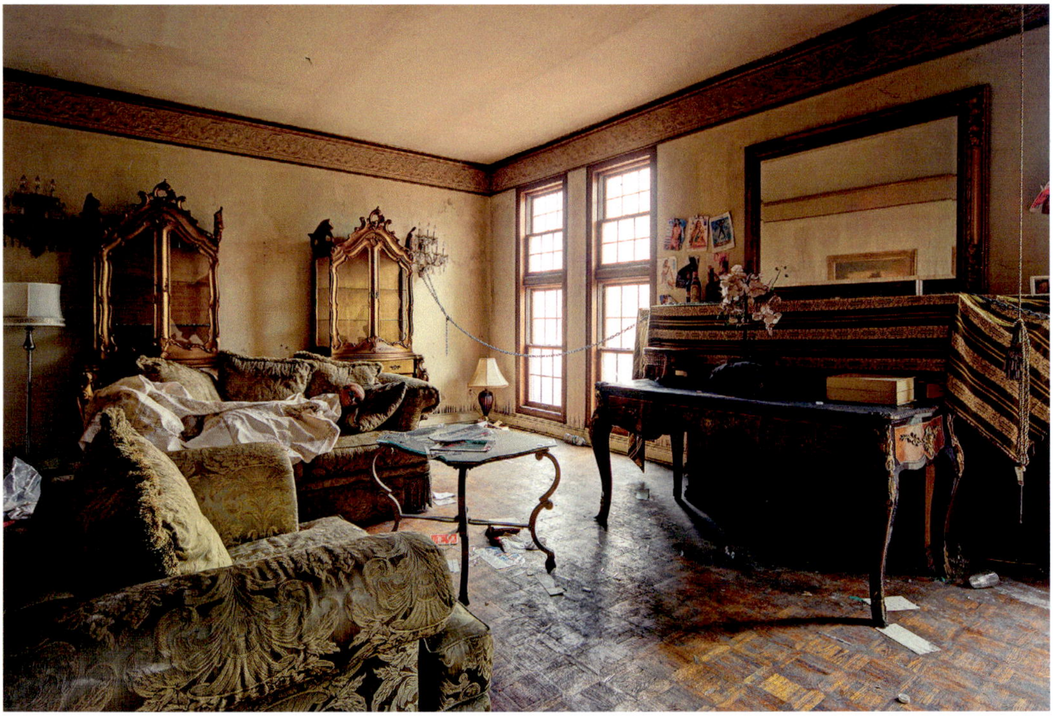

Luckily, there were some truly beautiful areas with the house, places where you could envision what life here must have been like in a time before the fire.

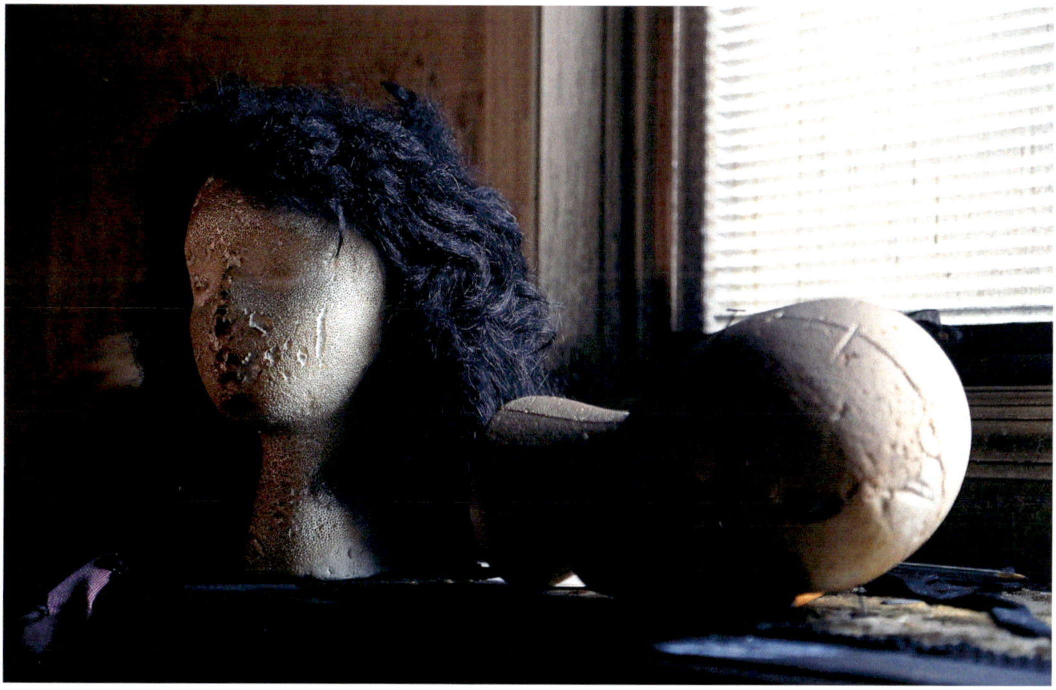

One of the more unusual elements were the numerous mannequin heads that lay scattered throughout the house. Dozens of them.

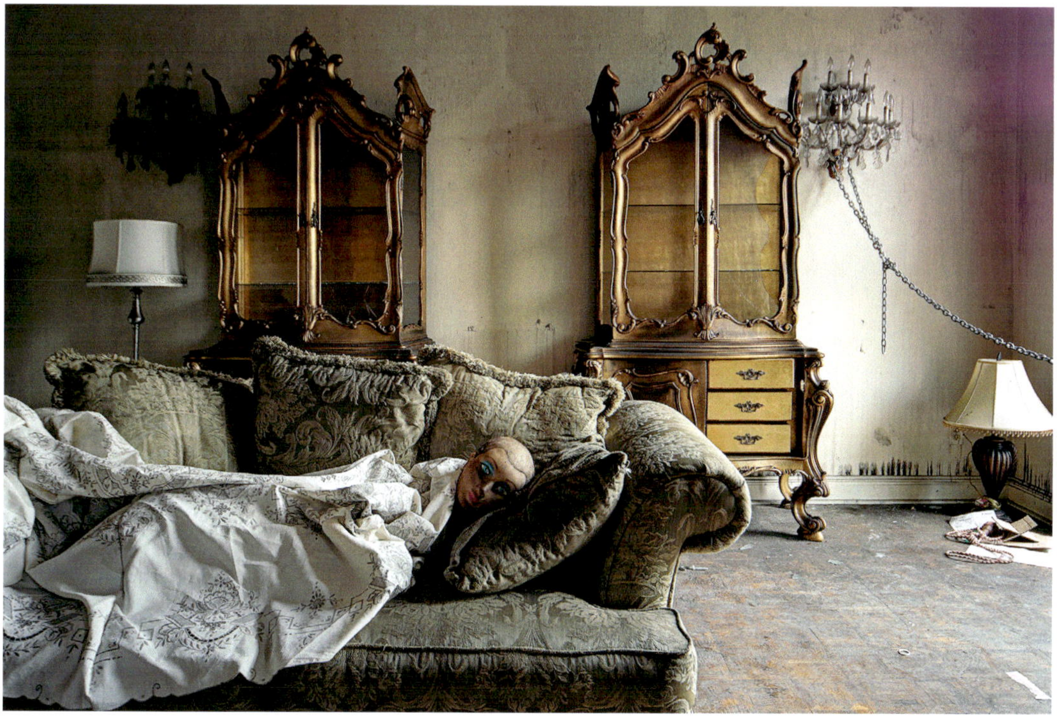

They stared out from the dark corners of closets and their perches on shelves, hiding away in nearly every room of the house.

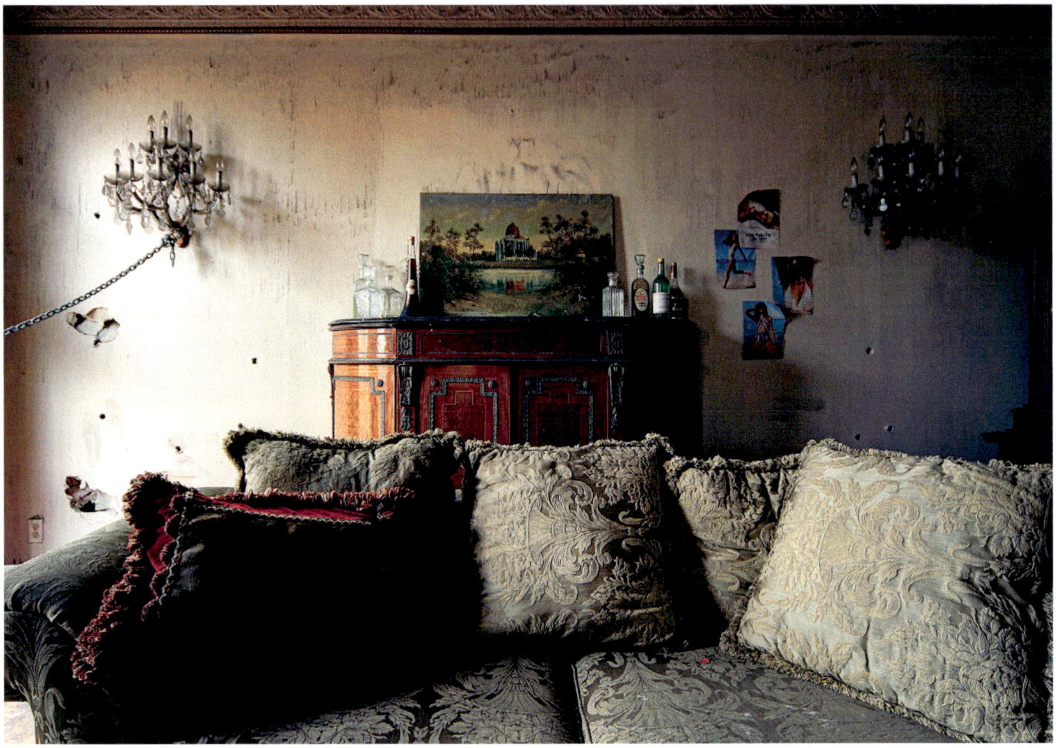

Above and below: Walking through the house felt almost indecent, and it's difficult to find the proper words to convey the feeling. Unlike most places we visit, where above all else a sense of awe and wonderment drive us to see what's around the next corner or hidden in the next room, here we simply felt pity for the displaced family.

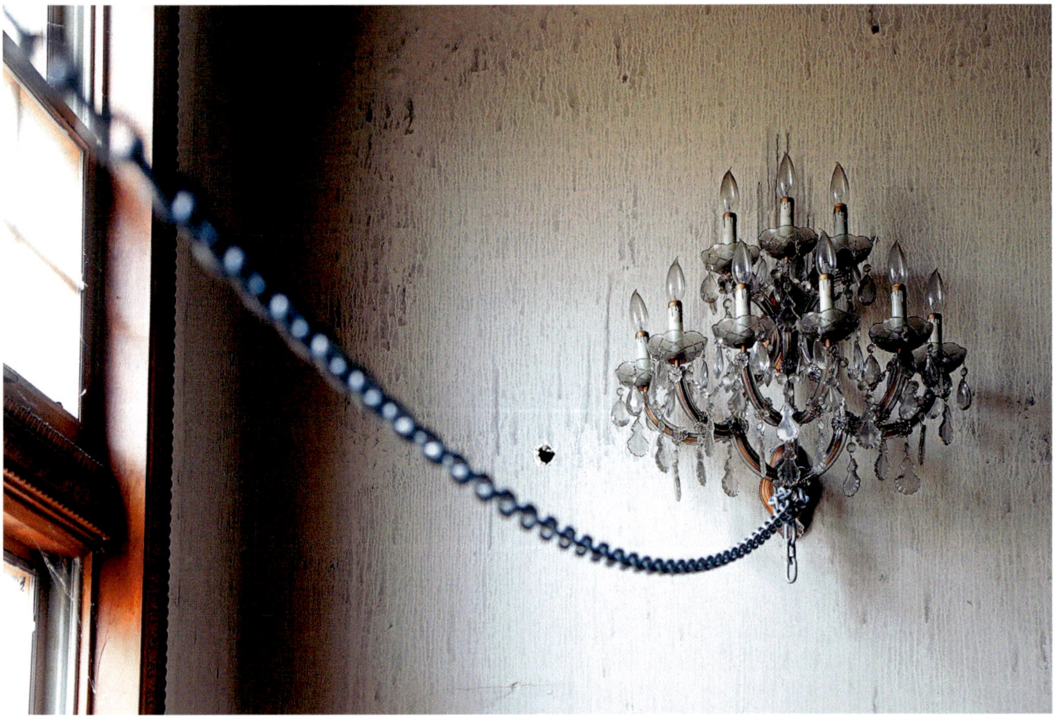

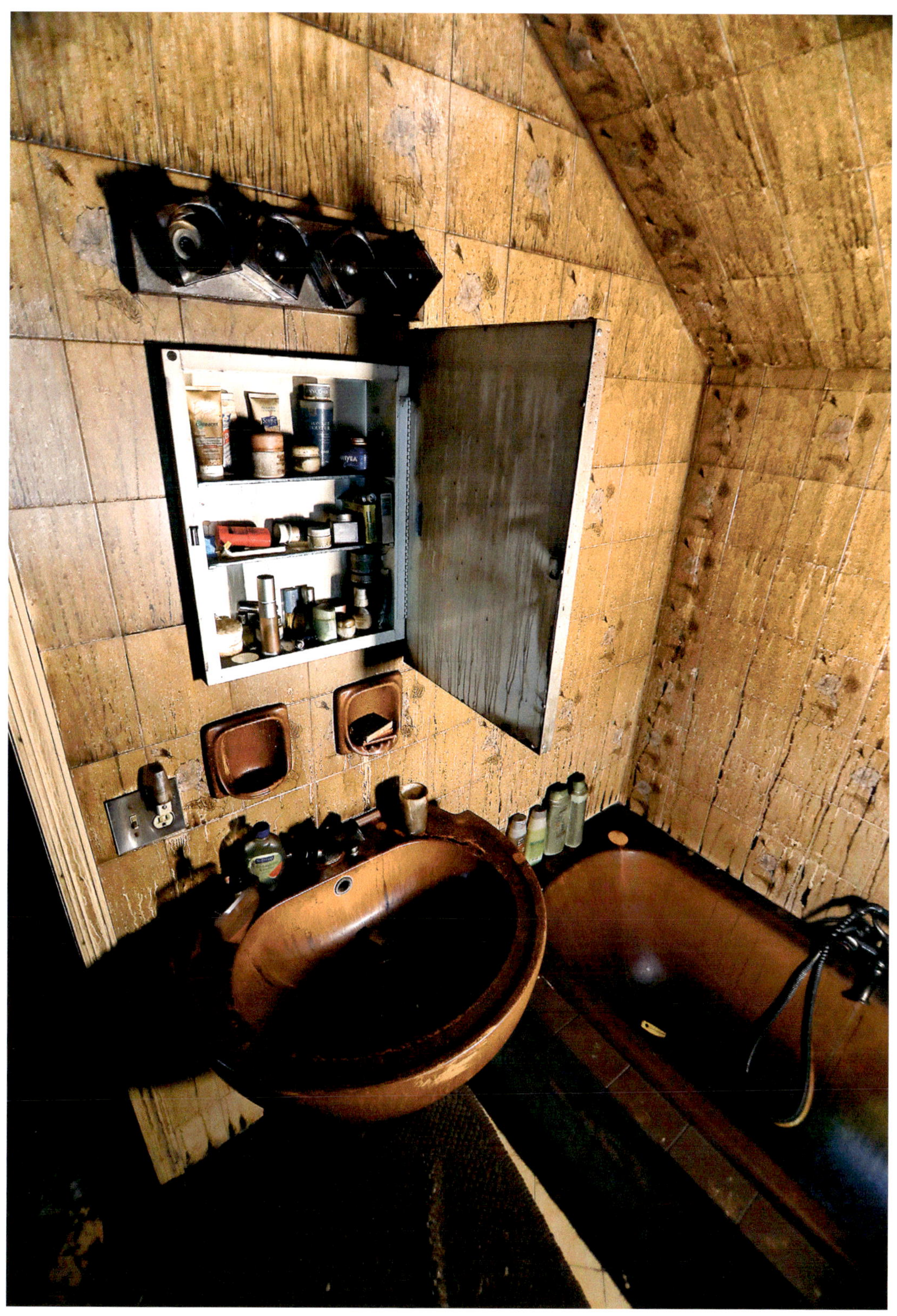

An upper-floor bathroom, every surface stained a sickly yellow from smoke damage.

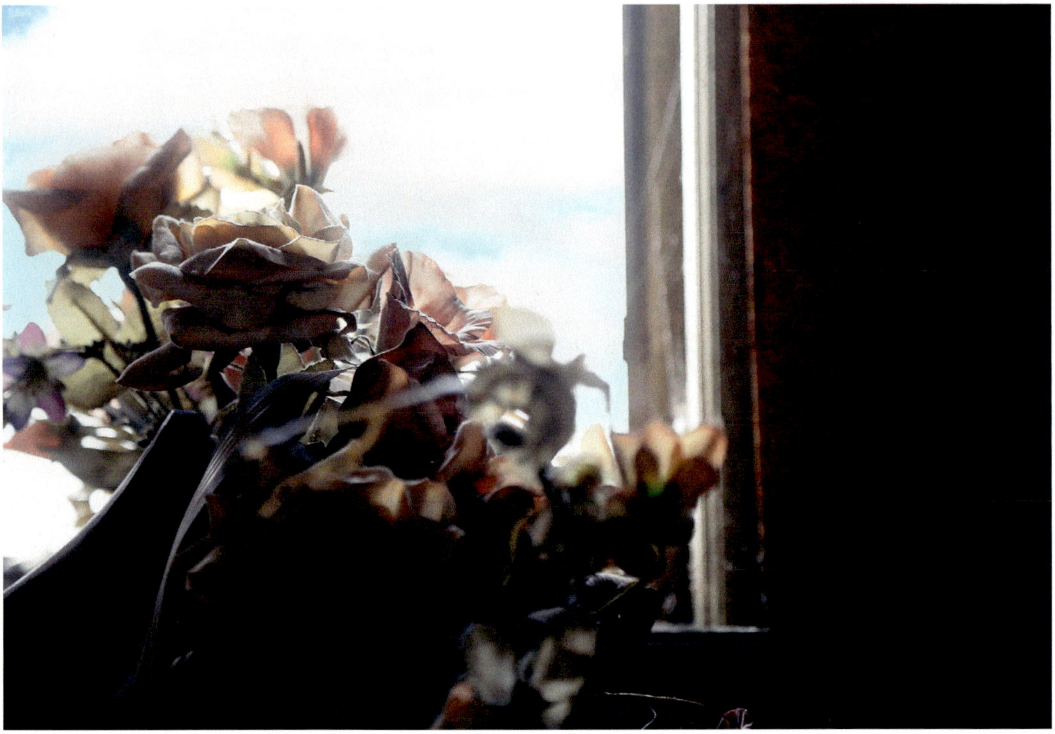

A silk flower arrangement sits by a bedroom window. A still life.

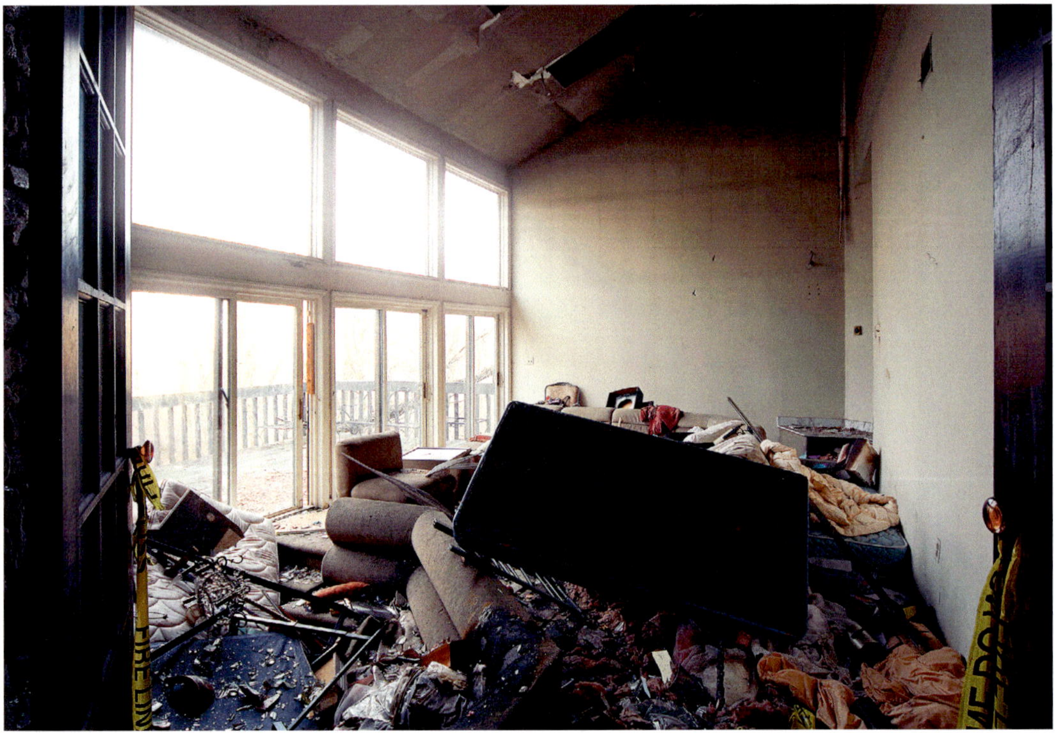

What was once a living room, now destroyed beyond recognition.

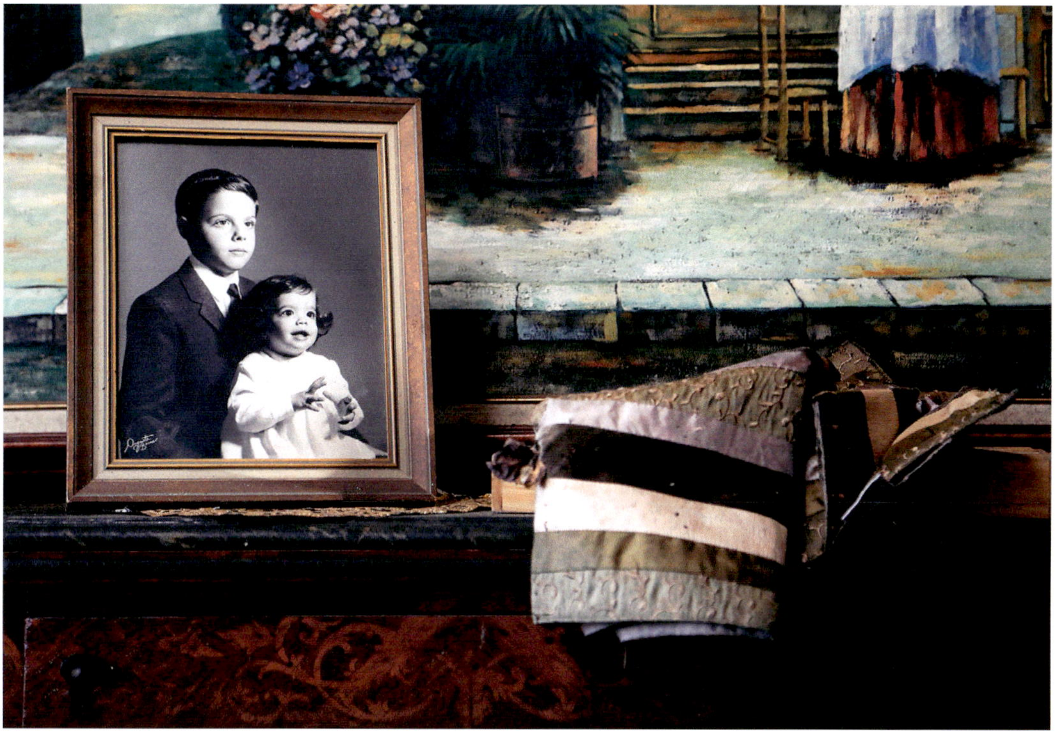

Above and below: Do these people staring out from the photographs still think about these things? Of their old home? Do they wish they had a chance to come back and retrieve these same items that people now throw from the balconies and trample underfoot?

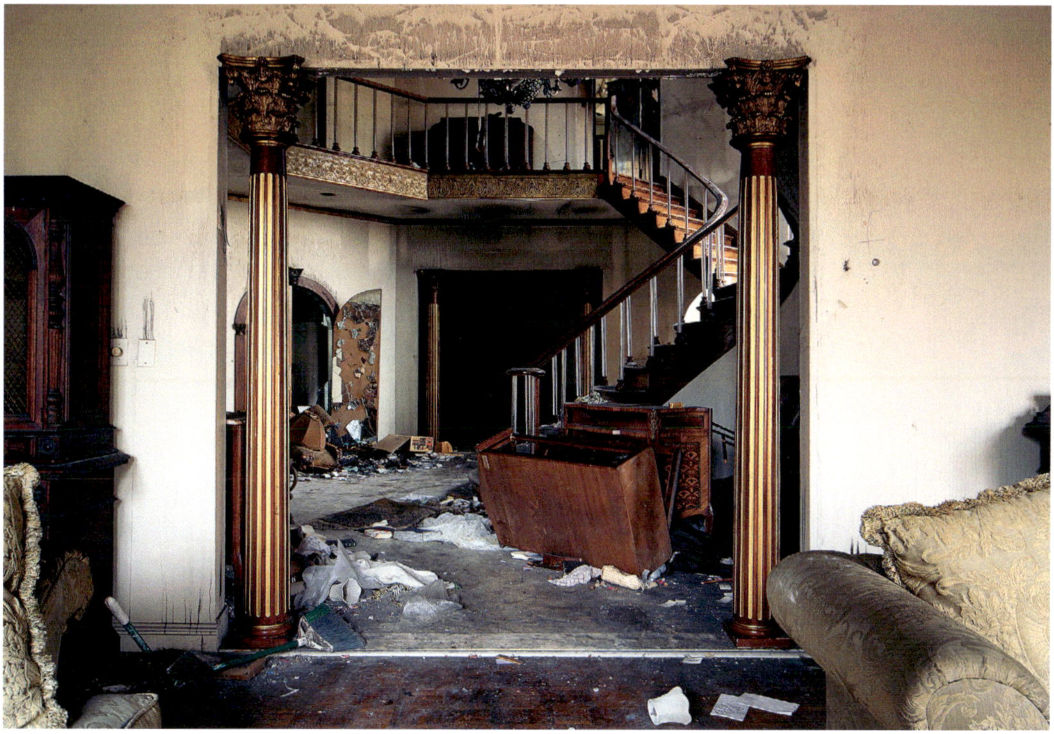

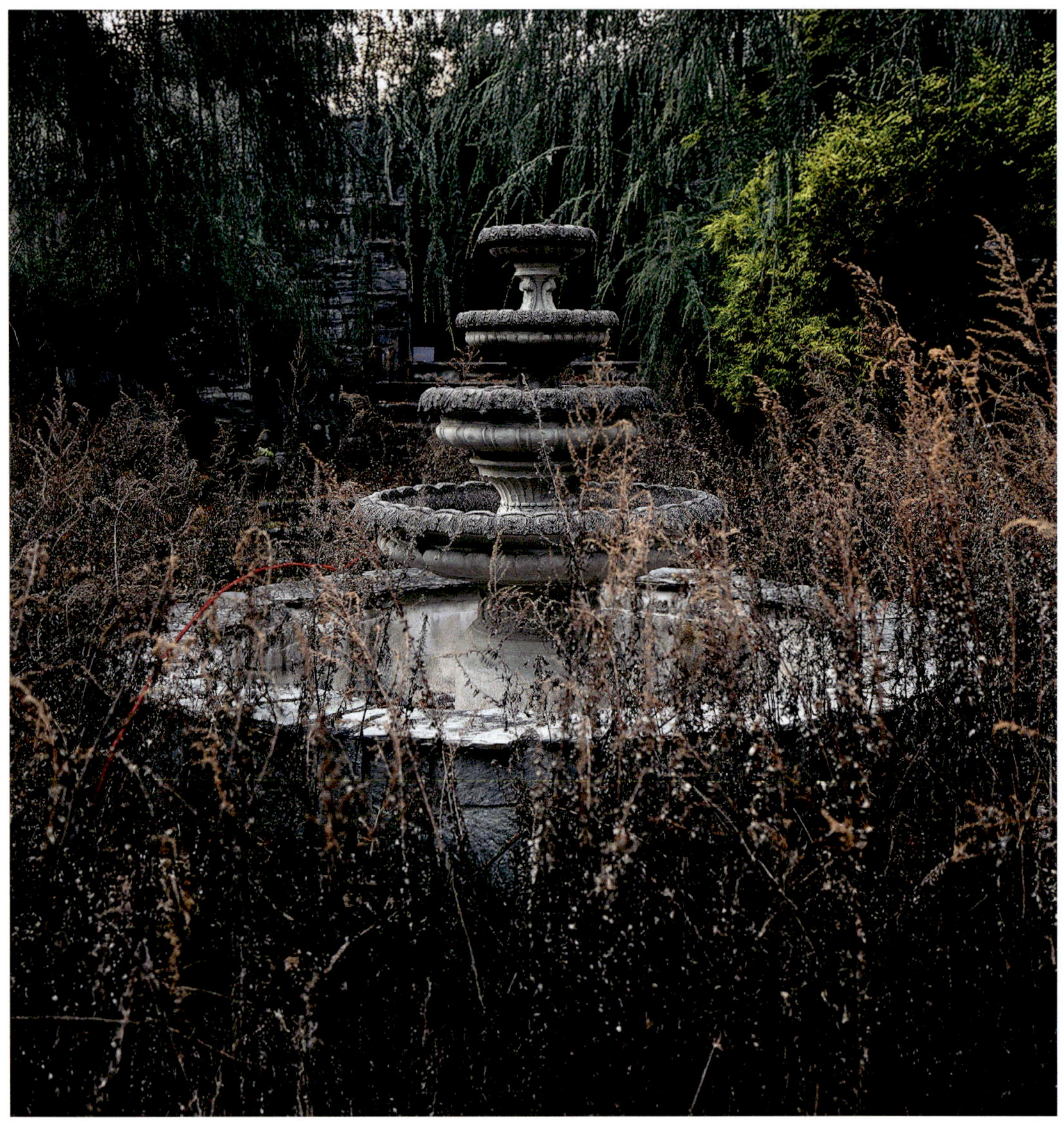

Maybe that's the lesson to be found here: Life can change overnight, and empathy is far less common than a kitchen fire.

10

AN UNQUIET SILENCE

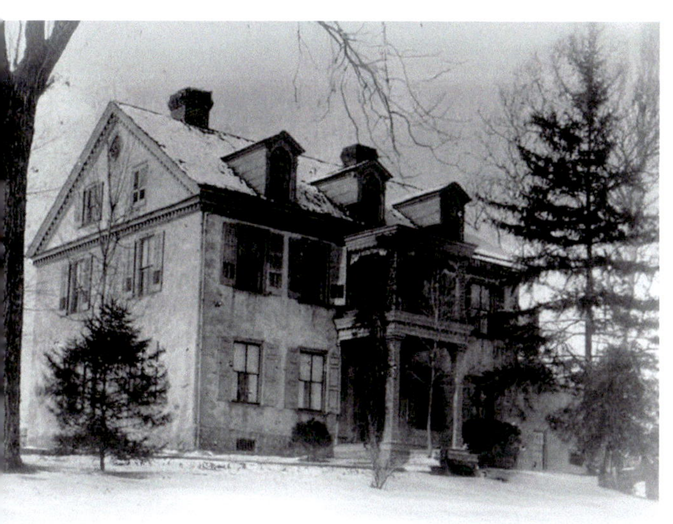

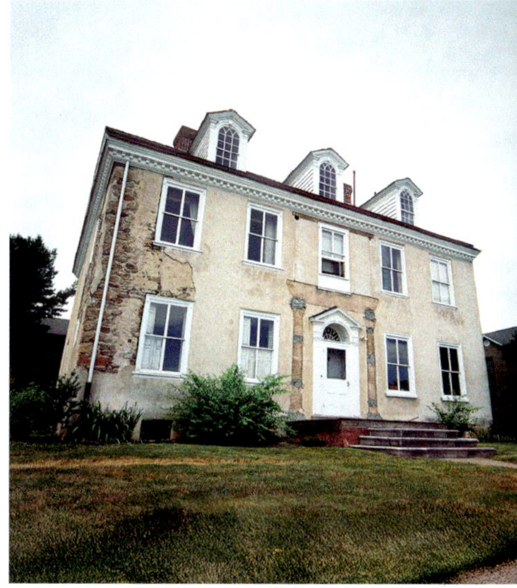

Above left Northwest of Philadelphia, about forty minutes from the New Jersey border, can be found the borough of Norristown, PA. It's a historic town, dating back to 1784, and serves as the seat of Montgomery County. Just driving through town, the age of the region is plain to see, as many beautiful old buildings, some dating back over 200 years, are tightly nestled between supermarkets and fast-food chains that have risen up since. The old and new worlds mix together here, and at times it's difficult to even picture the city of today as it may have looked when it was still a small rural town. One Norristown property in particular has come to be a symbol of the collision between modern life, and the quiet old town upon which the present-day city has grown: The Selma Mansion. (*Historic image courtesy of the Norristown Preservation Society*)

Above right: Grey clouds covered the sky. The quick-moving kind that you can sit and watch tumble and churn upon themselves, they stretched out forever like some inverted ashen sea. On a hilltop below that gloomy canopy stood the pale form of Selma Mansion. Just looking at the old place it was clear it had seen far better days than this one. A large marking covers the front of the old house, framing the entry door and extending to surround the window on the floor above. It looks not unlike a scar and marks the place where once a beautiful porch and balcony stood. In other places the original stonework, long concealed away behind a stucco facade, peers through in patches where rain and weather have eroded it away. The entire scene looked as if it could have been lifted from the pages of a ghost story, and rightly so.

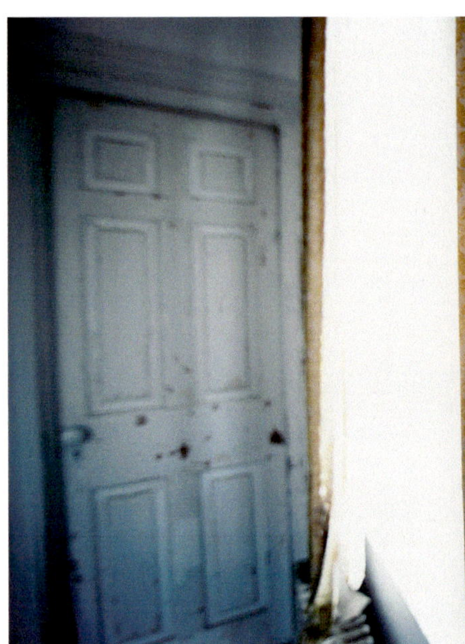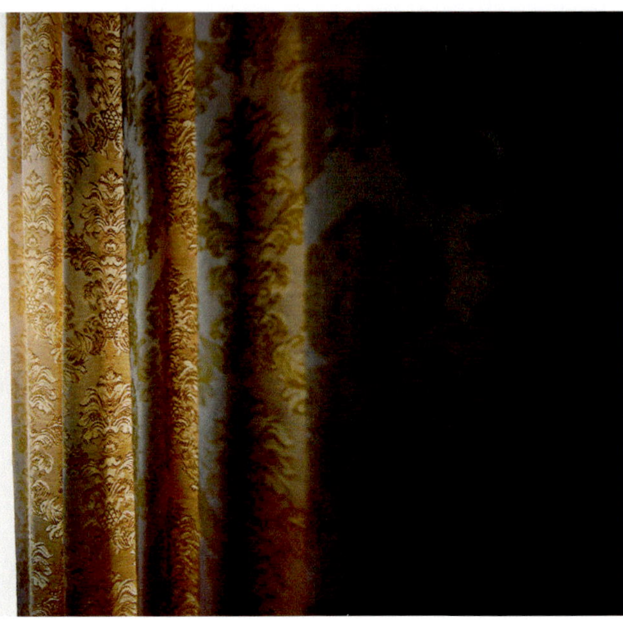

Above and below: Inside things are not much different. Peeling damask wallpaper runs the walls around large wood planked floors, upon which markings still remain of rugs and stair runners from lifetimes past. Long disused gas lamp fixtures extend from the wall, showing that even before electricity, Selma stood brightly upon its hill. To say things were different when Selma was built in 1794 would be an understatement. This knoll, now surrounded by apartment buildings, was once the peak of an open expanse of land, with a view that saw nearly all the way into the central parts of the city. The man behind its creation was a Mr. Andrew Porter. A name that, perhaps, many may not know. Most have surely heard of the United States Marine Corps, though, a branch of the armed forces which he helped found. Mr. Porter had four sons, all of which went on to have great influence, some of which on a national level. The most well-known of his linage, however, was his granddaughter, Mary Todd, who became wife to Abraham Lincoln.

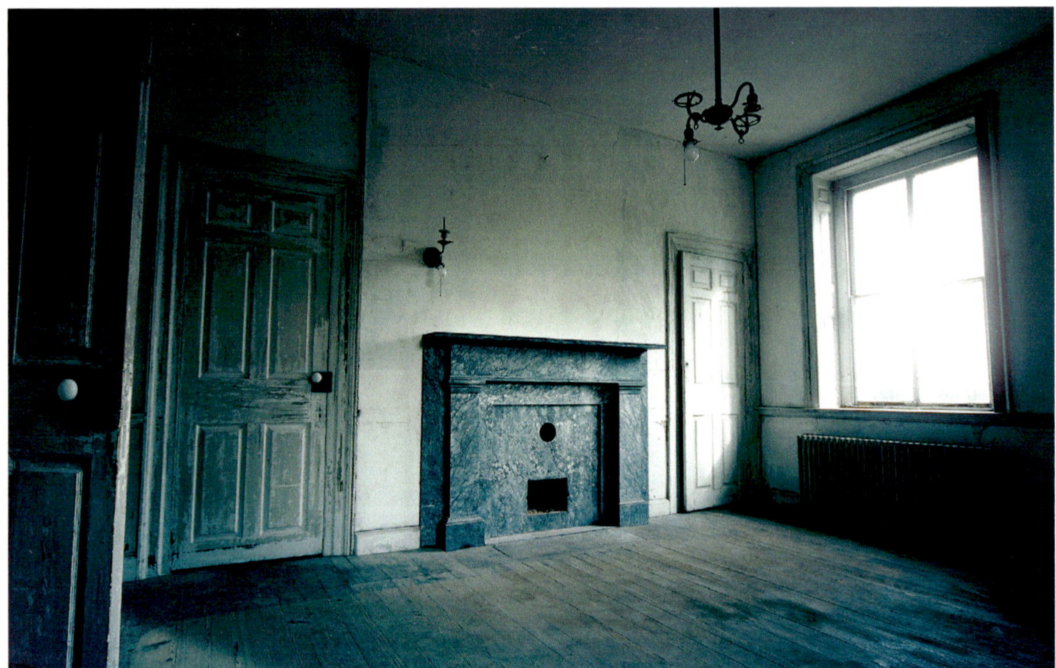

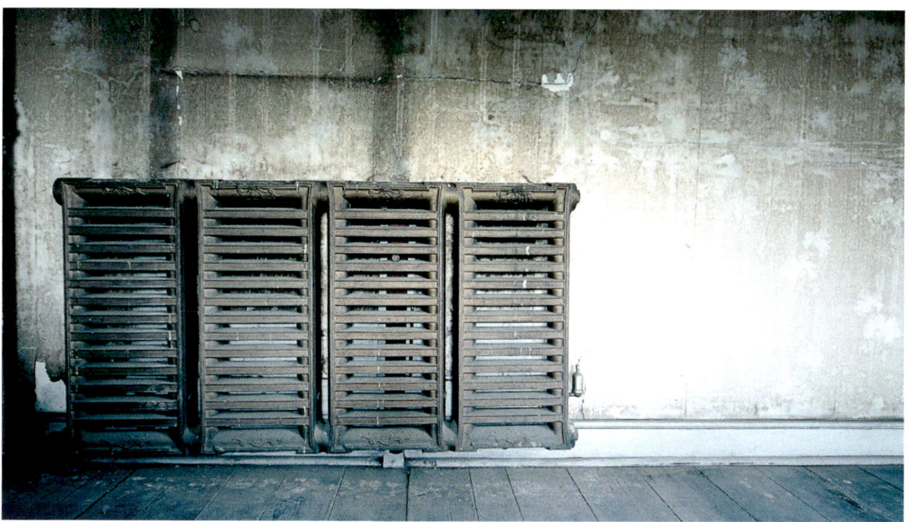

In 1821, Selma changed hands, coming into the ownership of the Knox family. It was passed down through the family for a couple of generations until it came into the hands of Joseph Fornance, husband of sole-surviving Knox family daughter Ellen. The Fornance family was the last family to own the mansion and called Selma home until the mid-1980s, when widow Ruth Fornance passed away. Upon her death the house was intended to be donated to Montgomery County, PA. Ruth even had a plaque made up that she proudly hung on the wall in the mansion stating such. Her caretaker who knew her during her final years said she would often point to the plaque when passing it, saying the home would be in good hands after her death. Sadly, this proved to not be the case.

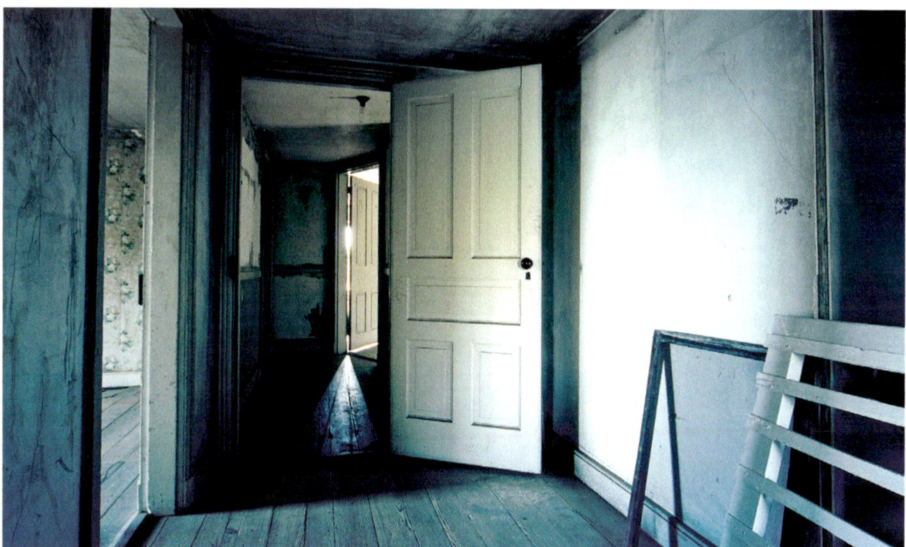

Both the county and township did not wish to take possession of the home after Ruth's death, and an estate sale was held on the property in the late 1980s which essentially liquidated the historic artifacts from the once-proud home. Even Ruth's plaque was not spared. The land was then sold to a developer, who quickly began erecting apartment buildings on the estate's outer perimeter. The intention was to convert Selma into a rec center after the apartments were complete, but those plans fell through. The developer then began weighing up the possibility of leveling the old mansion, to make room for a new construction or possibly additional parking for the complex. A fast-food chain was even vying for the property.

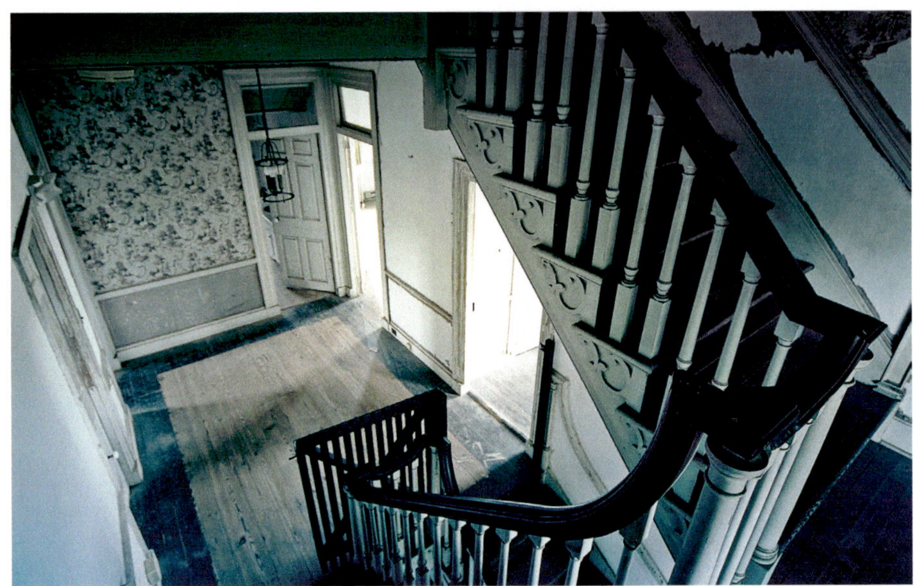

With such history tied to the old house, and the wrecking ball now seemingly winding up to give Selma an ill-deserved end, a group of concerned citizens banded together and formed the Norristown Preservation Society with the sole purpose of saving Selma. They succeeded and were able to purchase the old house and surrounding parcel of land from the developer in the 1990s. Maryann Buser, a one-time member of the preservation group, quoted a visitor who had come to see the aged mansion: "It is a house that wants to live … and we want to give it that chance".

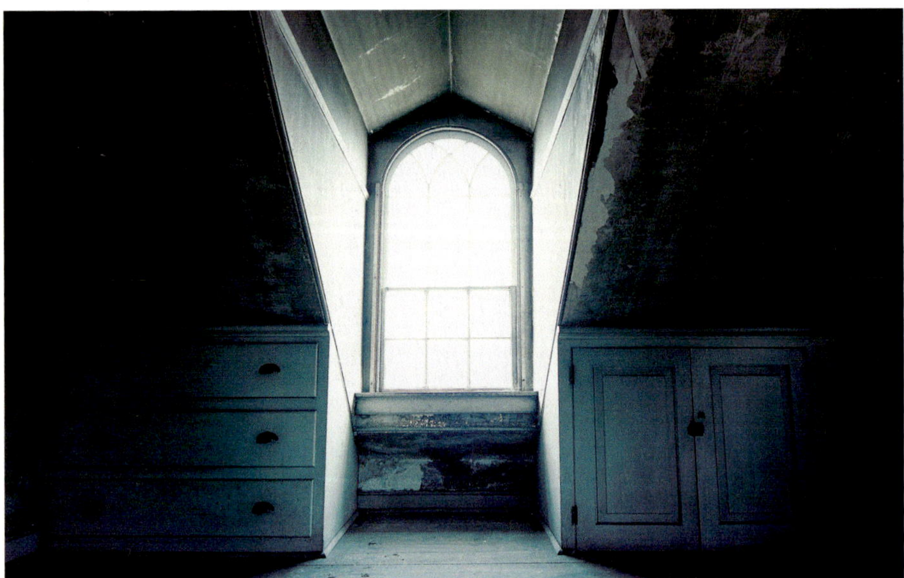

The Norristown Preservation Society often hosts events at the old Selma Mansion. What sets Selma's public tours and events apart from many other historic sites is the fact that here they openly embrace the possibility that the old house is not quite as empty as it outwardly appear. Public ghost tours and after-dark paranormal investigations are a popular attraction at Selma. Beyond allowing guests to pierce the veil of death on a nightly basis, these events also help generate revenue for the much-needed repairs which the two-century-old mansion needs.

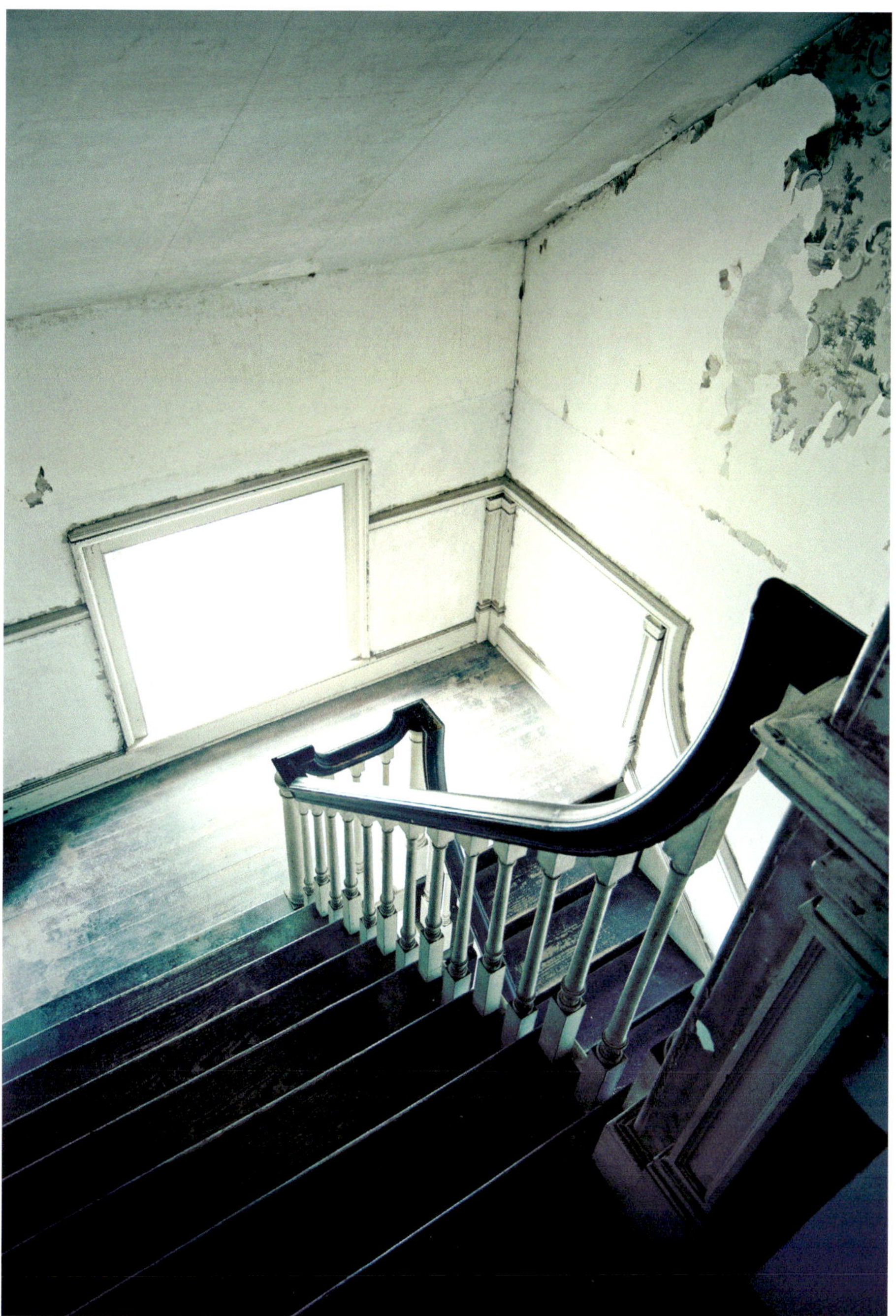

These paranormal events at Selma have involved many groups, though one—Pennsylvania Underground Paranormal Society (aka PUPS)—had a particularly interesting tale to tell. First, however, some context; members of their group also volunteer at the historic Fort Mifflin in Philadelphia. An old fort with deep ties to Selma. Andrew Porter was, himself, an officer in the Continental Army during the American Revolution, and thus would have frequented the fort during his military career. Years later, in the early 1800s, his youngest son, James Madison Porter, went on to manage a militia at Fort Mifflin. Selma and the historic fort share a lot of memories, and it seems this mansion remembers them well. It was around midnight, and the group had gathered on the uppermost floor of the house.

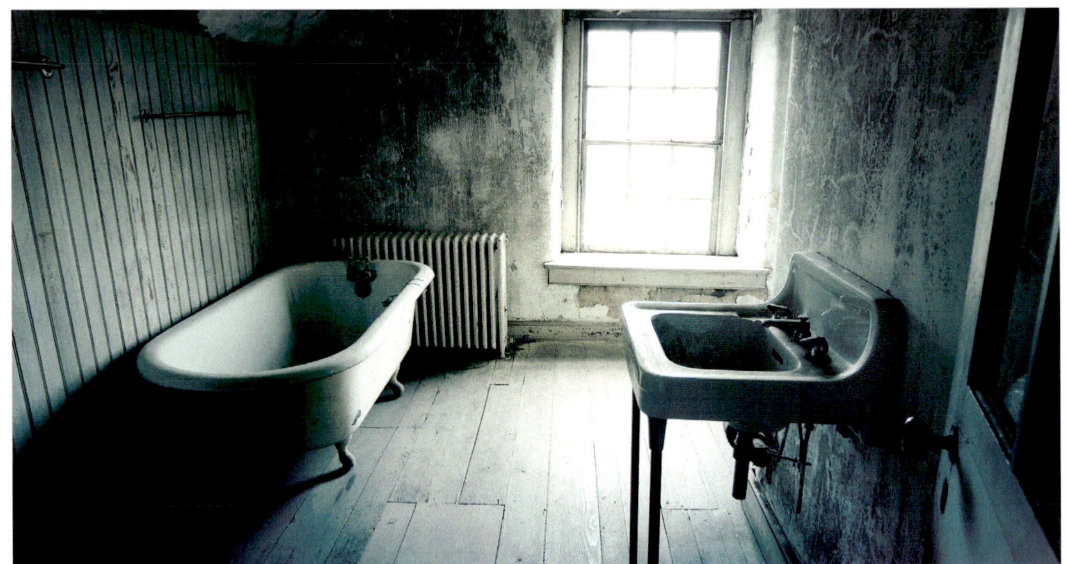

Above and below: On that floor, there is an old bathroom at the end of the hall; within that old bathroom, against a wall, stands a very old cast-iron bathing tub. It is here where the events of that evening begin; Lisa Terio, founder of PUPS, was the first to take note of it. She described the sighting as a murky black mass which was emanating from the bottom of the tub. Altering the others in the group, everyone present cautiously congregated around the tub. The mass was seen by everyone present and was described as rising and slowly lowering back into the tub. As the group gathered closer the mass grew and writhed over the sidewall of the antique tub. Lisa described it as "When you see a horror movie, and someone drags a dead body out of a bath … it looked just like that." The mass took no form other than what was described as a loosely formed blackish haze. Maryann was also there that night, she described the inky mass as eventually "blotting out all vision in the room" before spreading across the floor and down the hall a distance. After some time of observation, the mass began to recede, eventually returning to the old bath. Then it was no more.

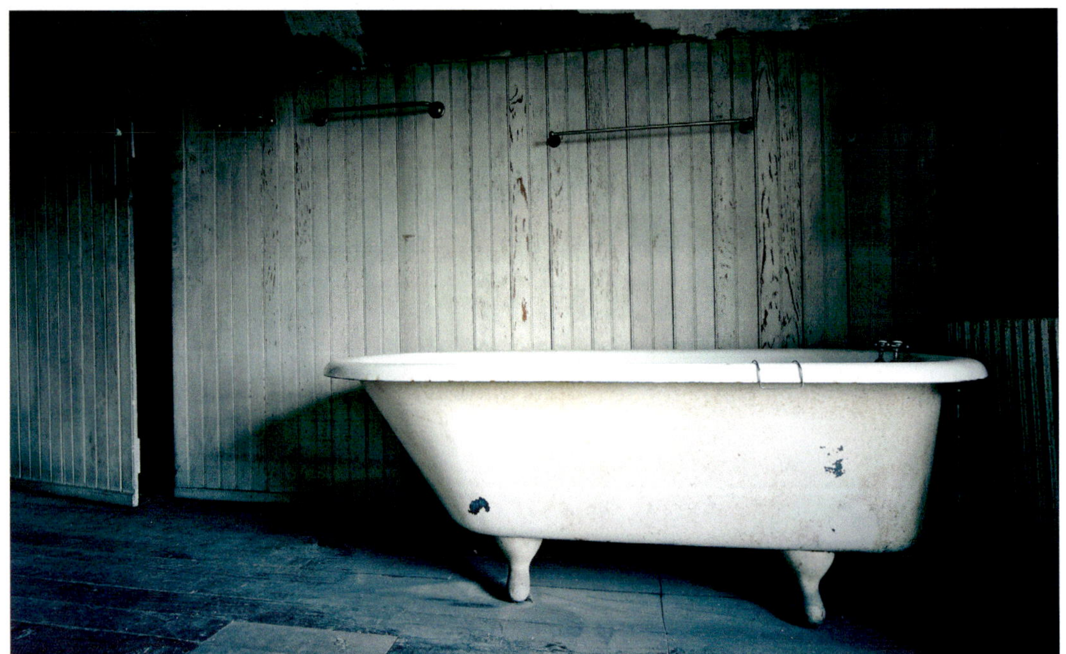

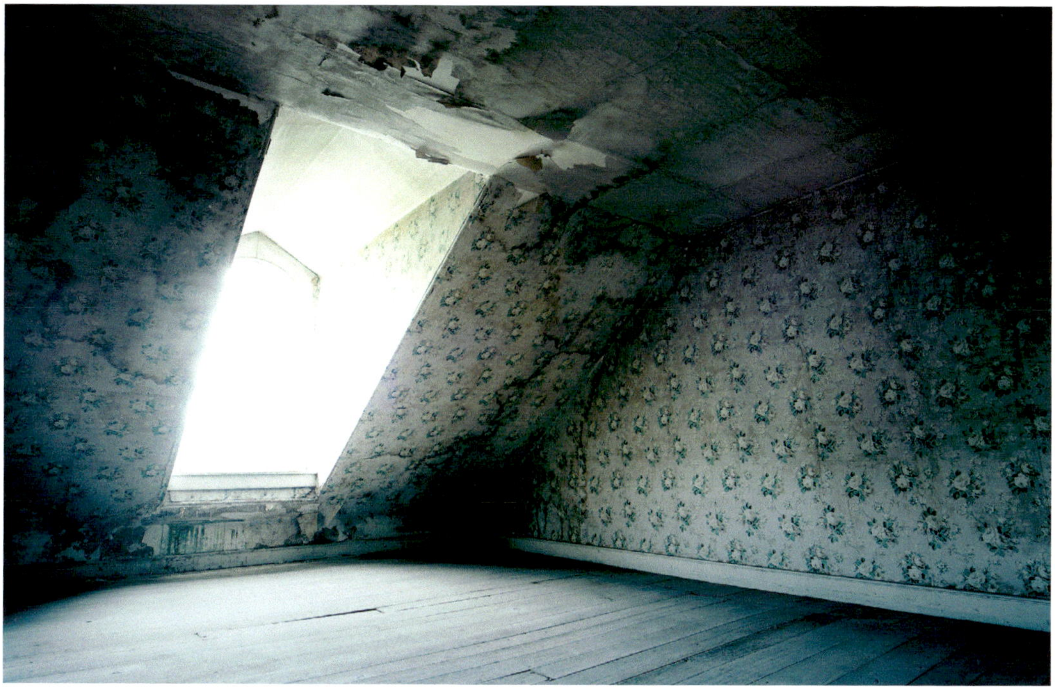

For most people, that singular occurrence would have been more than enough to remove any doubt of otherworldly forces, and it is surely a story that will forever haunt all those involved, but the night was just beginning.

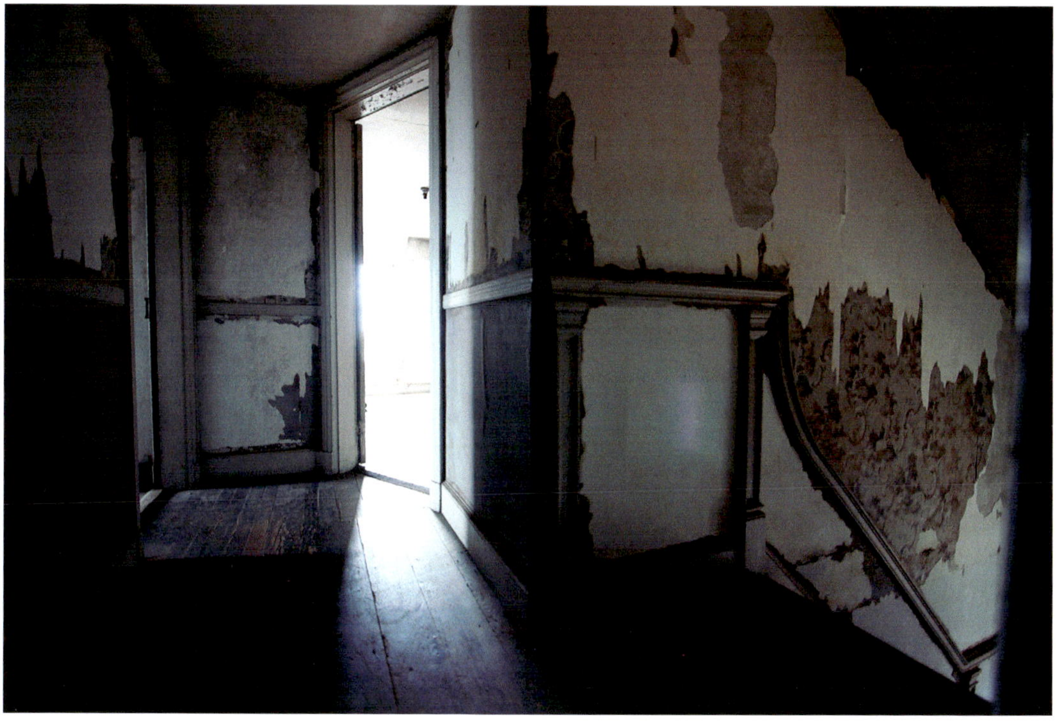

After the events with the blackish mass from the tub, the PUPS group proceeded to hold a spirit box session on the second floor.

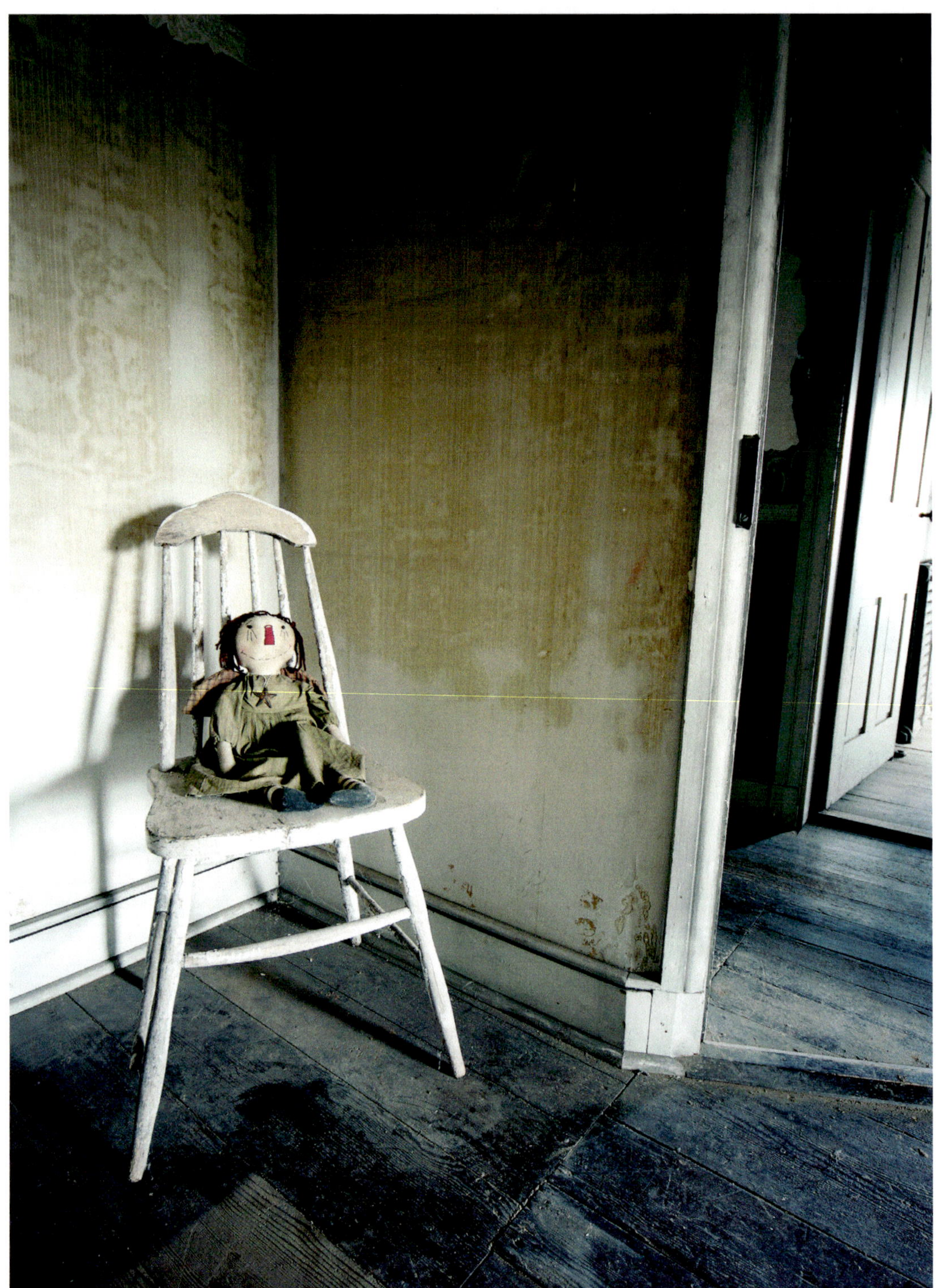

For those who may not know, a spirit box is a device paranormal researchers use to communicate with spirits, via radio frequencies and white noise. In effect, it is designed to allow people to attempt real-time conversations with those who have gone beyond. A message did indeed come through the static that evening, and though seemingly enigmatic at first, it was later proven to be eerily clear.

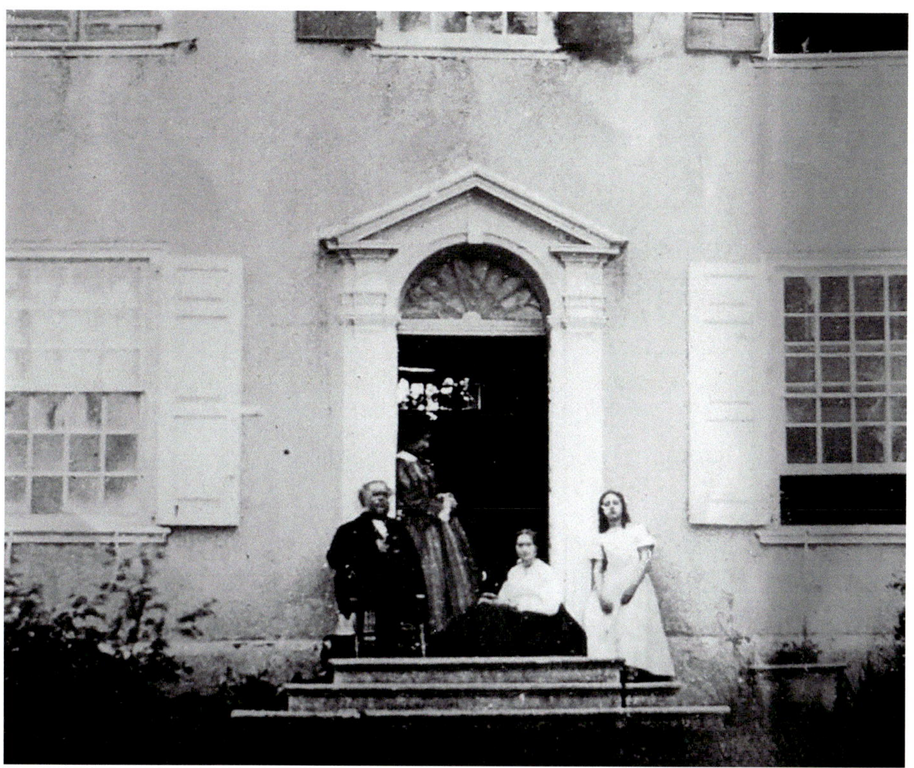

It was around midnight on the darkened second floor of the old mansion when the first words gargled forth from the box: "Wake up Wayne." "Wake up Wayne" it repeated, between static hisses. Lisa knew who the box was speaking of. "Wayne was the caretaker at Fort Mifflin," Lisa explained. "He wasn't here with us that night," she continued, "so we thought the spirits were looking for him." (*Historic image courtesy of the Norristown Preservation Society*)

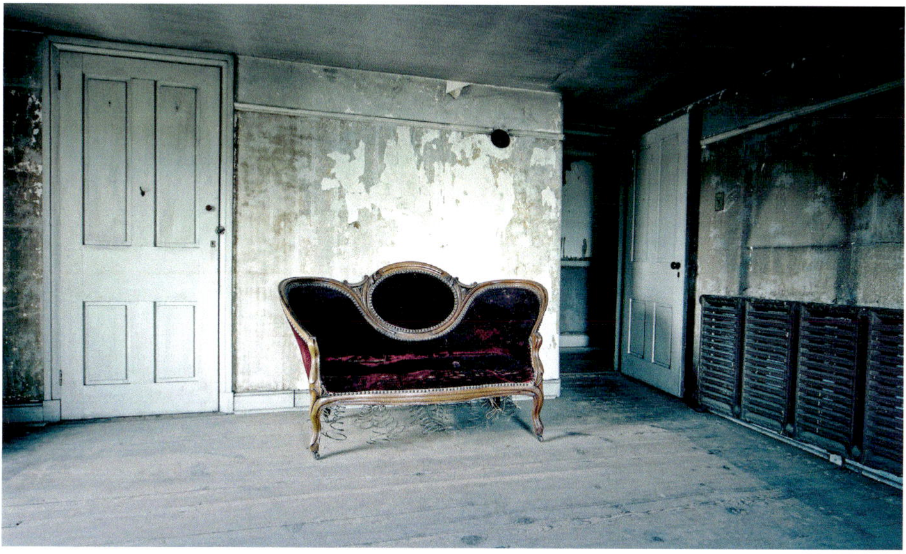

"Wake up Wayne" continued to be repeated from the box numerous times through the night. Its meaning is not understood until hours later.

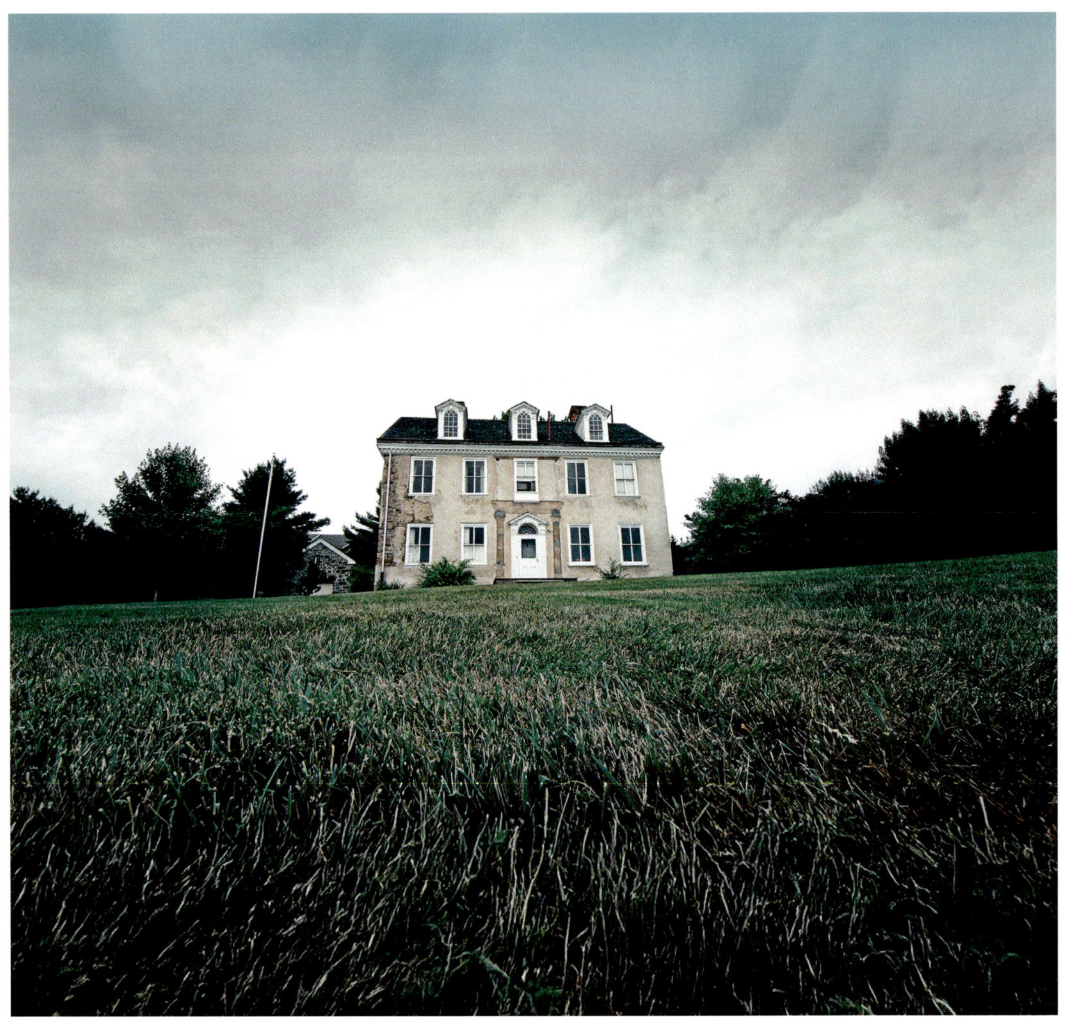

Lisa arrived home in the early morning, "I was home no more than a minute when I get a call." "Maryann called me, she's told me the fort's on fire!" Lisa was panicked. As fort caretaker, their friend Wayne lived on the grounds. "A Boy Scout troop saw smoke and called the fire department. They saved Wayne." "Firefighters woke him out of bed." As it turned out, Wayne was fast asleep just down the hall from the fire. It has been estimated that the blaze ignited around midnight, the same time the box had been gargling its cryptic message.

THE CRYPTIC KEEP

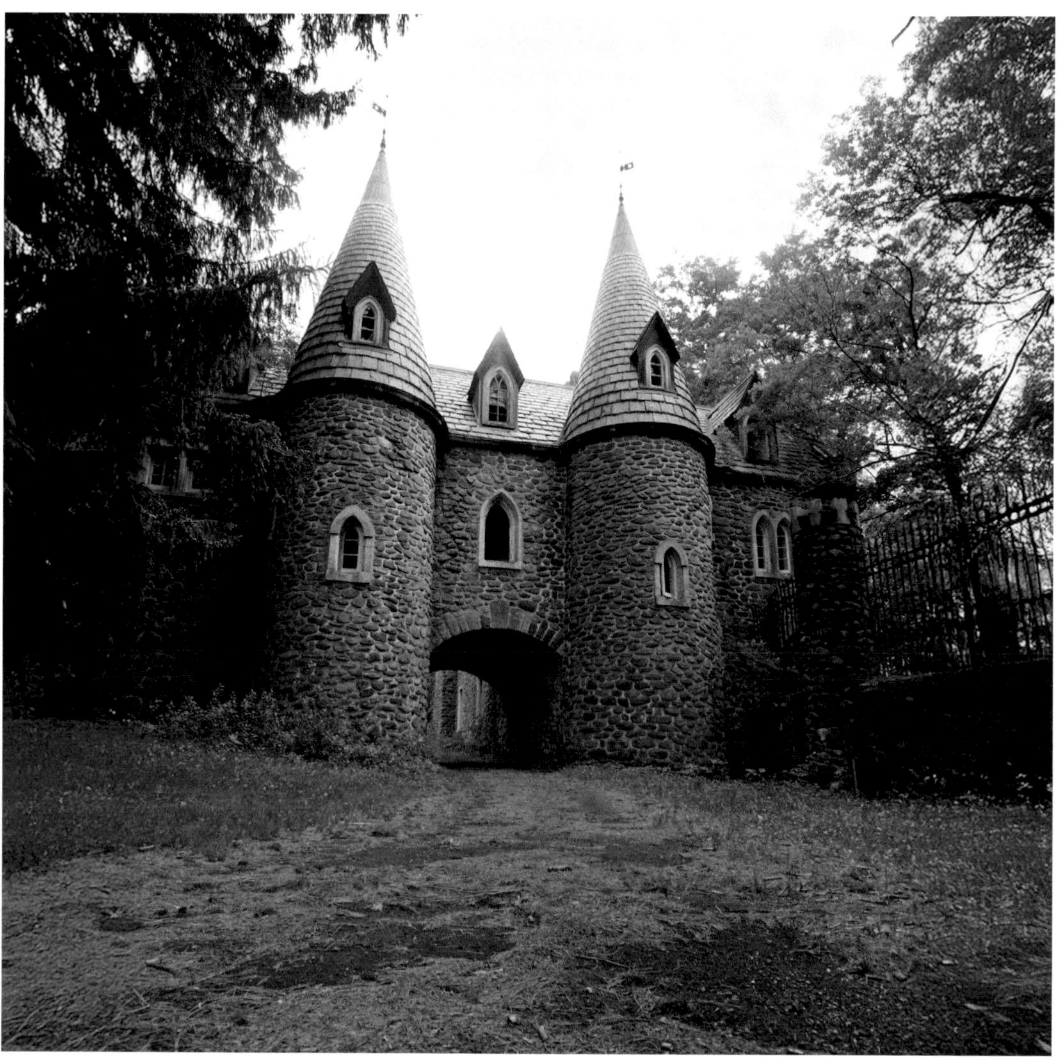

As you stand among the tall grasses of the courtyard, black birds fly overhead before swooping in to their nests thorough the missing second-floor windows. So what is the story behind this forsaken castle, if not a tale penned by the Brothers Grimm? As it turns out, fiction and reality are sometimes hard to differentiate.

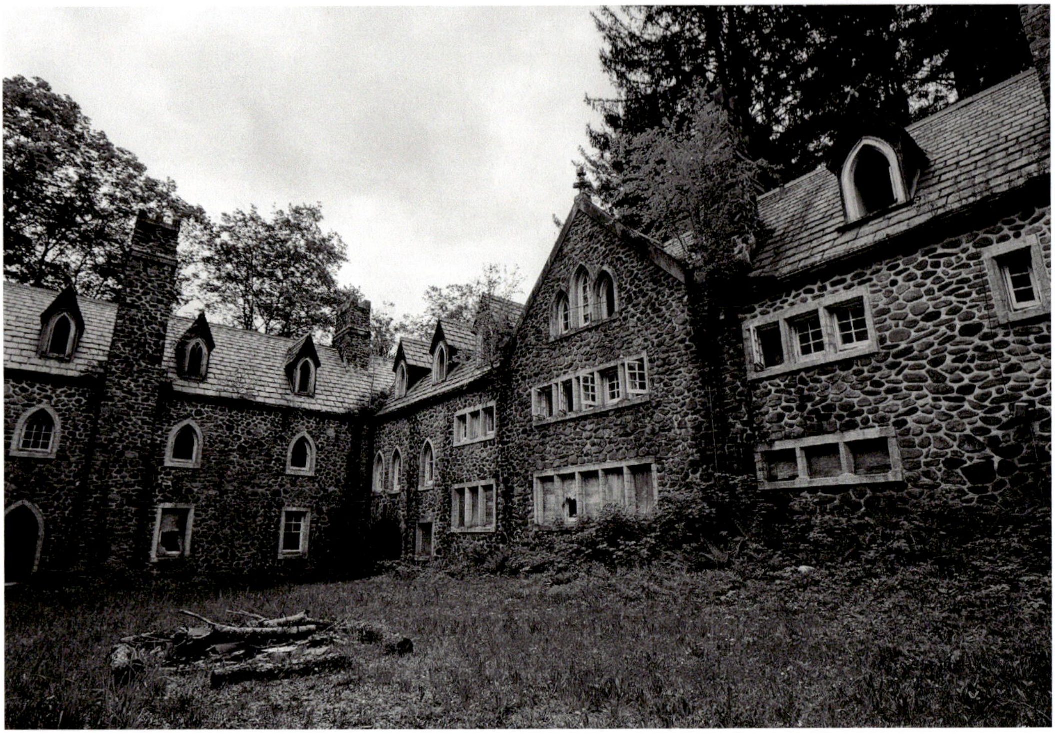

The exact origins of the place and detailed history prior to the late 1940s is enigmatic at best, with several research points displaying conflicting information. An air of mystery clings about this place almost as tightly as the ivy upon its stone walls.

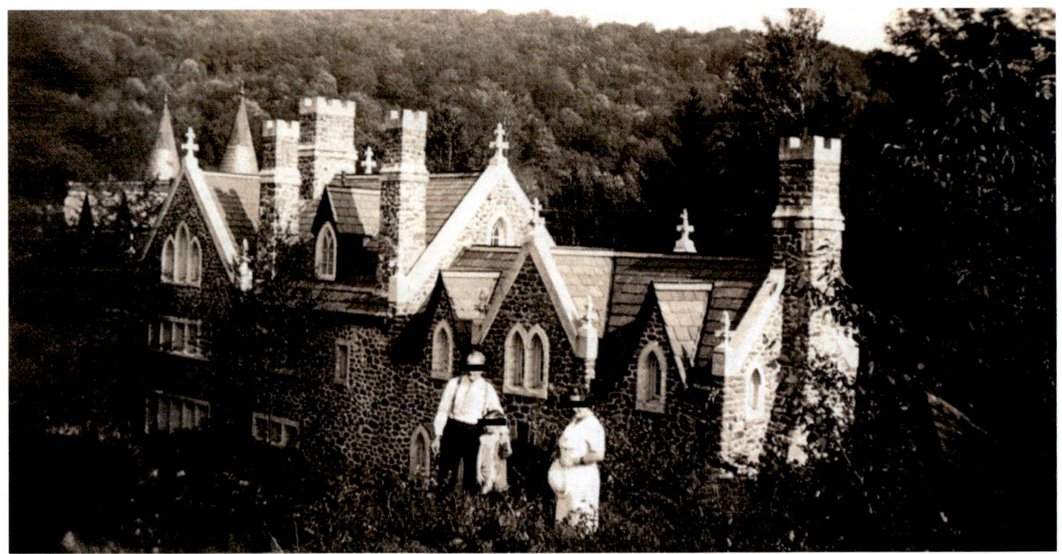

A point of certainty in a sea of unverified information is that the construction of the home occurred some time prior to the year 1920. From what little information was available to us, it seems that the designer of the home may have been Bradford Lee Gilbert, a notable architect of the era. Having passed away in 1911, this places the castle, at least in the early design stages, within the range of dates agreed upon by sources. (*Historic image courtesy of Obscure Vermont*)

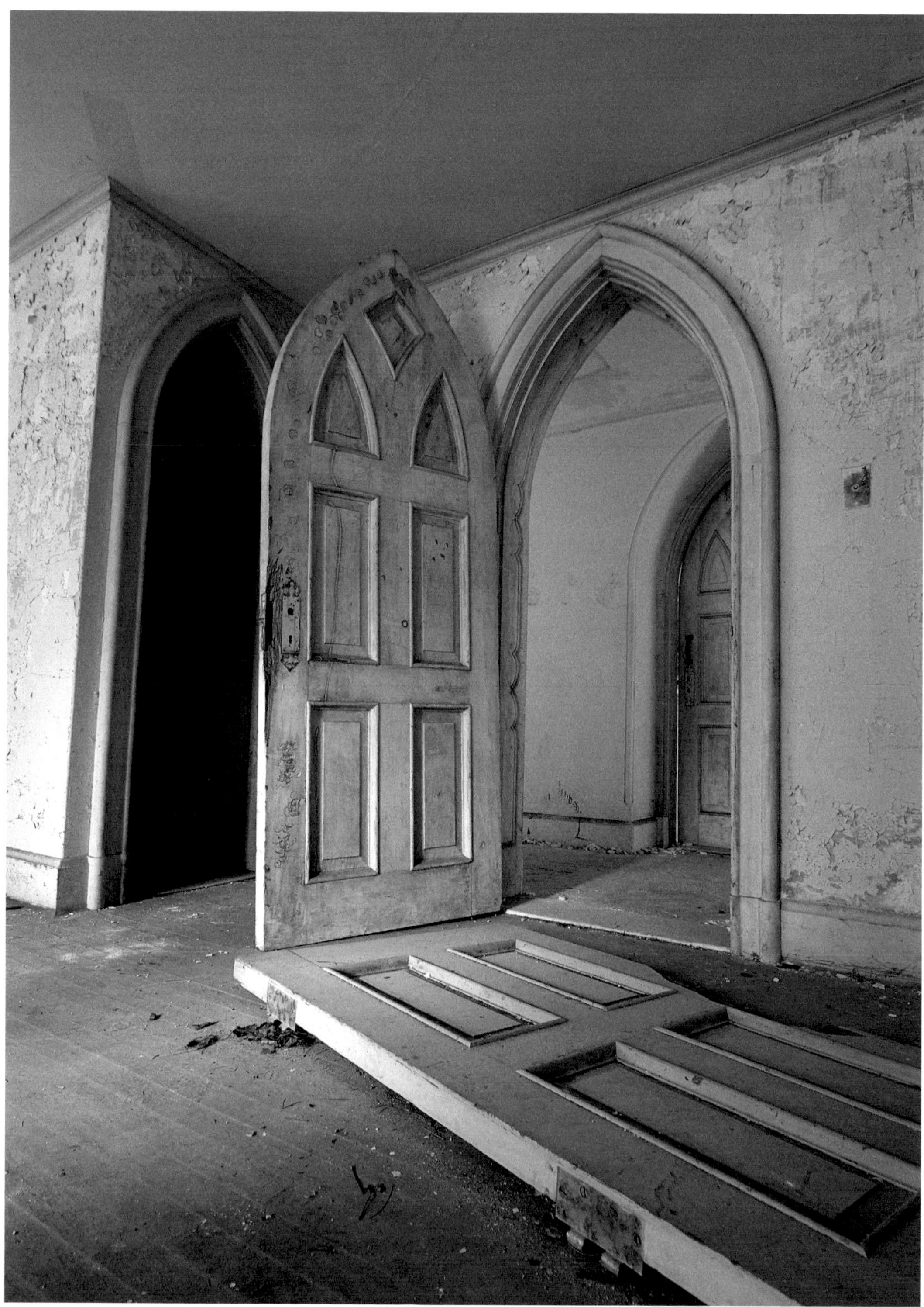

The estate was to be built upon a plot of some 1,000 acres of forestland, far from any neighboring structures. Some claim that the design plans called for roofing slate imported overseas from England, and marble floor tiles from Italy. Wherever the bits and pieces came from, they culminated in the creation of an astounding home.

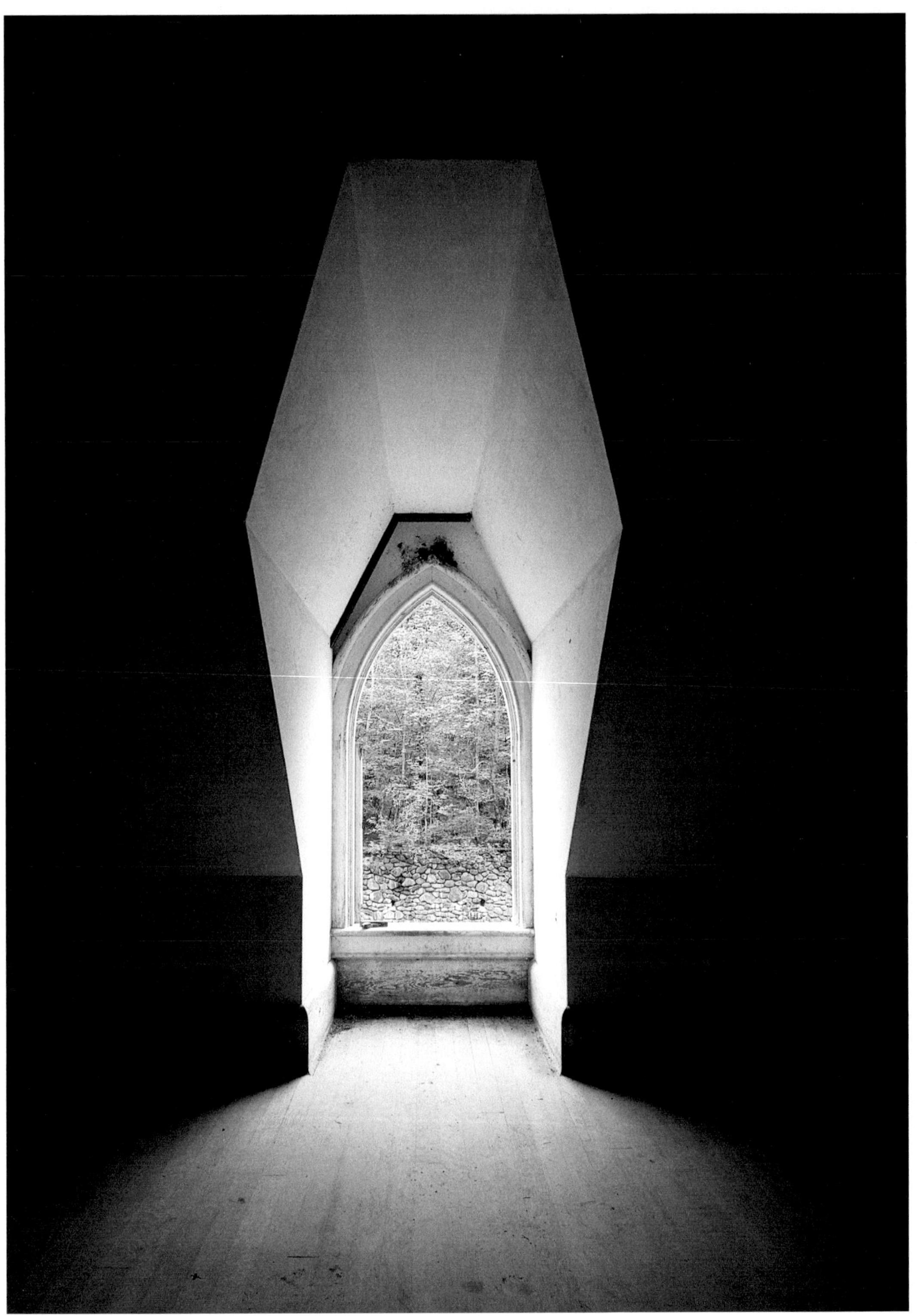

Sadly, the would-be resident of the castle was never to see it for himself, as he passed away before its completion, leaving behind his wife and daughter.

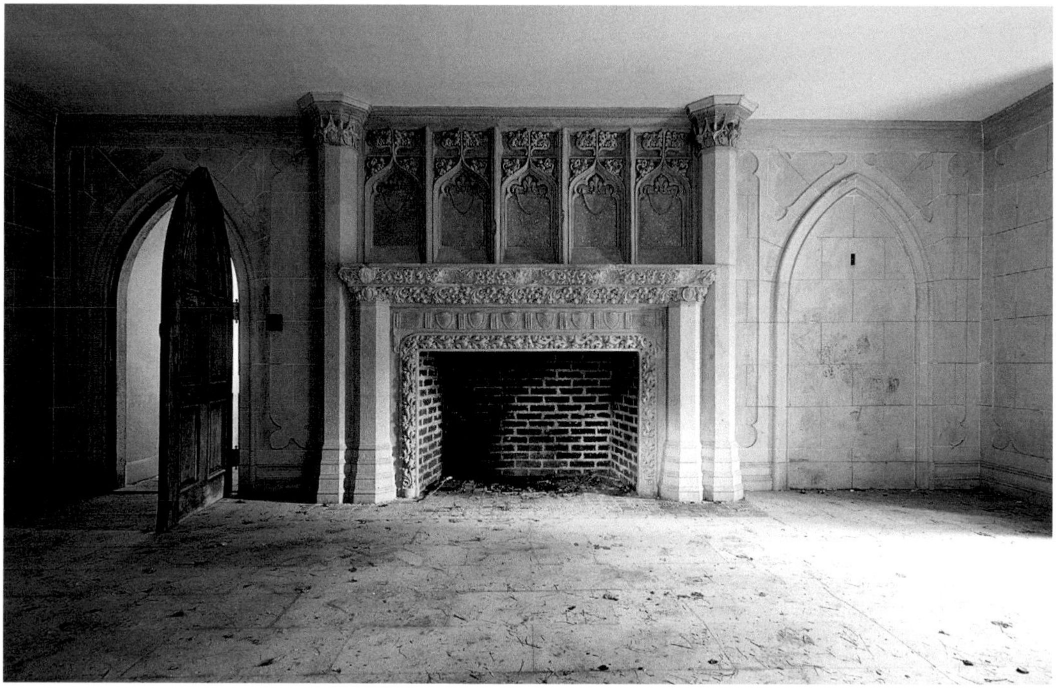

From here on out, historical accounts begin to muddy, with fact mixing with urban-legend in a way that is difficult to unravel.

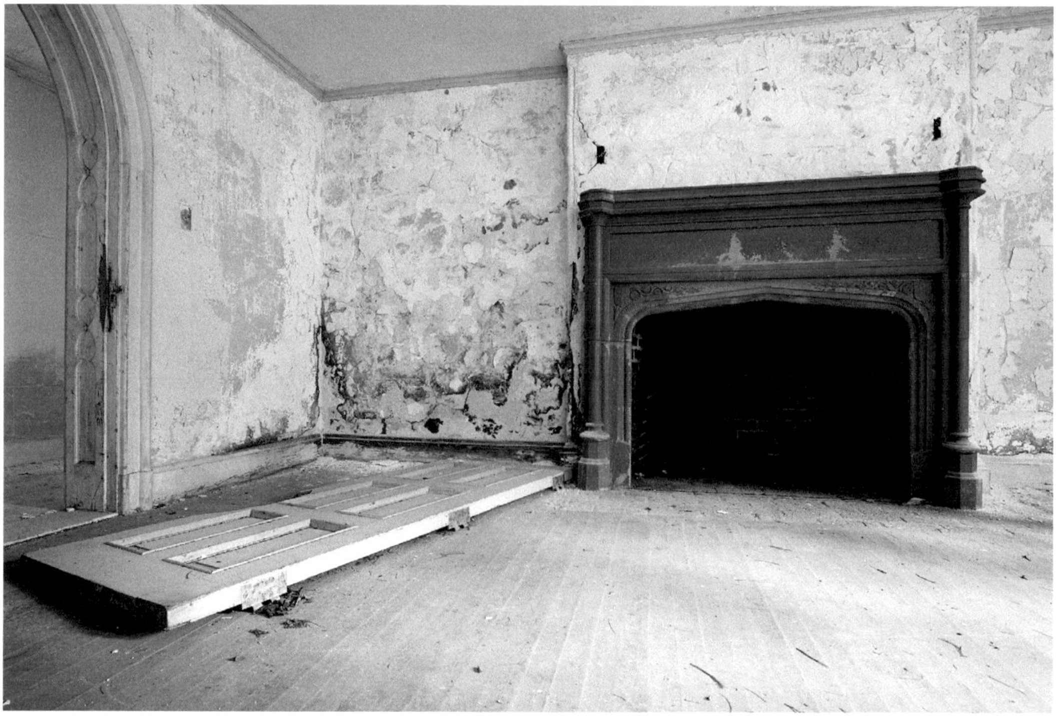

It is seemingly agreed upon that during the years that followed, his wife slowly sank into some poorly documented form of madness, likely dementia, and that she was subsequently sent away to a sanatorium for treatment.

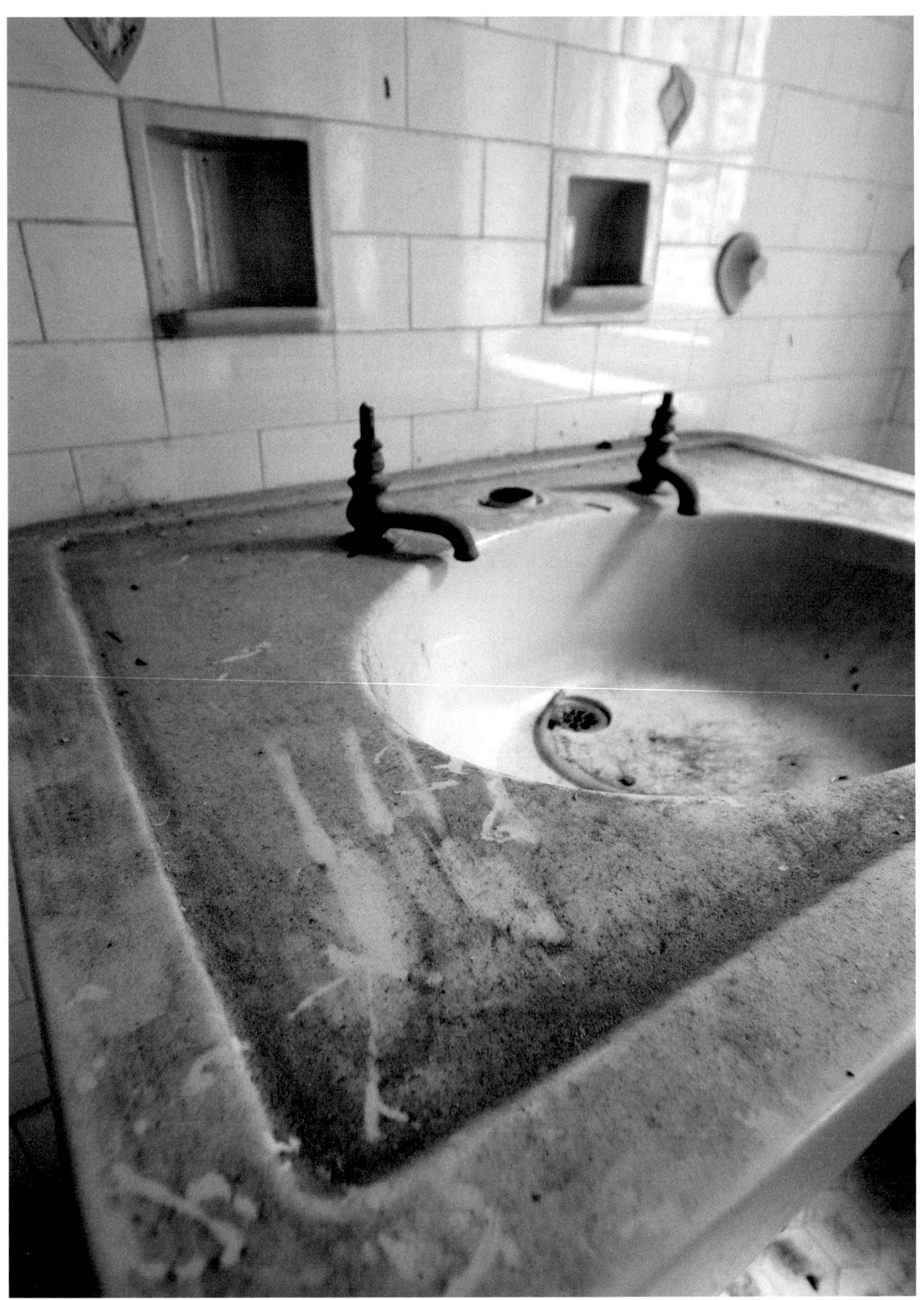

How the time between the death of her husband and her commitment to the sanatorium was spent is not clear, though. Some of the more bizarre accounts tell of her being held as a captive within the castle itself. Sealed away in a portion of the home, behind doors that had no interior knobs.

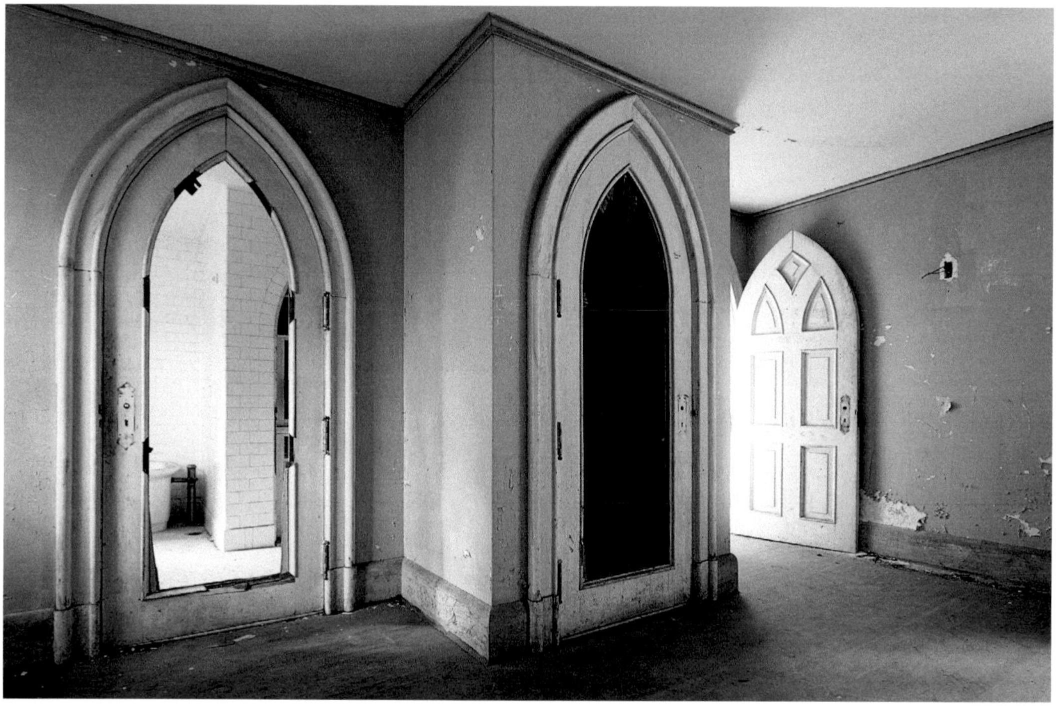

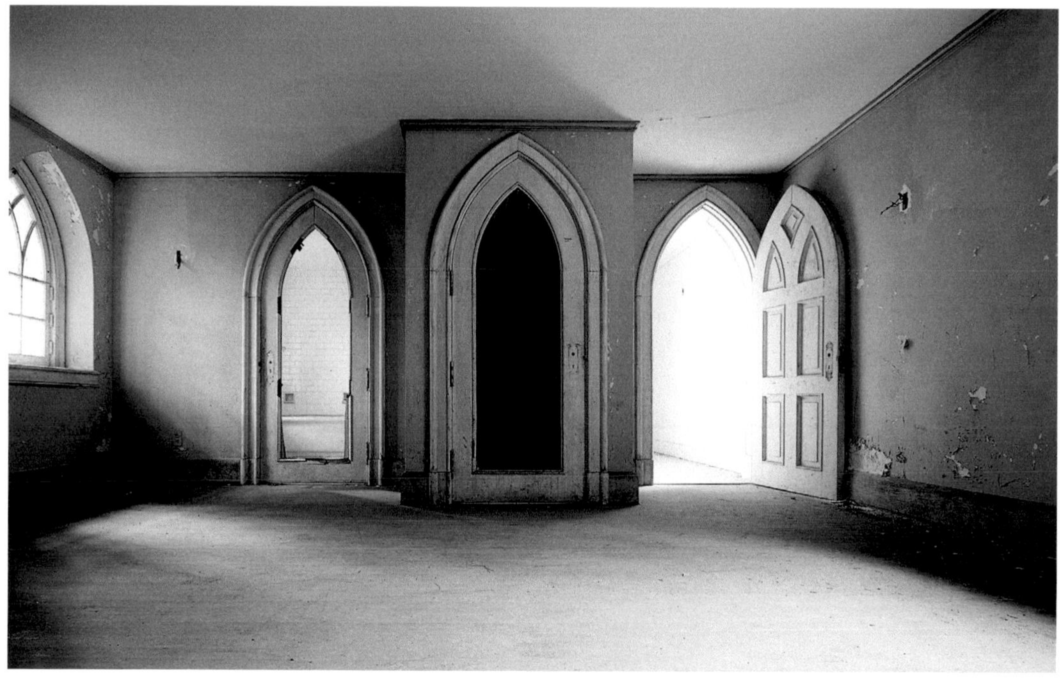

Being as this is a true-life castle on a hilltop, the story of a maiden held against her will seems eerily suiting, though tragic if indeed true.

Whatever the truth may be, after her eventual commitment, it appears that the daughter set off on her own, married, and moved away with their husband. This likely transpired in the early 1930s and has left the castle without a proper tenant ever since.

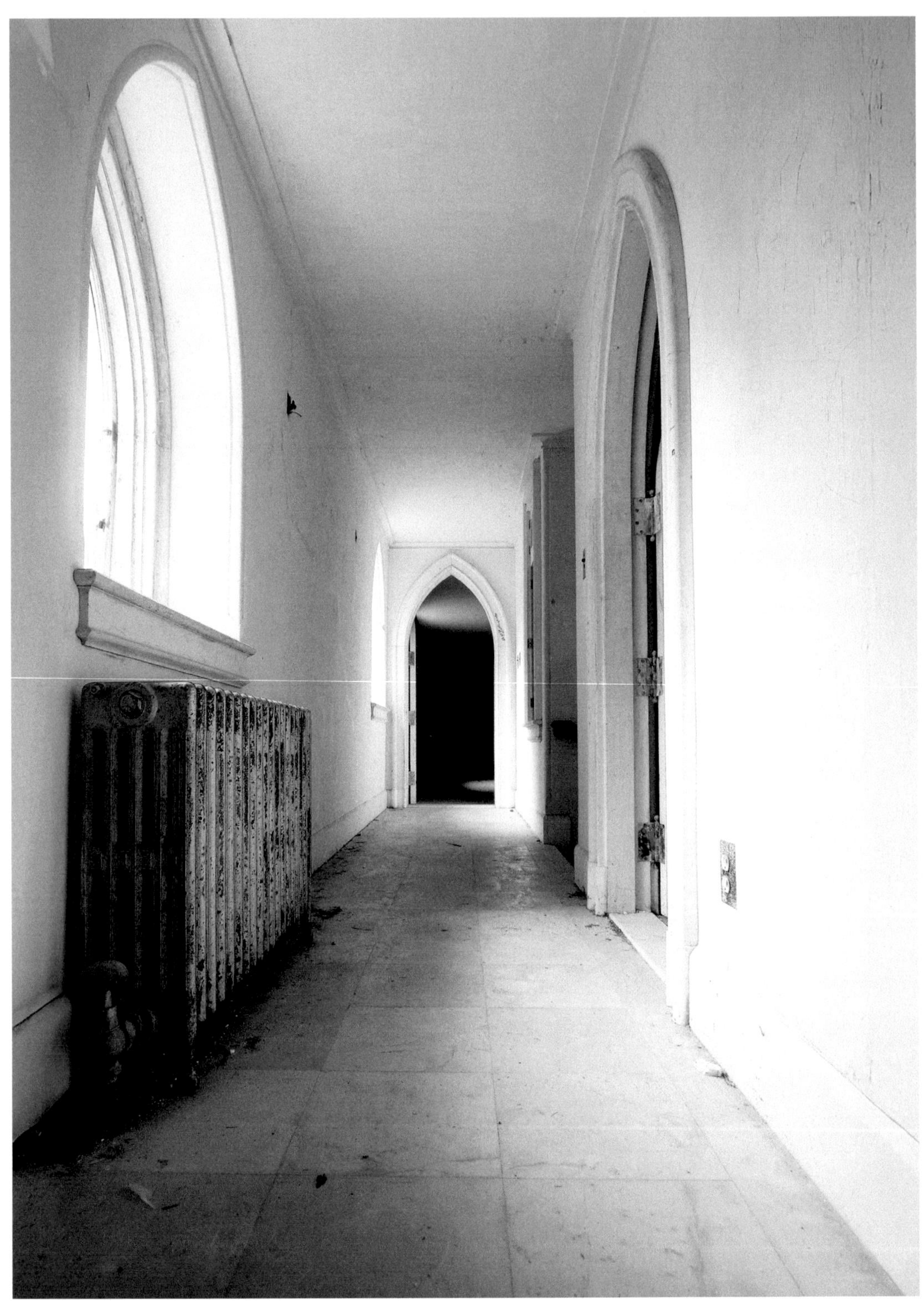

Supposedly a groundskeeper once resided in a sectioned-off portion of the castle, and watched over it for some time thereafter, but he has long since left as well. In 1947, the castle was purchased by an order of the Freemasons, but to what end is yet another mystery.

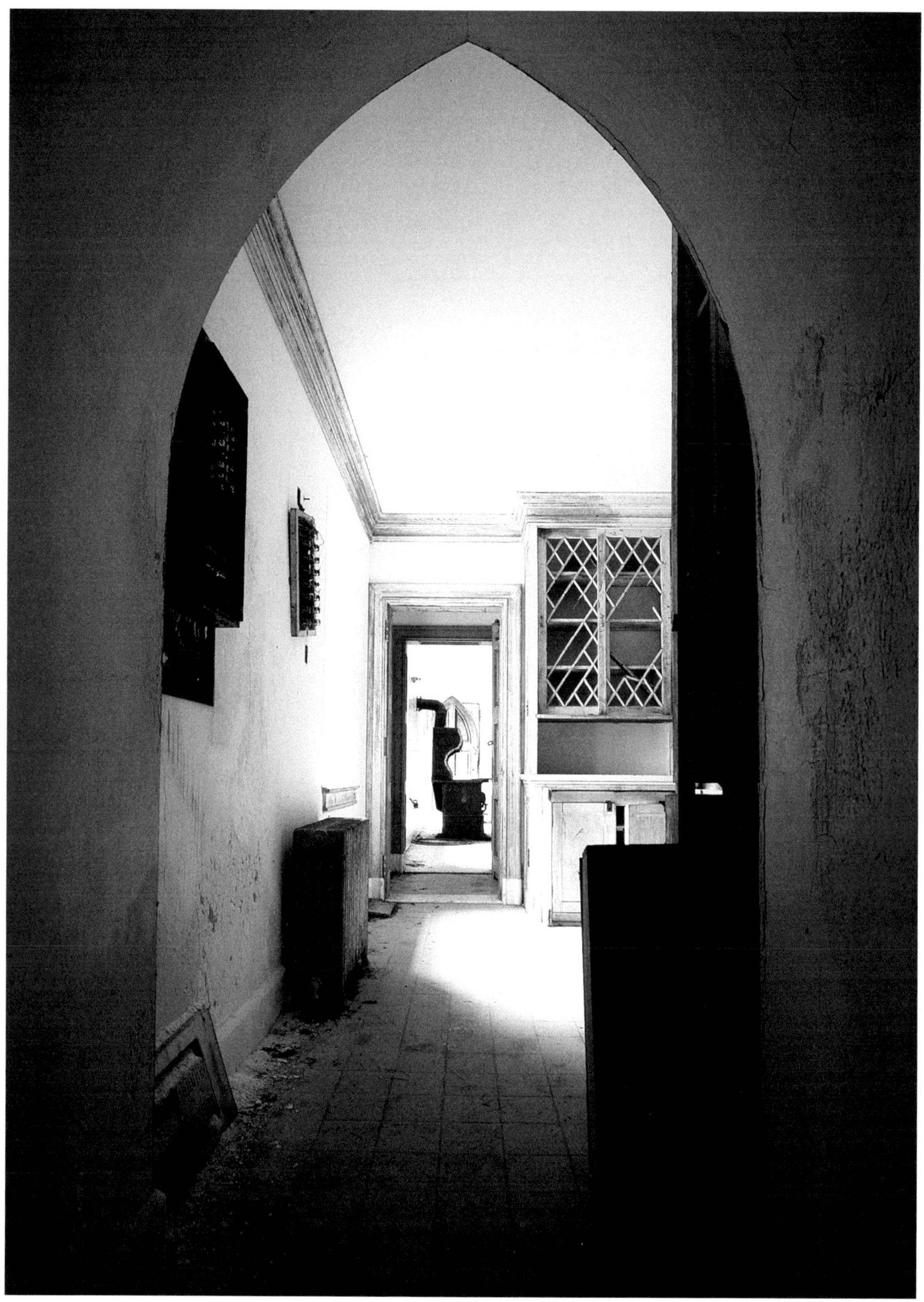

The strangely sparse, conflicting, and at times surreal backstory gives the property an unsettling ambiance, even on the brightest and warmest of summer days.

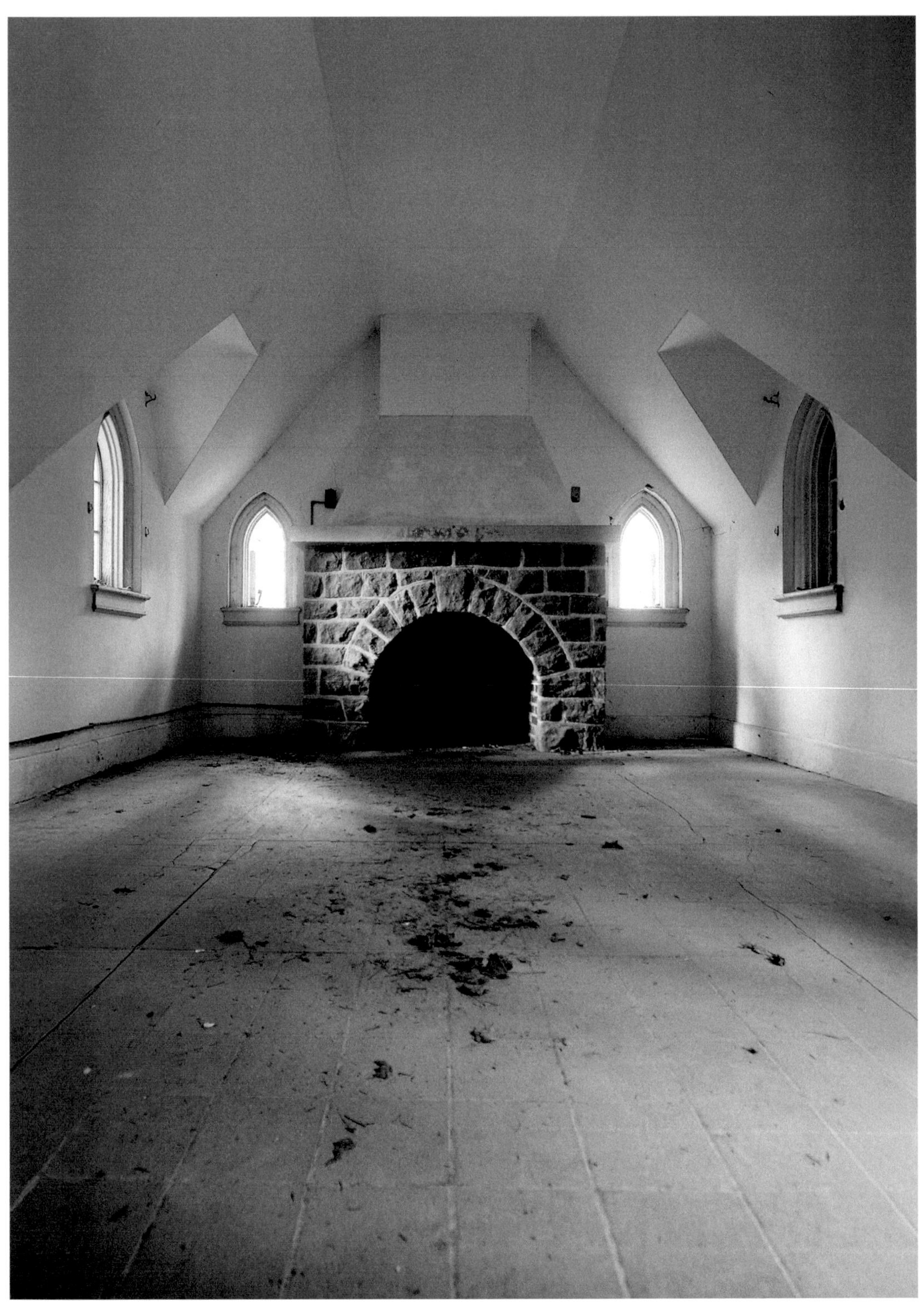

The urban-legend status which the castle has acquired over the decades has turned the castle into something else entirely. Only the walls themselves truly know exactly what transpired within them, and they seem to enjoy keeping secrets.

12

LYNNEWOOD HALL

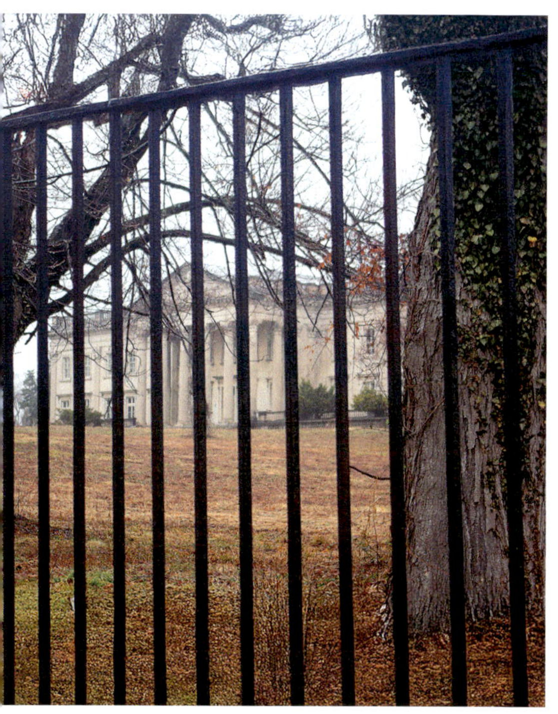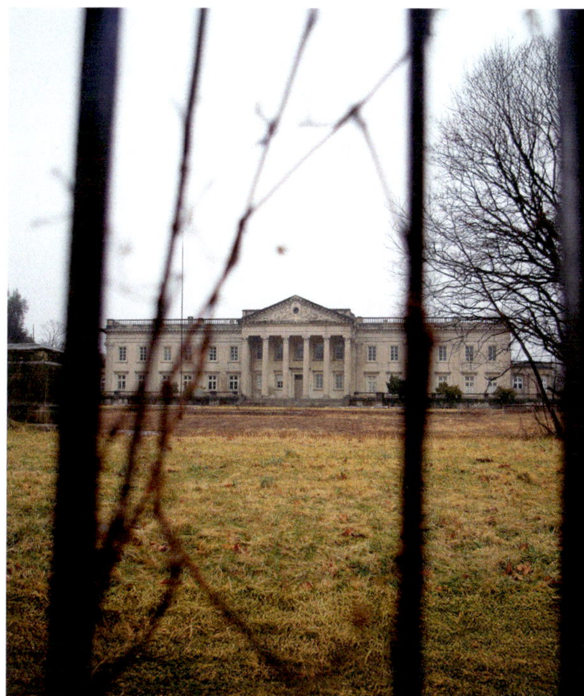

Above left and right: Just outside the city of Philadelphia can be found the second-largest mansion in the United States. Constructed in 1899, it has not housed a proper tenant in decades. Crafted as equal parts memorial, art gallery, and family estate, the property has long been draped in a cloak of mystery. Fiction blended with fact through the years that the edifice stood vacant, but one thing was an agreed-upon truth: Lynnewood Hall was one-of-a-kind architectural gem, and it was slowly wasting away in plain sight beyond wrought-iron fencing.

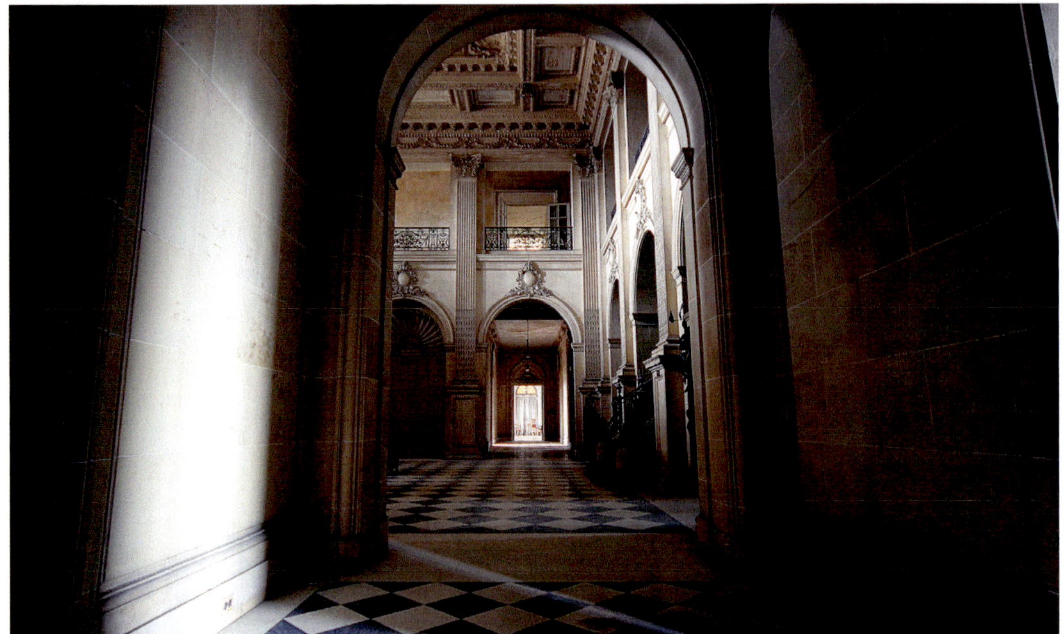

Inside the vacant mansion was dark, cold, and unnaturally quiet. Every sound echoed countless times off the stone walls and marble floors. To see such grandeur left in a state opposite of its constructed purpose was unnerving on a base level. This was a place quite literally built to be shared with others; to have its halls filled with guests, art, and music. Yet it languished in a chilled silence, devoid of what gave it purpose.

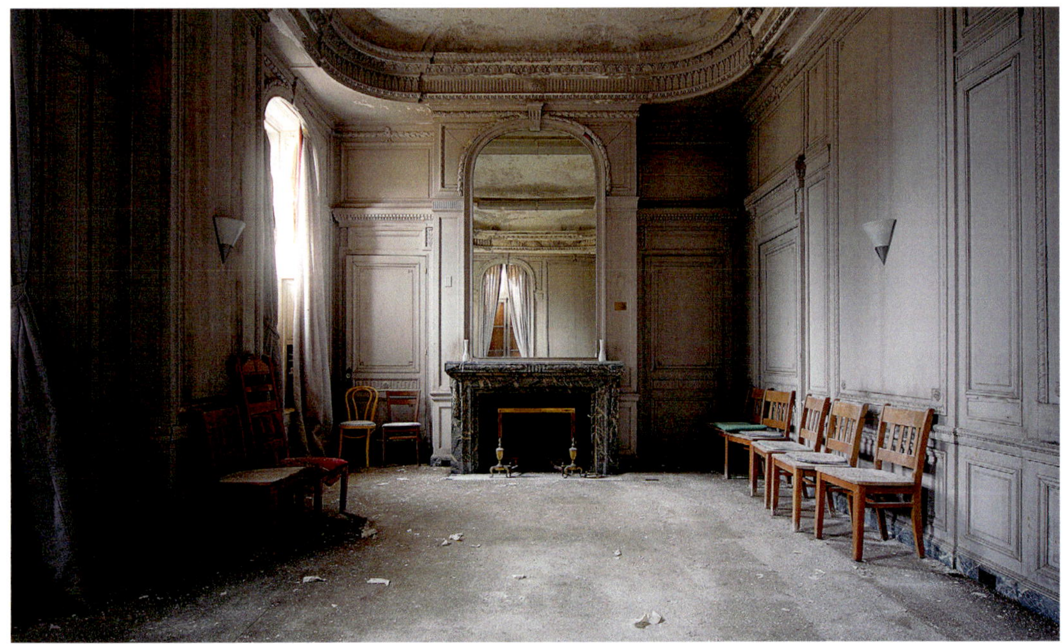

Though Lynnewood Hall sat for decades, neglected and without use. But there were always people watching, people who cared and had hopes and visions for the increasingly weathered mansion. In 2019, the Lynnewood Hall Preservation Foundation formed in an attempt to ensure a future for the aging mansion, and set about pulling it back from obscurity and ruin.

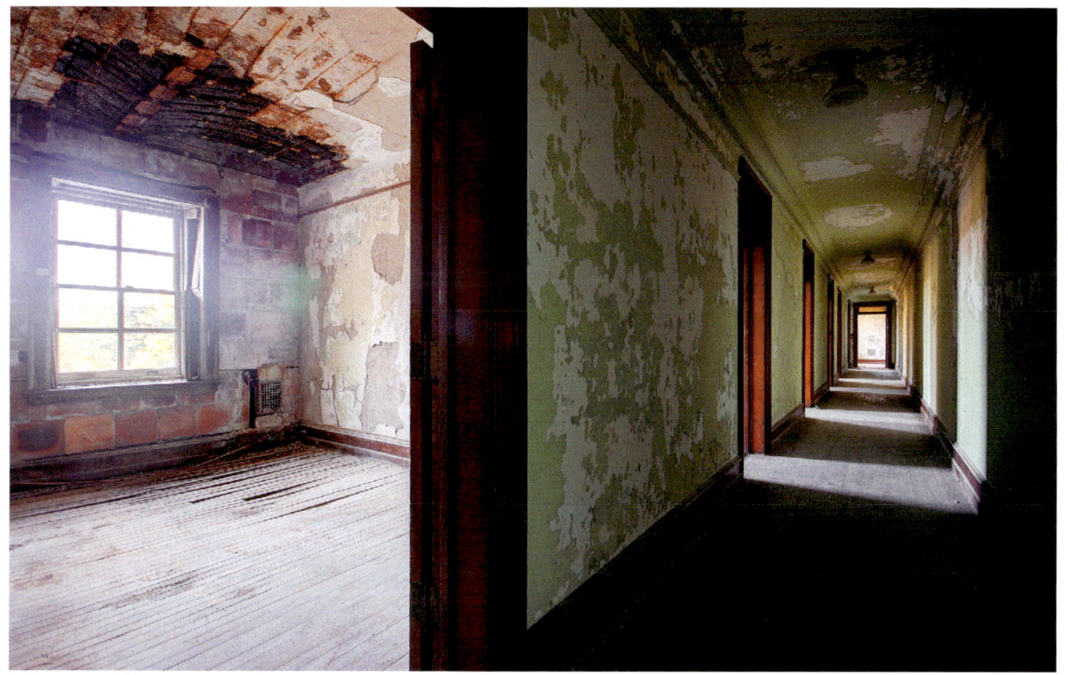

"We formed our nonprofit in 2019 with no money, a lot of aspiration, a lot of ambition, but no money … and we spent several very rough years trying to find it," explained Edward Thome, CEO & executive director of the Lynnewood Hall Preservation Foundation.

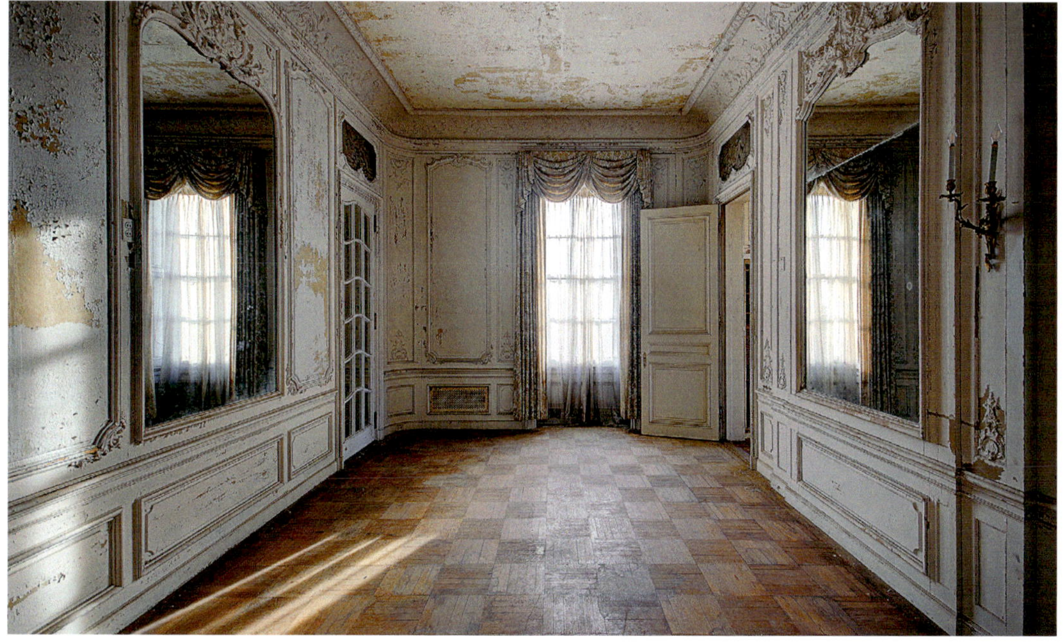

"First and foremost, this was a home and an art gallery. It was built as a memorial to Peter Widener's wife, but it was also built to celebrate family now and in the future. This was to be the family compound for centuries to come. It lasted about 46 years. This was supposed to be the family shrine and compound forever," Thome added, explaining the intent behind Lynnewood Hall's creation.

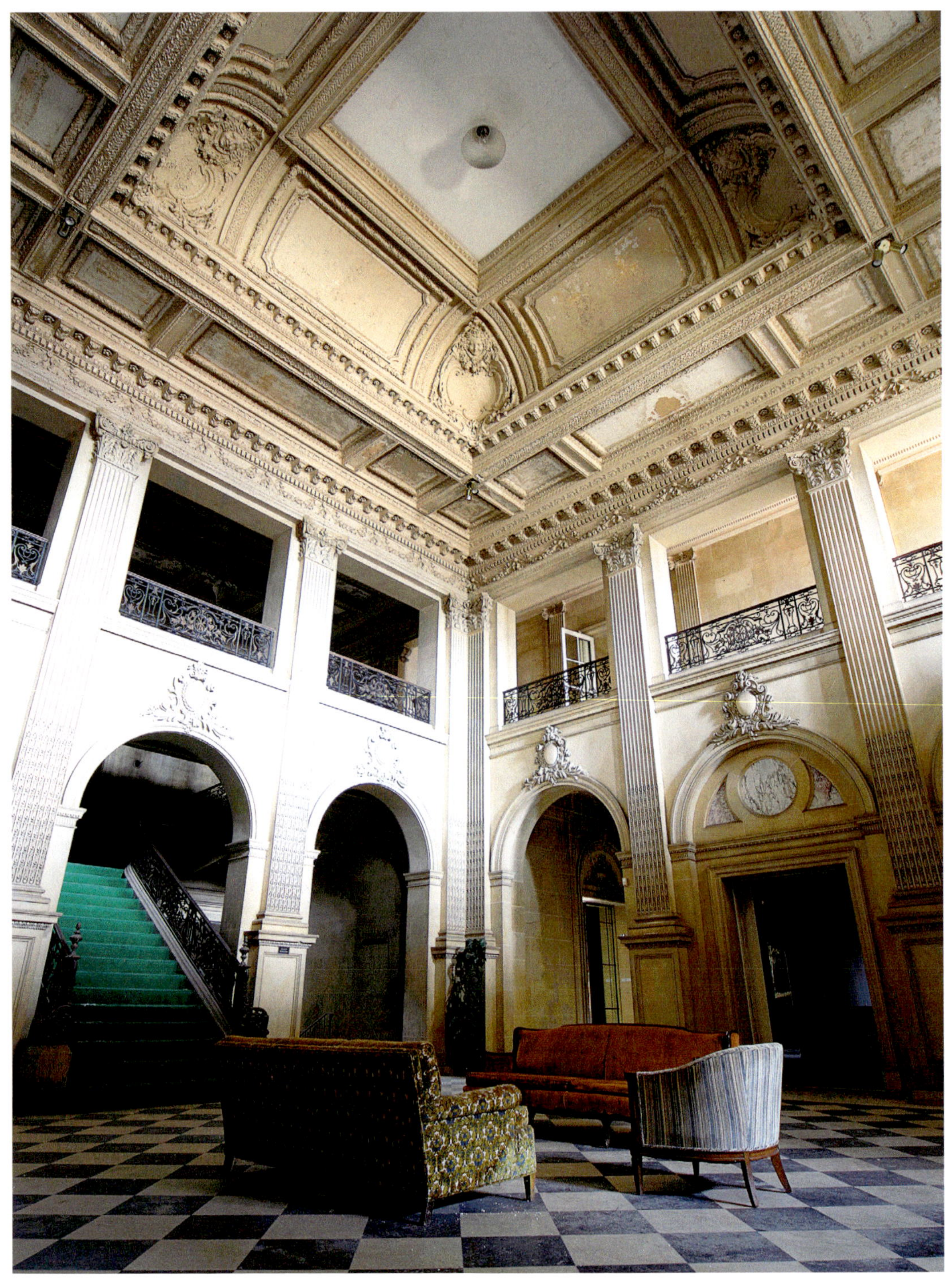

The cavernous entry hall of Lynnewood Hall in an abandoned state. Enormous, cold, and dark, it had transformed from a room meant to instill awe, wilting over time into something more akin to a dark and lifeless cave.

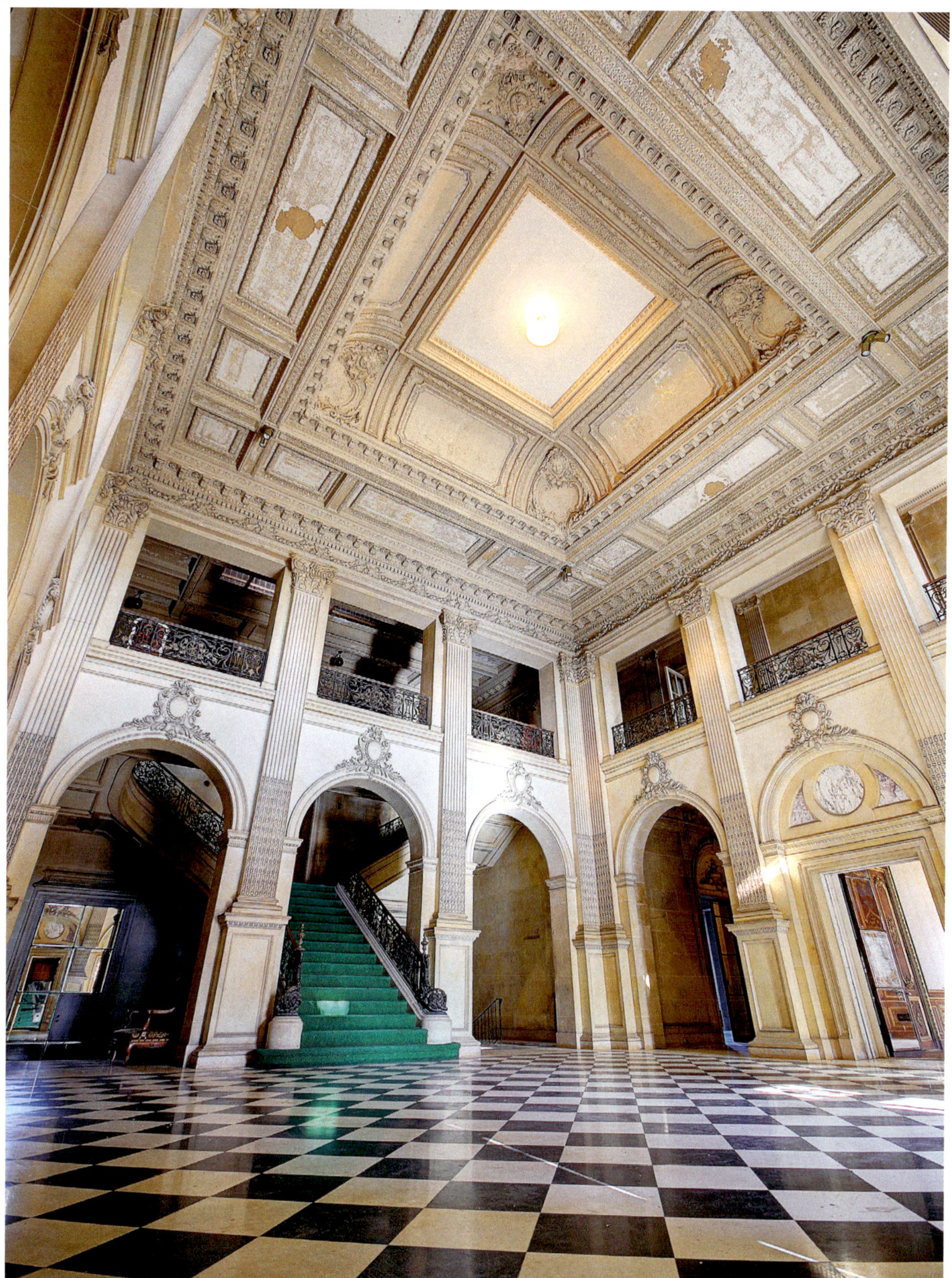

The very same room now that the Lynnewood Hall Preservation Foundation has begun to breathe life back into the old edifice. "The building itself is, it's a icon of an age that America will never see again, the great American gilded age.… It was a time for philosophy and enlightenment and progressiveness and bringing back the neoclassical ideals and arts and culture from hundreds and hundreds of years ago, not thousands of years ago," said Thome regarding the mansion's national significance.

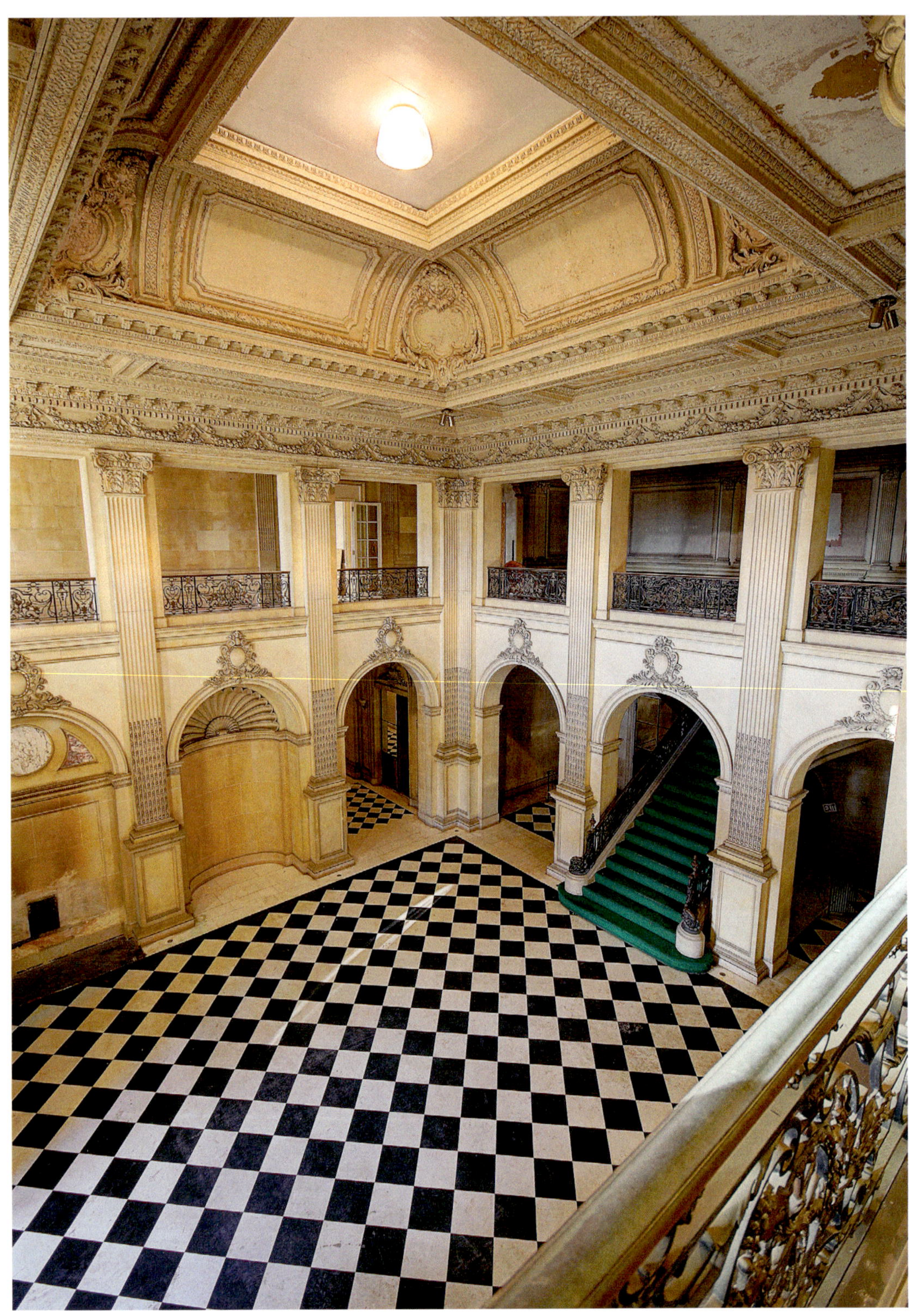

Thome continued: "This building, this is the epitome of neoclassical beauty and grandeur. It's a work of art. And it is just such a testament to the care and pride that people put into everything that they did at that point in time."

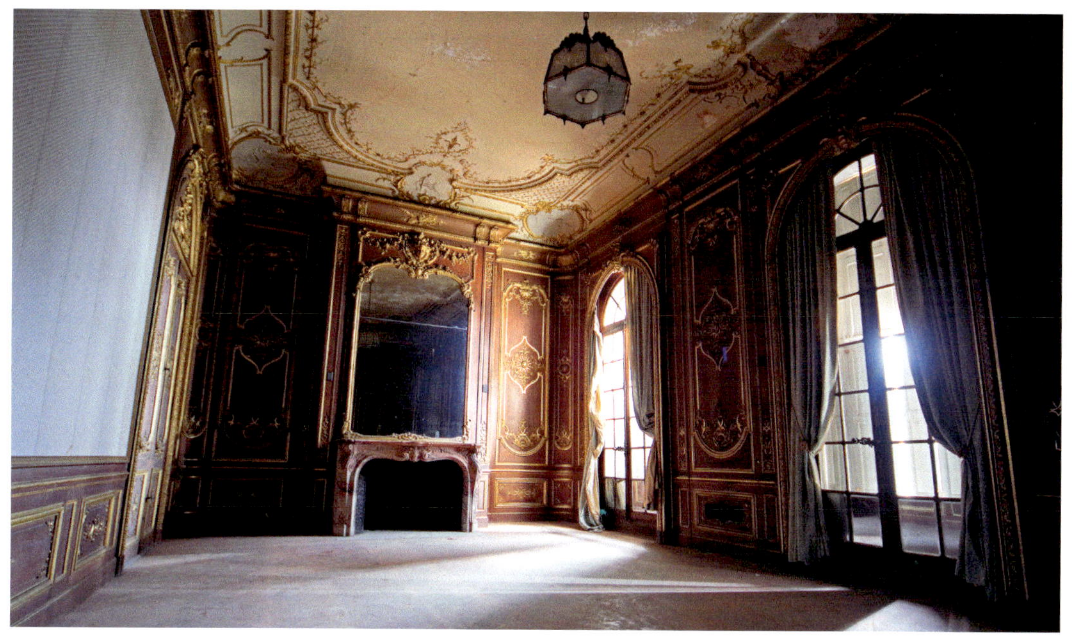

Tyler Schumacher, facilities site manager of the foundation, mused about the task they have collectively undertaken with Lynnewood Hall: "It's a privilege to be able to work on a building like this. You need to understand the importance that the building has; this is not just an ordinary stone structure. This was a home for a very wealthy family that were great philanthropists, great people."

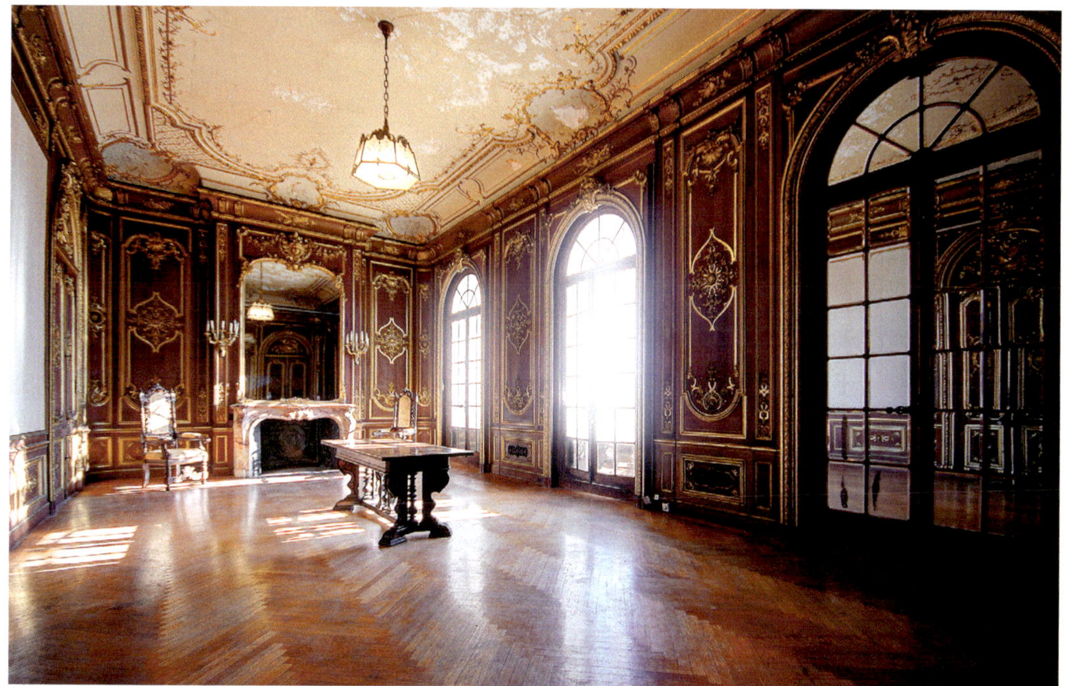

Schumacher continued: "As you approach the restoration, you need to keep in mind that history that the building holds and not just haphazardly do things. It needs to be done with care and respect to the Wider family and to their legacy, and to what this house means."

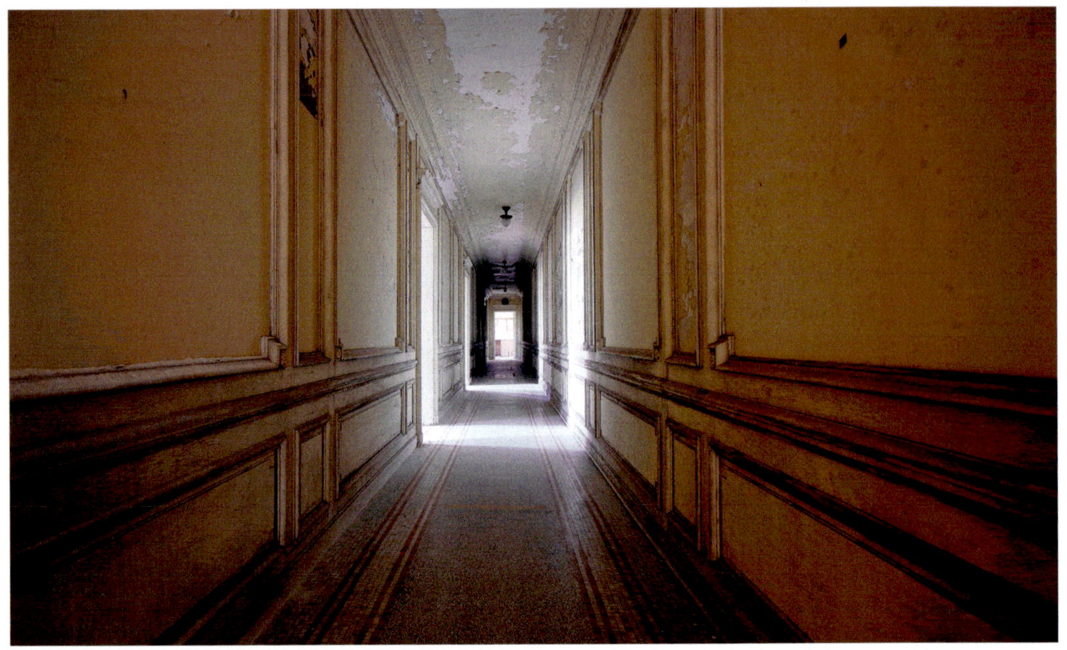

Thome touches on the mysterious air that the mansion had during its lengthy vacancy: "I would say at that time there was an aura of mystery surrounding this house unlike a lot of other abandoned mansions. Nobody had been in here for decades. No one even had updated pictures of the interior. There were all sorts of rumors that it was burned out and destroyed, that the interiors were non-existent, and that the house wasn't worth saving. Nobody really knew much."

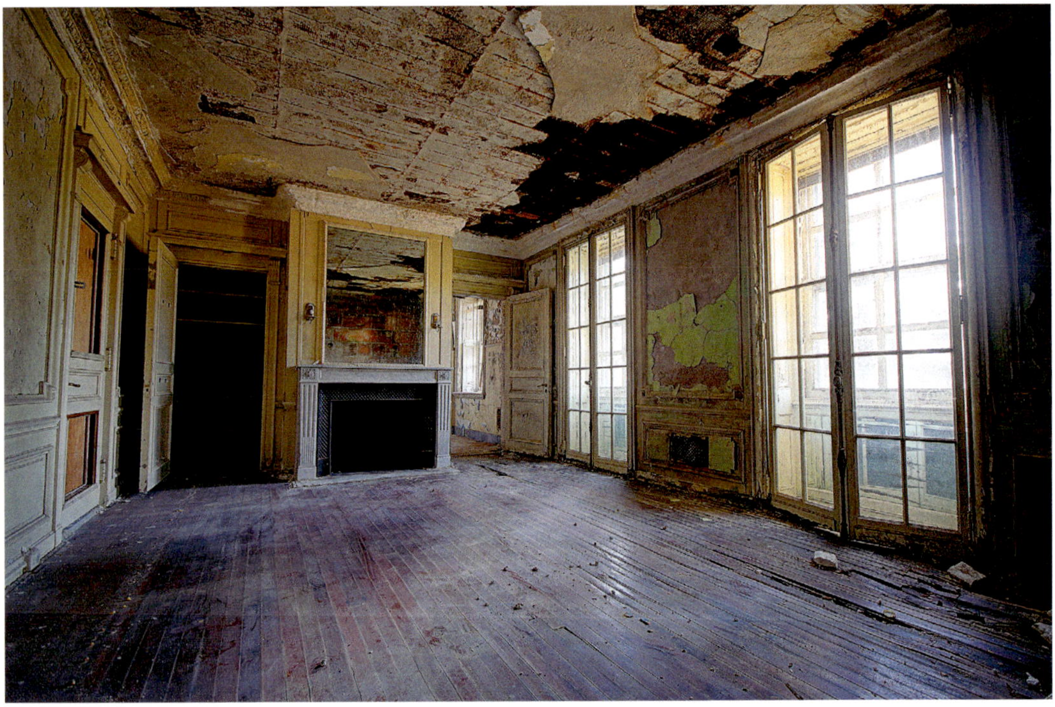

Thome continued: "Personally, I treat it with a reverence as though they're still here. This is still their house. I think having that mindset that this is a home has changed my perspective on a lot of things."

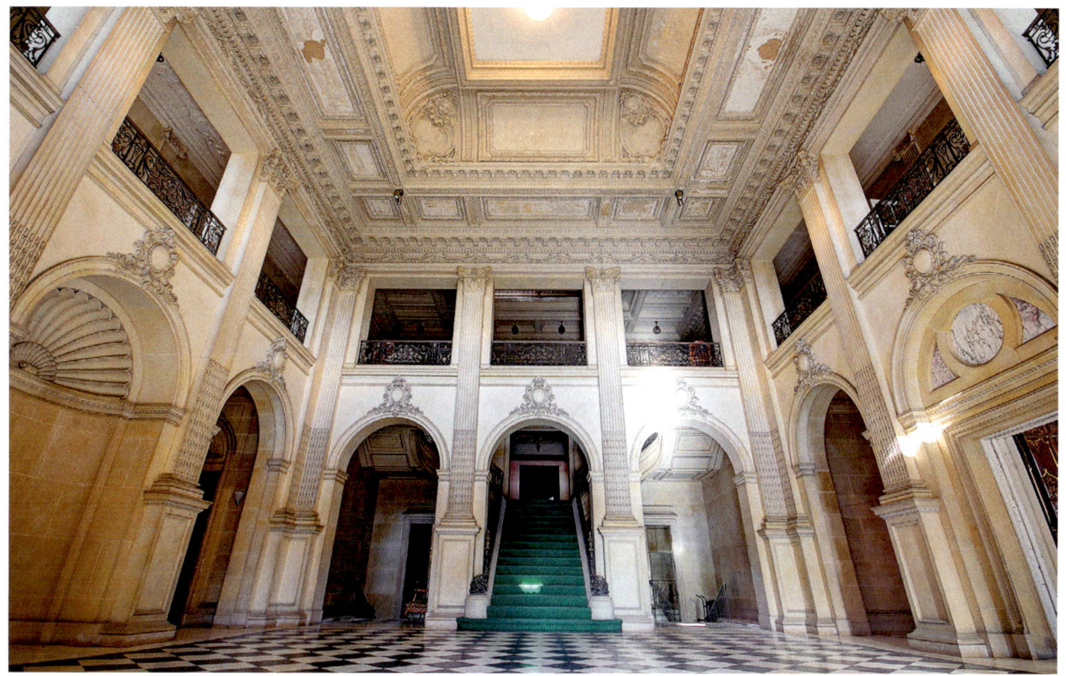

Angie VanScyoc, chief operating officer, vividly recalls her very first steps inside the historic hall: "When I walked inside of this building for the first time … you look around and you see the craftsmanship, the beauty. You know, we have that in government buildings to a degree, but it's not personal. This was a home."

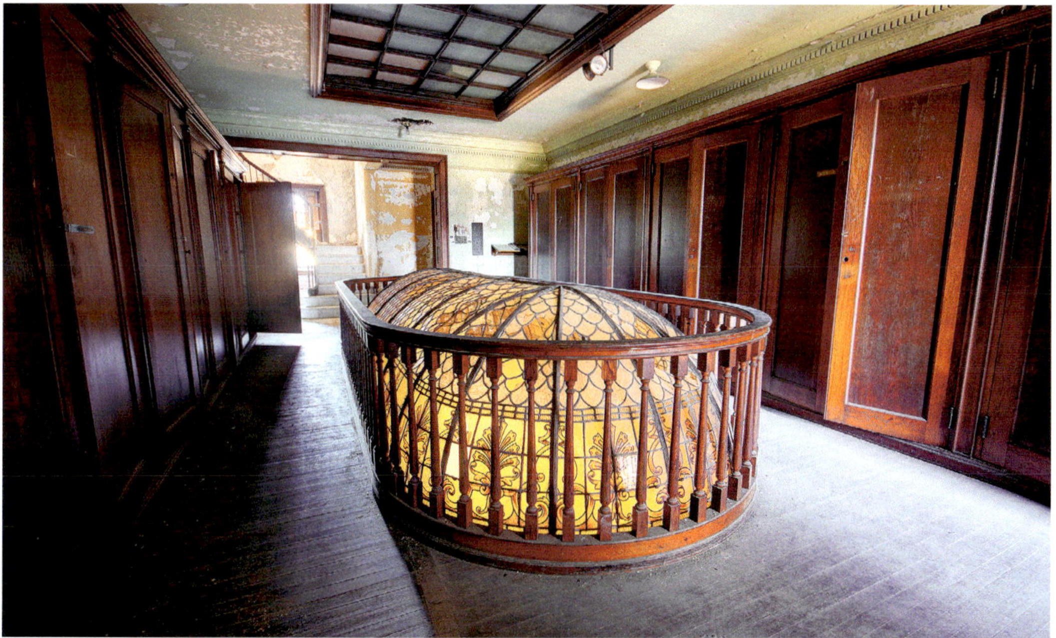

VanScyoc continued, speaking on the future of the home which had been left without purpose for decades: "Everybody wants to know; what is Linwood Hall ultimately going to be? We want it to be a multi-use facility. We want it to be cultural center, and an art museum again, you know … to all the different things that can activate to sustain this property. But our first use is really of being an active educational preservation project."

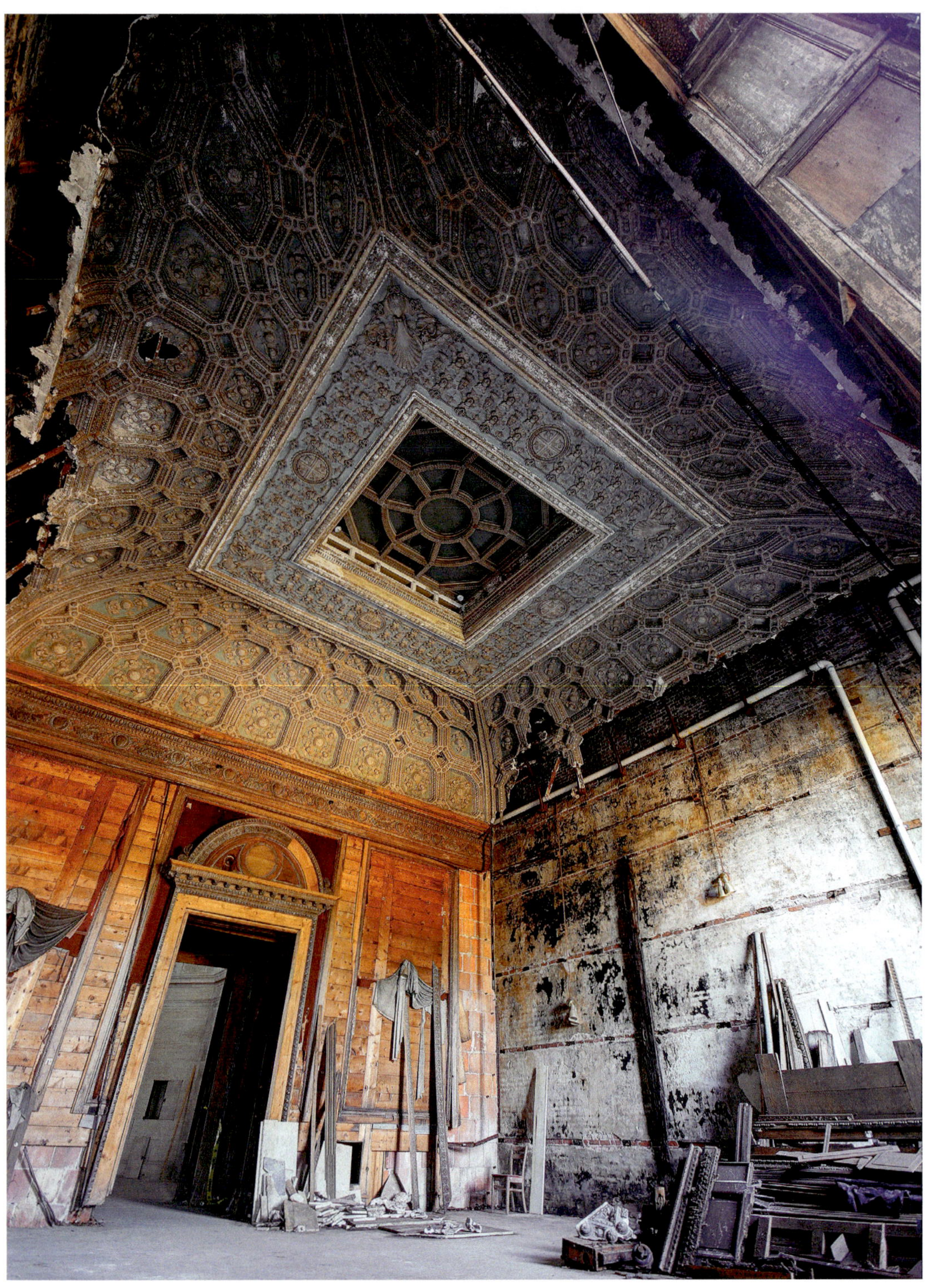

VanScyoc added: "You know you have a lot of people will come in here and they'll say it's really a shame that it's been left go to this degree, or that that is in the state it's in. My response is that therein lies the opportunity, because we have 110,000 square feet of space to implement educational programming to bring [Lynnewood Hal] into a learning space, through the process of bringing it back."

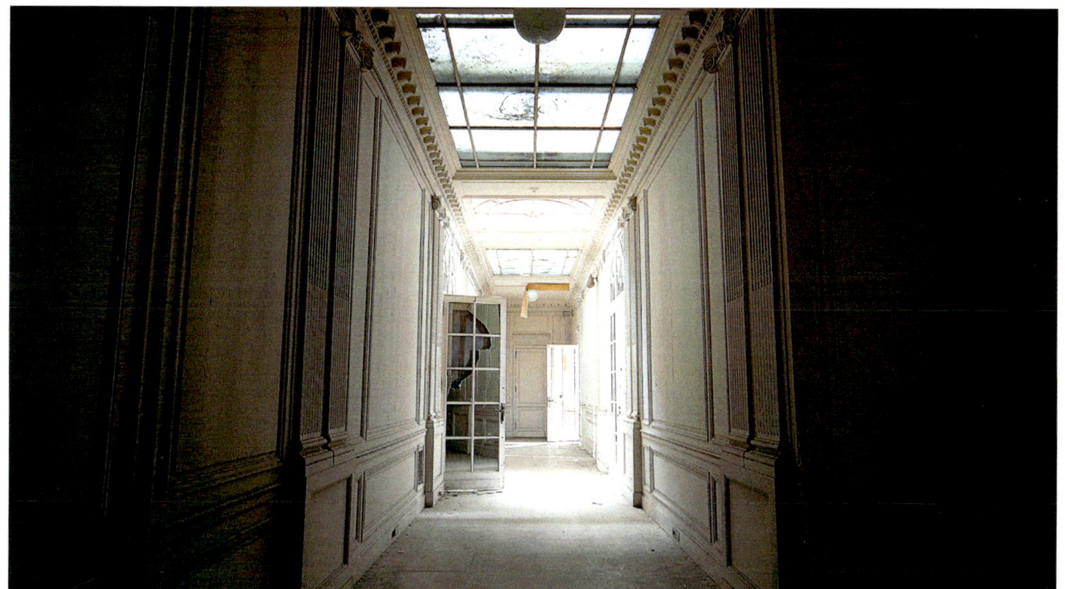

Thome echoed VanScyoc's sentiments regarding the restoration process being utilized as an educational tool: "We don't want to just have the master craftsmen come in and fix all this. No one is going to be hired if they don't bring students with them. I don't care if they're high schoolers, trade school students, college students, or adults that are 40s and 50s that are like, 'Hey, I'd like to learn how to do carpentry or masonry or tile work'. Every aspect of this restoration has to be an educational component in the skilled trades to make sure that these skills live on."

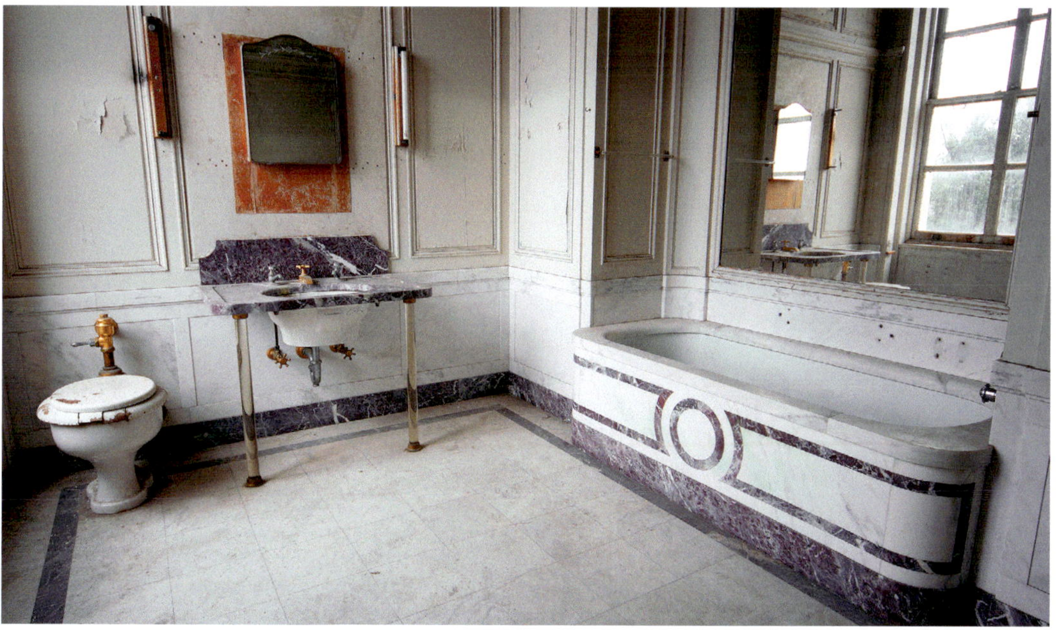

"I have talked with different people with different memories of this house, but I haven't found a single person with a bad memory. The oldest [individual] I could think of was 93.… And it's just, it's so interesting. People who are no longer here, they've written stories about what was like living here, or working here. To talk to people that are still alive and hear that the house means something just a little bit different to each one, but it's been special to all of them. That's what gives a building purpose and meaning," said Thome, with reference to the layered history of the old mansion.

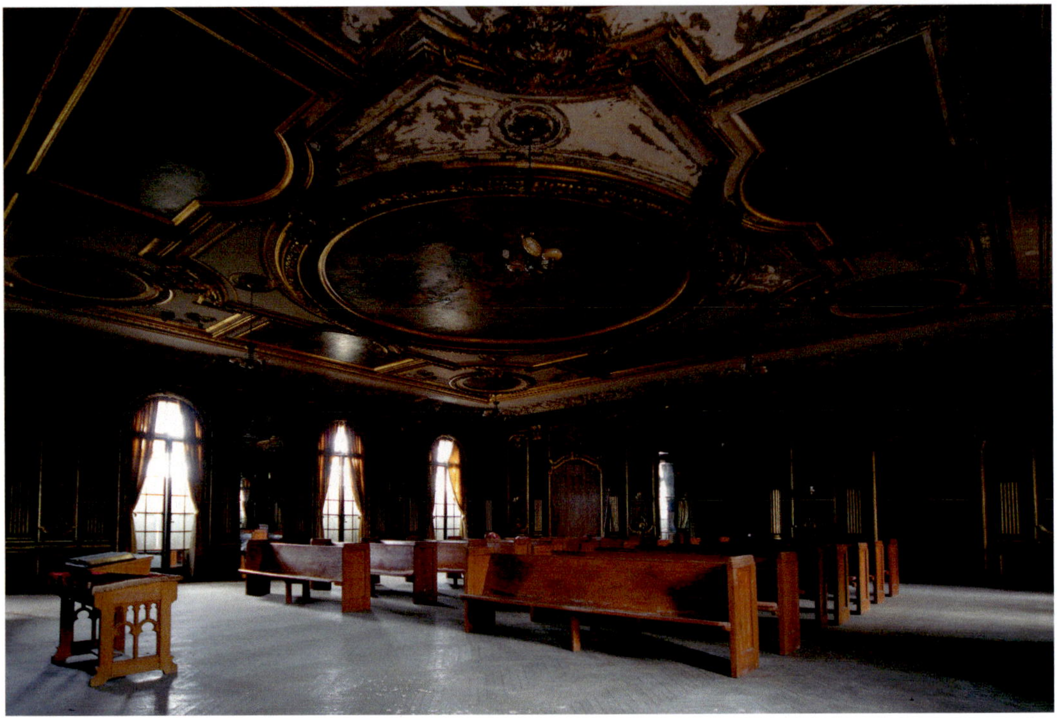

Above and below: For a time, Lynnewood Hall had been utilized as a seminary school, with its ballroom having been converted into a chapel. This photo, taken during the mansion's state of abandonment, shows the space as it existed until the preservation foundation took control of the property. In the years since, the former ballroom has been cleared back to its original state and the pews donated to local schools.

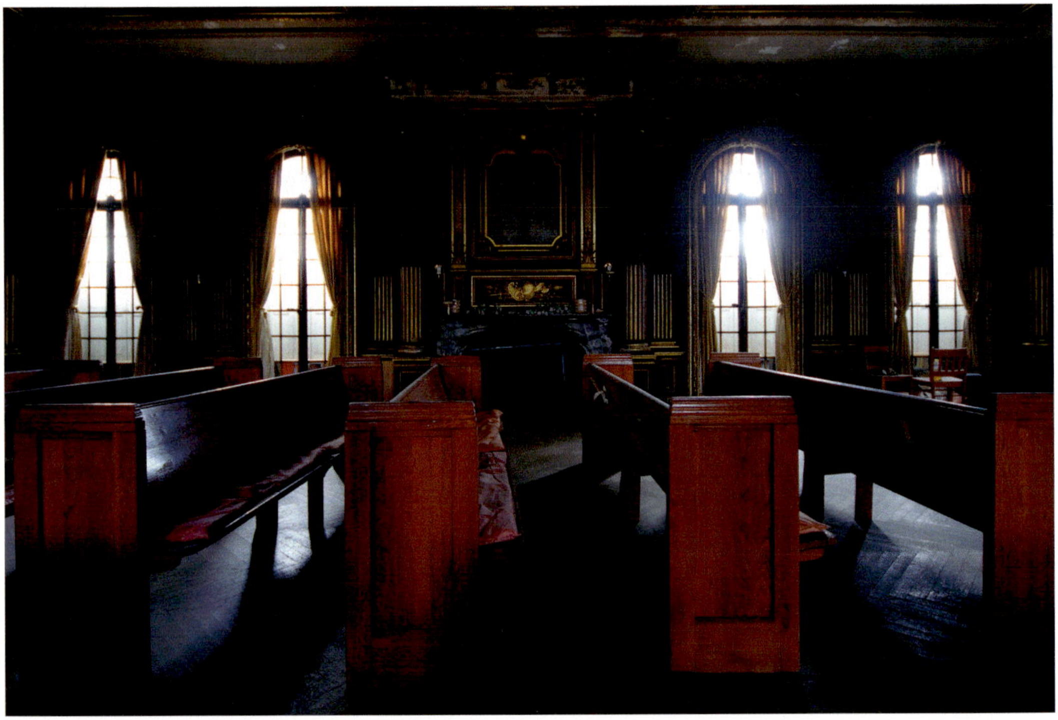

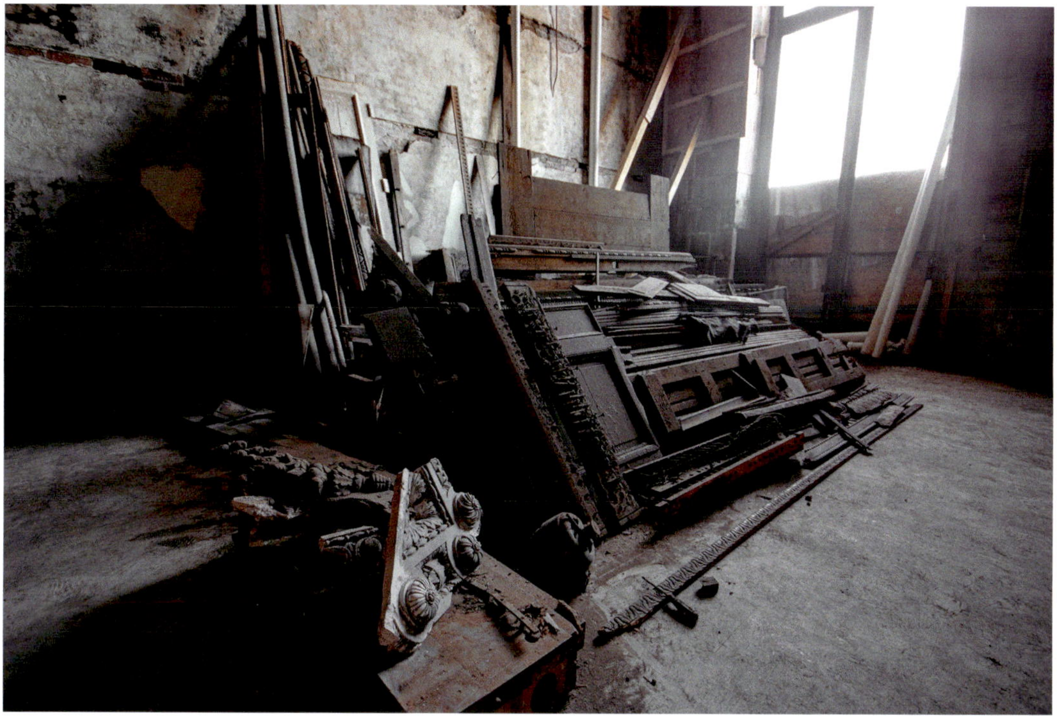

Fallen and removed details from the interior of the mansion, collected and organized for future use.

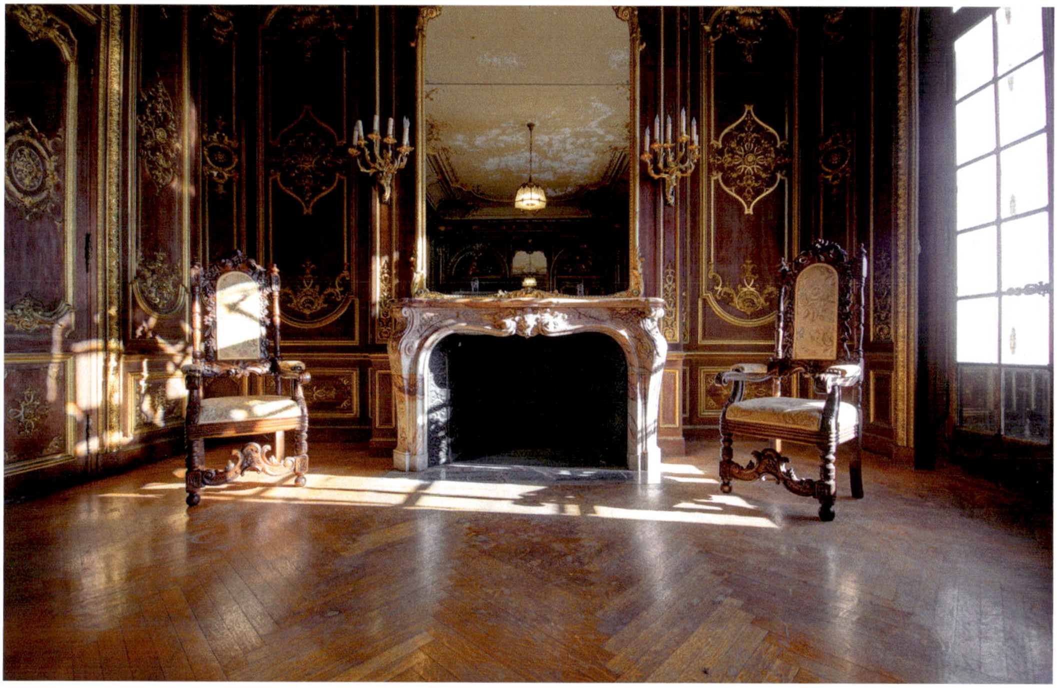

"The whole building is a work of art. And you don't really see that much after 1950, but especially after the Great War in 1914. And this is a picture in time that you'll very likely never see again. And that point from a cultural standpoint is very important," said Thome, speaking on the national significance of Lynnewood Hall.

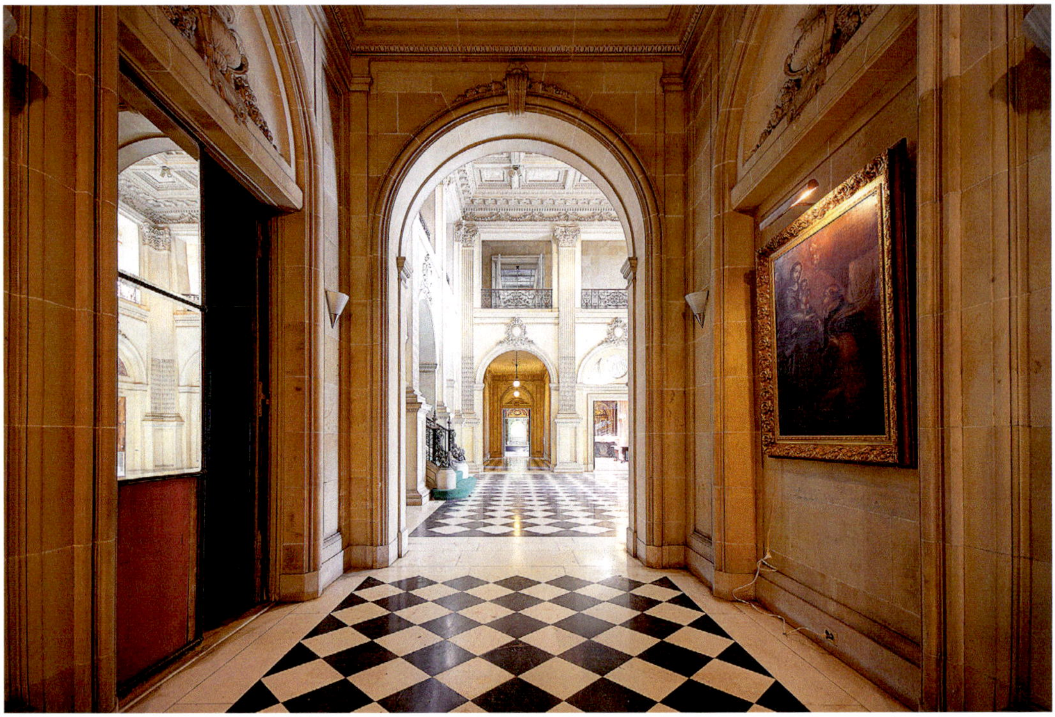

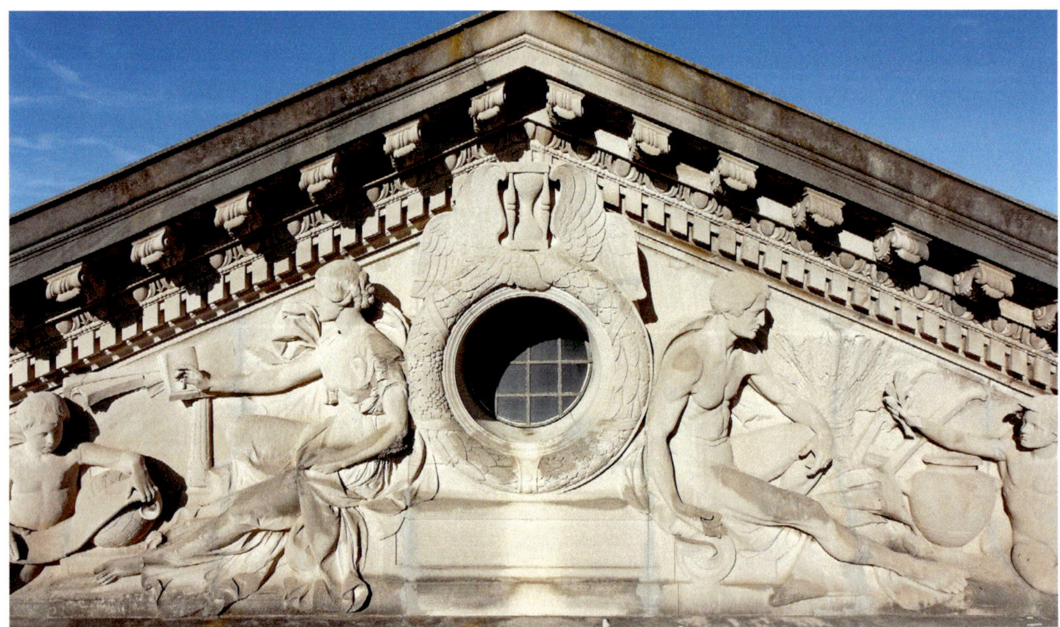

Above and below: Vanscyoc reflects on the greater purpose which Lynnewood Hall may serve: "Just like a painting with a blank canvas; you're be able to come here and find out what speaks to you, what inspires you. And we can all be inspired together, even if what that is for one person or the next person is different. Because we all have an understanding that we're in a special place, that we can come together and create, heal, you know, communicate with one another. That might be a beautiful thing, coming together and just experiencing something great alongside another person…. There's so much negativity in this world. If we can come in here and do that, and do it in a positive manner, that would be profound."

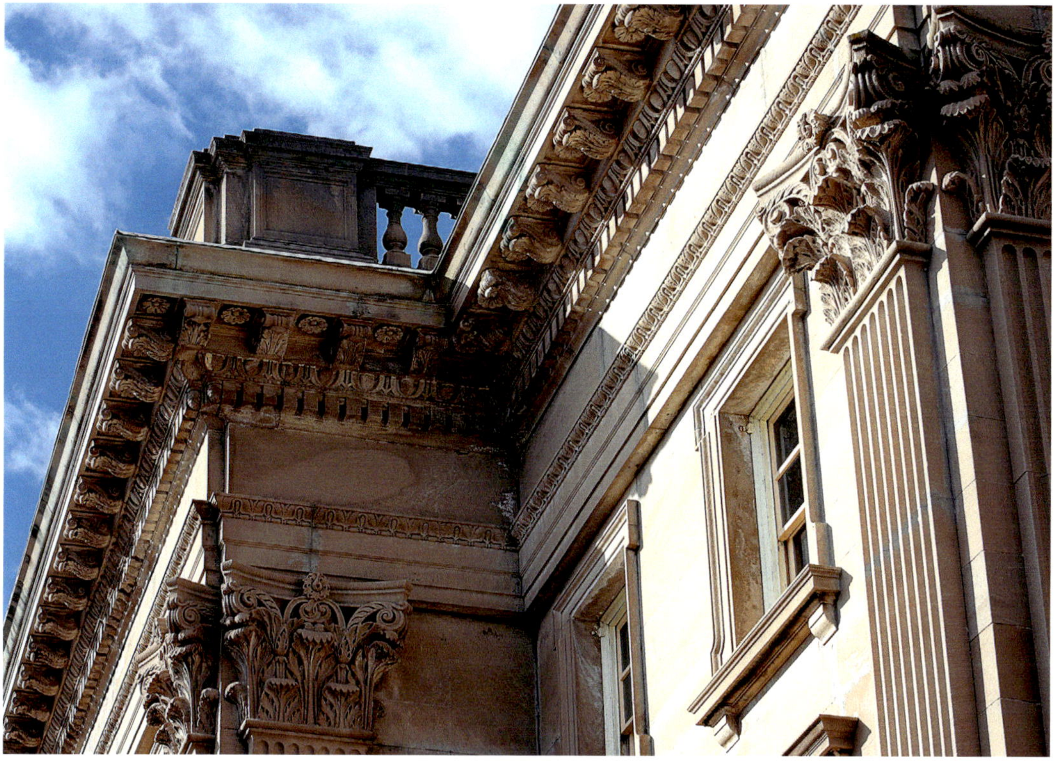

Above and below: With respect to the broader importance of architectural preservation, Thome spoke on his personal perspective: "I read it a long time ago, and I've never been able to find who it's attributed to, but it said that architecture is the most public form of art. It's true. I think one of the most beautiful forms of art, but it's also often the most forgotten."

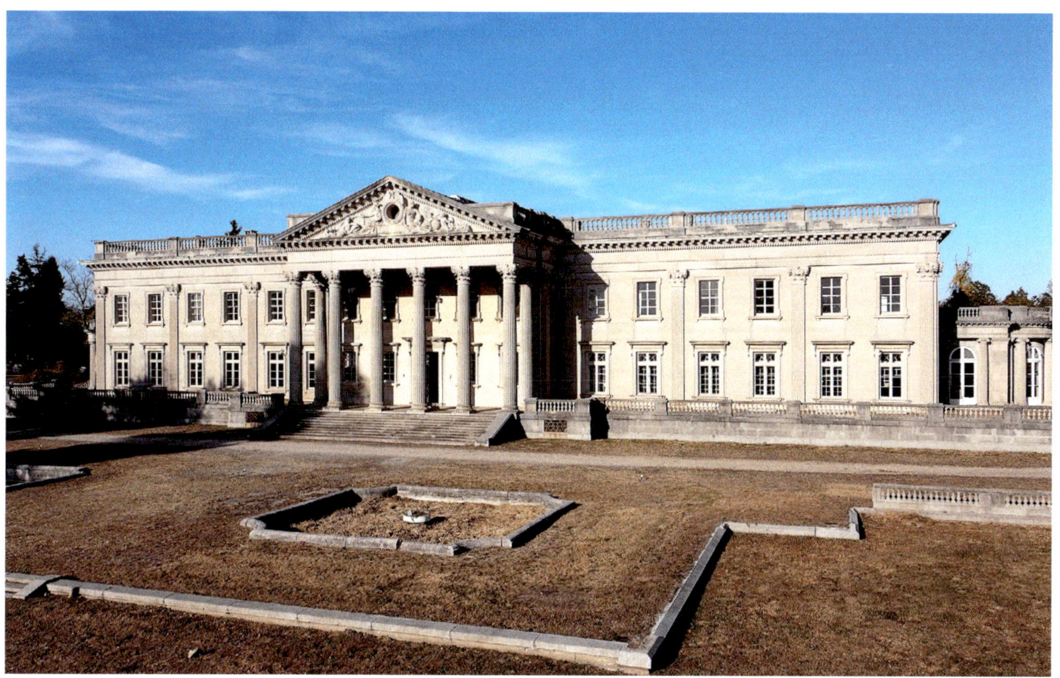